SEVEN SEAS ENTERTAINMENT PRESENTS

NEW GAME!
-THE SPINOFF!-
story & art by SHOTARO TOKUNO
VOLUME 5

TRANSLATION
Jenny McKeon

ADAPTATION
Jamal Joseph Jr.

LETTERING AND RETOUCH
Courtney Williams

COVER DESIGN
Nicky Lim

PROOFREADER
Danielle King
Christina Lynn

EDITOR
Jenn Grunigen

PRODUCTION ASSISTANT
CK Russell

PRODUCTION MANAGER
Lissa Pattillo

EDITOR-IN-CHIEF
Adam Arnold

PUBLISHER
Jason DeAngelis

NEW GAME! VOLUME 5 -THE SPINOFF!-
© Shotaro Tokuno 2016
First published in 2016 by Houbunsha Co., LTD. Tokyo, Japan.
English translation rights arranged with Houbunsha Co., LTD.

Seven Seas books may be purchased in bulk for educational, business, or promotional use. For information on bulk purchases, please contact Macmillan Corporate & Premium Sales Department at 1-800-221-7945 (ext 5442) or write specialmarkets@macmillan.com.

Seven Seas and the Seven Seas logo are trademarks of Seven Seas Entertainment, LLC. All rights reserved.

ISBN: 978-1-64275-014-0

Printed in Canada

First Printing: March 2019

10 9 8 7 6 5 4 3 2 1

W9-ADJ-469

FOLLOW US ONLINE: www.sevenseasentertainment.com

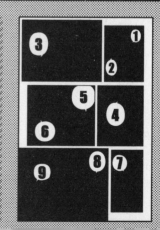

READING DIRECTIONS

This book reads from **right to left**, Japanese style. If this is your first time reading manga, you start reading from the top right panel on each page and take it from there. If you get lost, just follow the numbered diagram here. It may seem backwards at first, but you'll get the hang of it! Have fun!!

Watermelon (2)

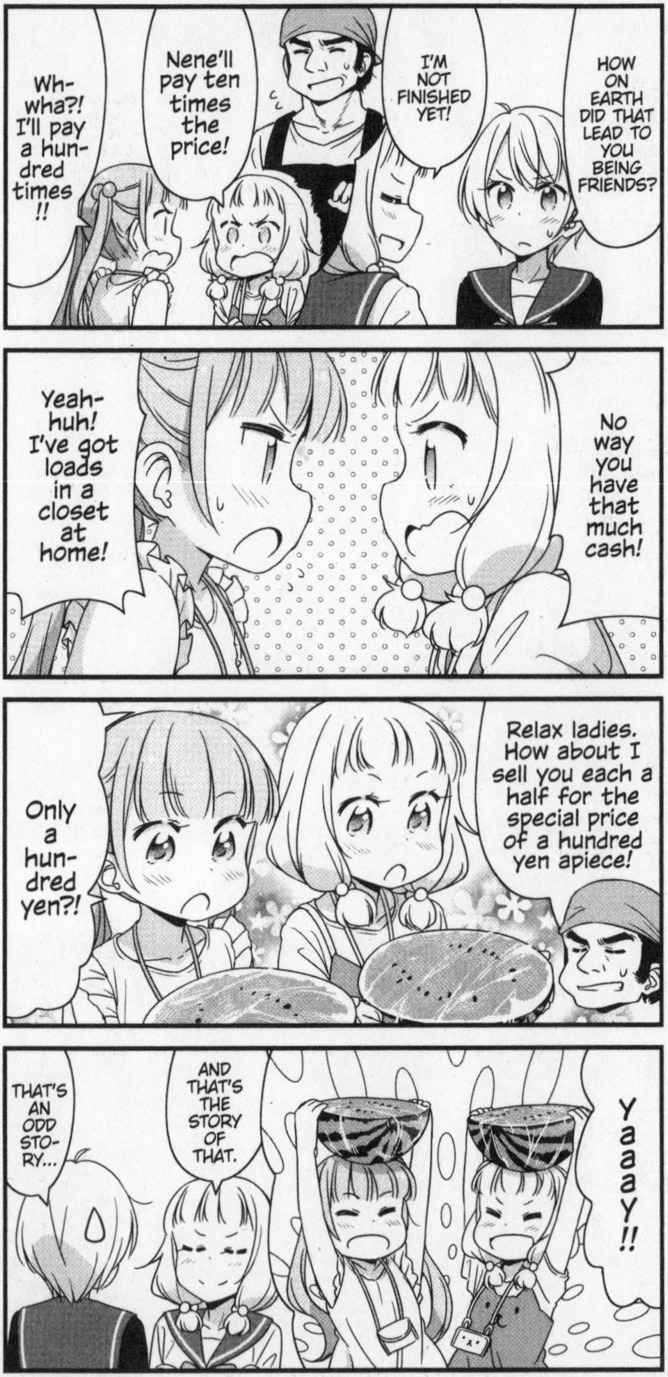
HOW ON EARTH DID THAT LEAD TO YOU BEING FRIENDS?
I'M NOT FINISHED YET!
Nene'll pay ten times the price!
Wh-wha?! I'll pay a hundred times!!
No way you have that much cash!
Yeah-huh! I've got loads in a closet at home!
Relax ladies. How about I sell you each a half for the special price of a hundred yen apiece!
Only a hundred yen?!
Yaaay!!
AND THAT'S THE STORY OF THAT.
THAT'S AN ODD STORY...

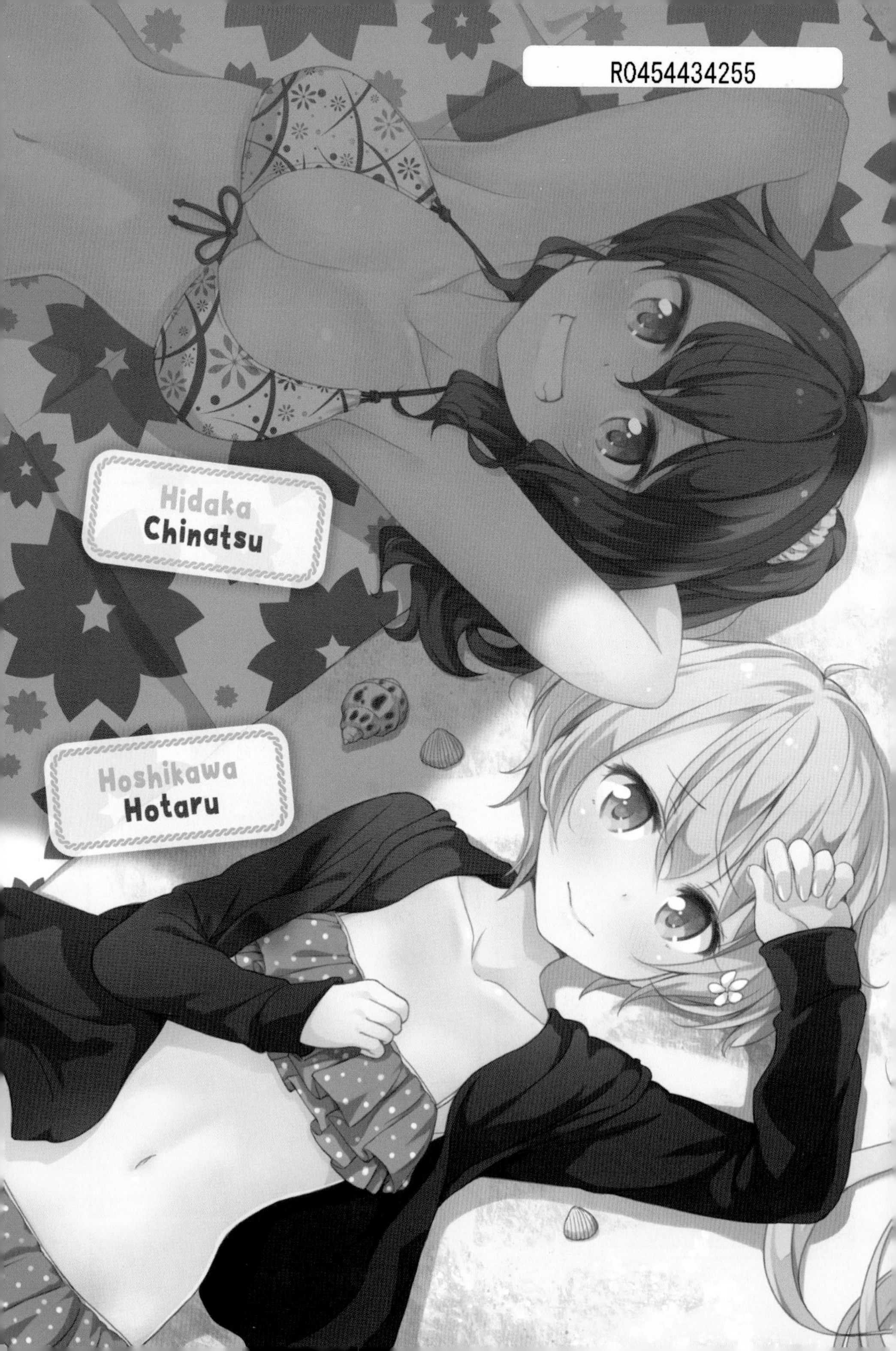
Hidaka
Chinatsu
Hoshikawa
Hotaru

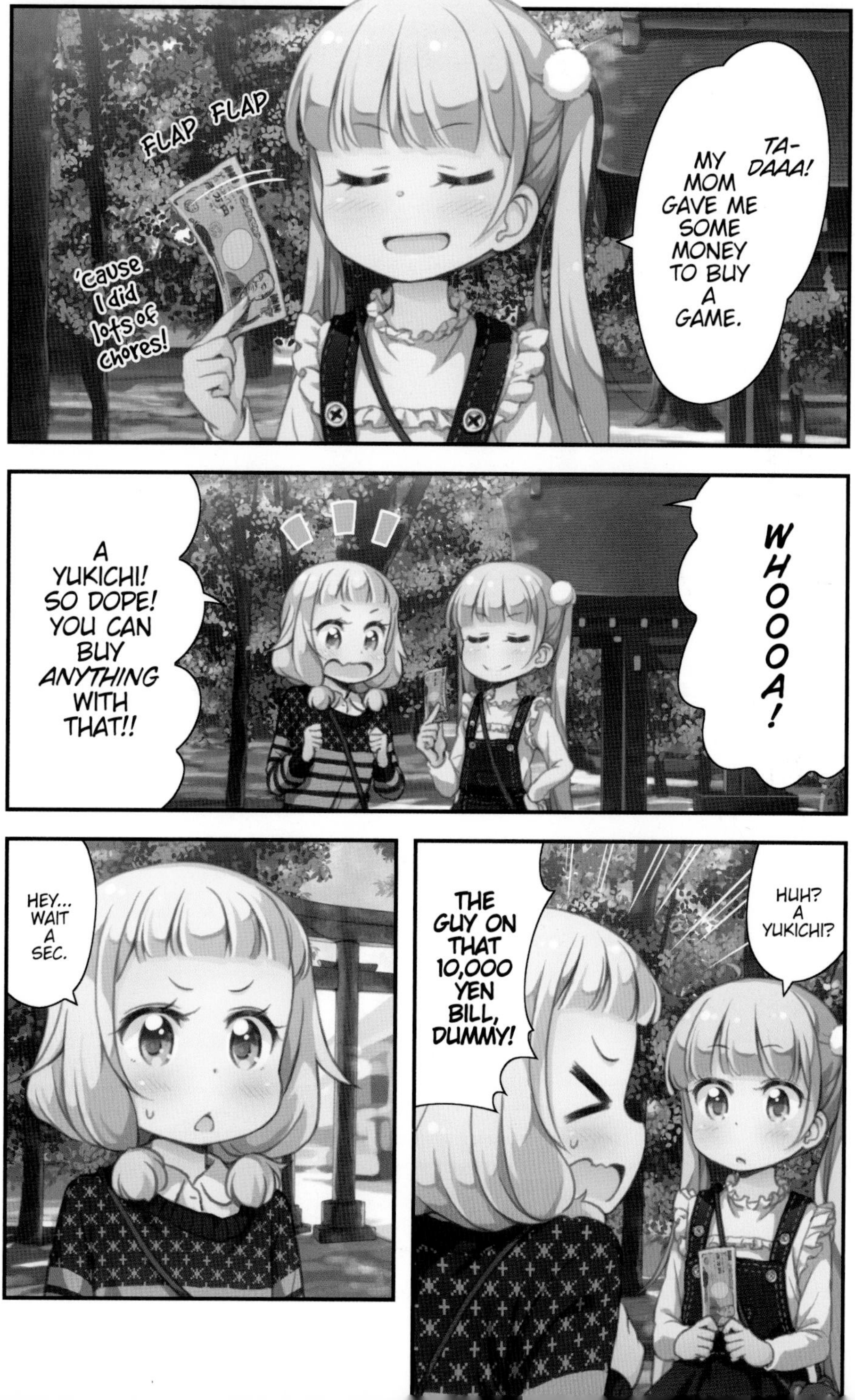
TA-DAAA!
MY MOM GAVE ME SOME MONEY TO BUY A GAME.
FLAP FLAP
'cause I did lots of chores!
WHOOOOA!
A YUKICHI! SO DOPE! YOU CAN BUY ANYTHING WITH THAT!!
HUH? A YUKICHI?
THE GUY ON THAT 10,000 YEN BILL, DUMMY!
HEY... WAIT A SEC.

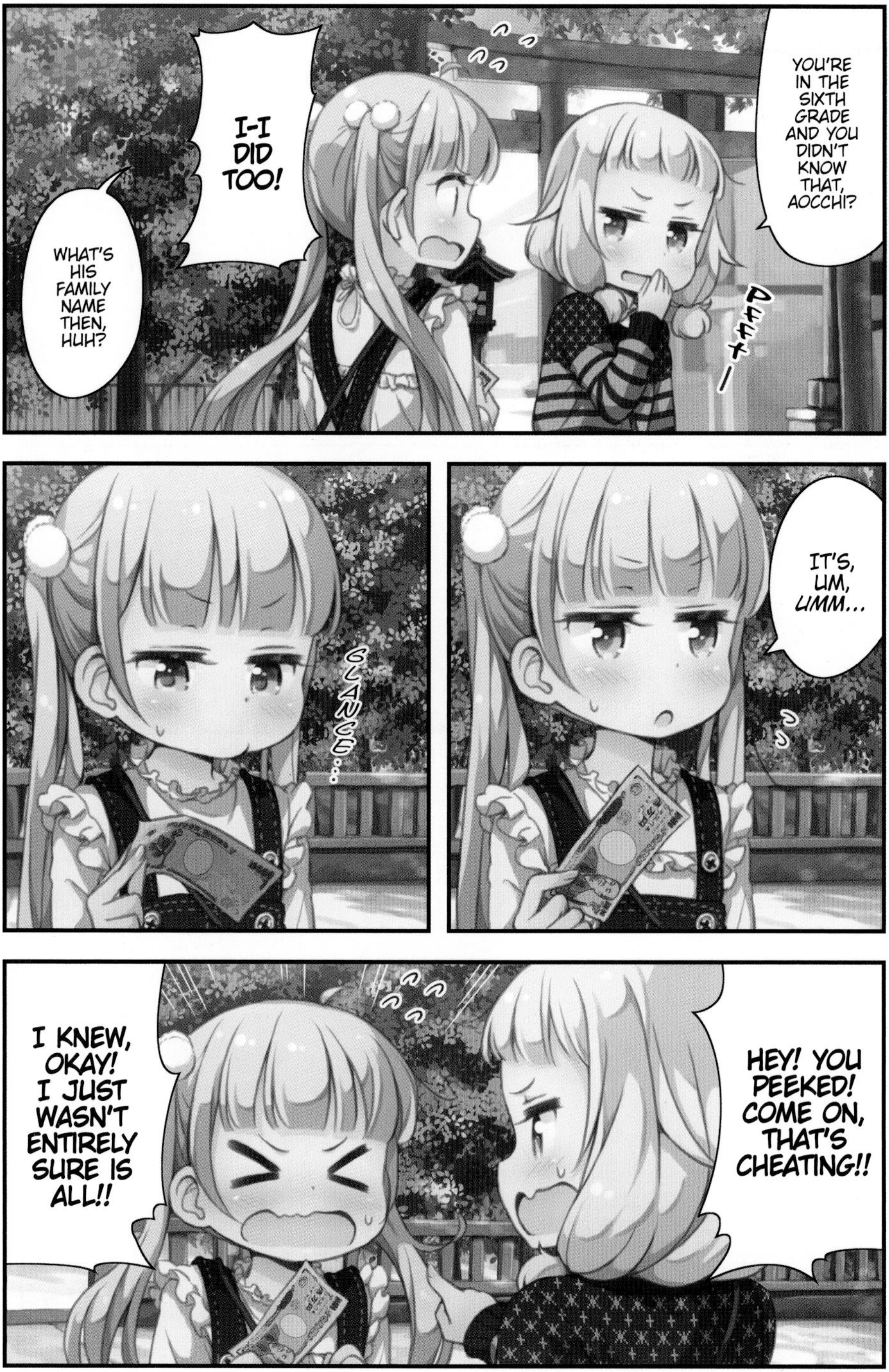
YOU'RE IN THE SIXTH GRADE AND YOU DIDN'T KNOW THAT, AOCCHI?
PFFT—
I-I DID TOO!
WHAT'S HIS FAMILY NAME THEN, HUH?
IT'S, UM, UMM...
GLANCE...
HEY! YOU PEEKED! COME ON, THAT'S CHEATING!!
I KNEW, OKAY! I JUST WASN'T ENTIRELY SURE IS ALL!!

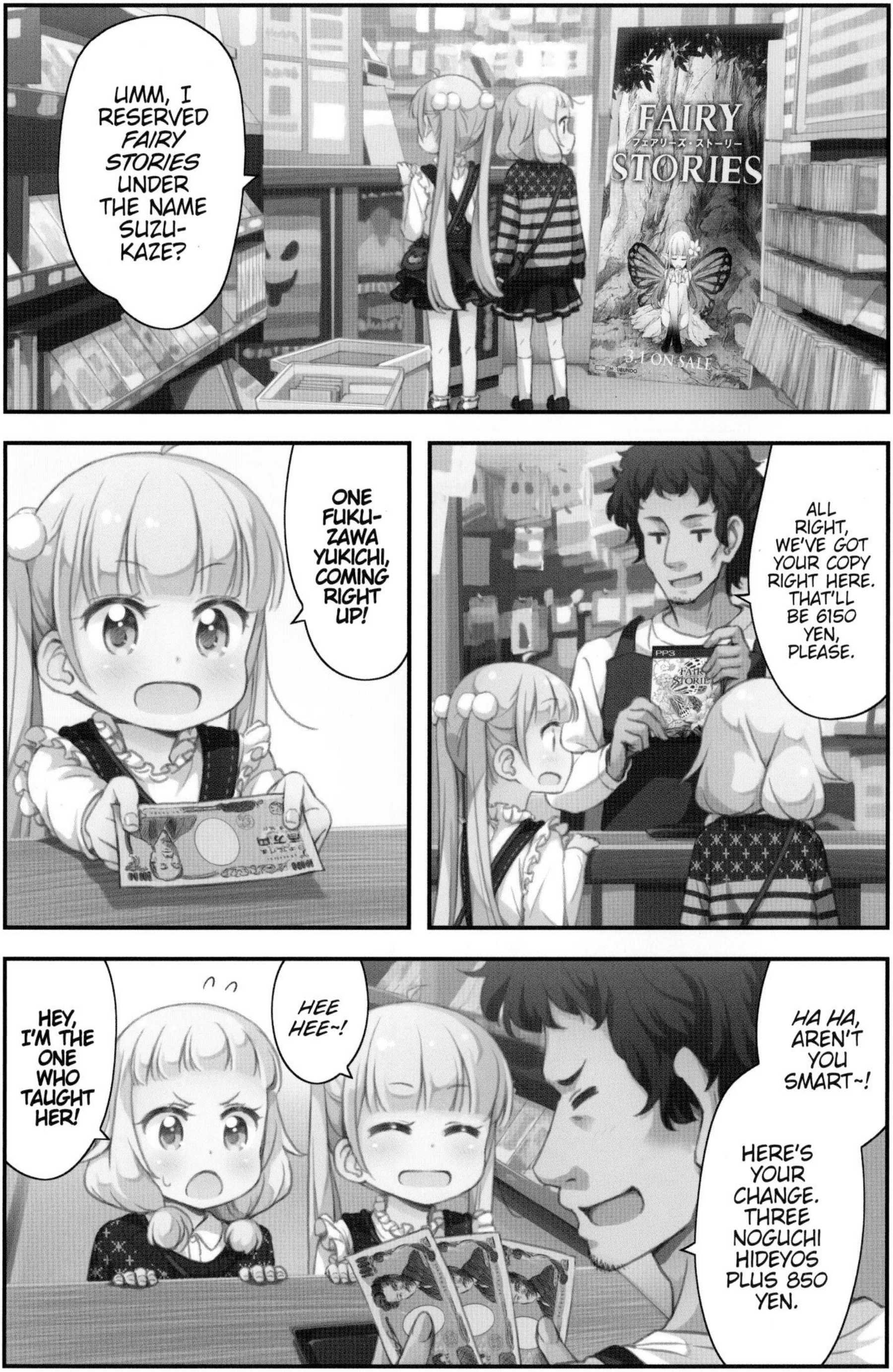
UMM, I RESERVED FAIRY STORIES UNDER THE NAME SUZU-KAZE?
FAIRY
フェアリーズ・ストーリー
STORIES
3.1 ON SALE
ALL RIGHT, WE'VE GOT YOUR COPY RIGHT HERE. THAT'LL BE 6150 YEN, PLEASE.
PP3
ONE FUKU-ZAWA YUKICHI, COMING RIGHT UP!
HA HA, AREN'T YOU SMART~!
HERE'S YOUR CHANGE. THREE NOGUCHI HIDEYOS PLUS 850 YEN.
HEE HEE~!
HEY, I'M THE ONE WHO TAUGHT HER!

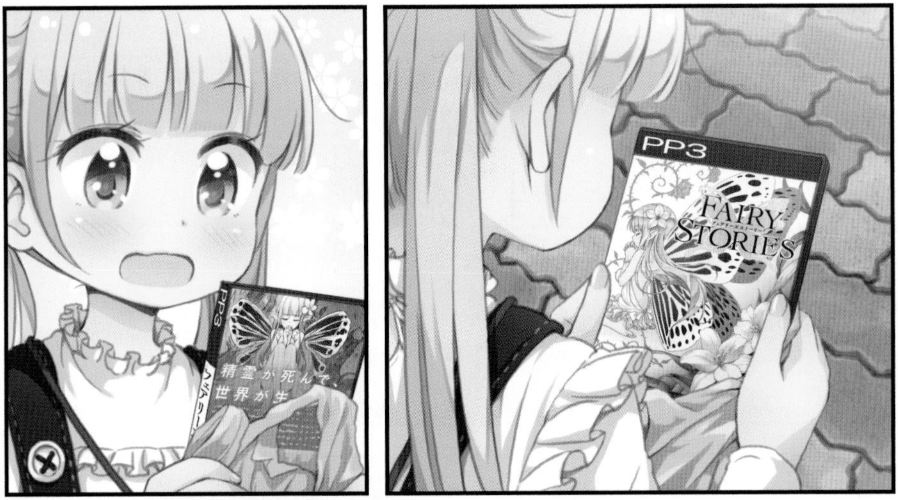
PP3
FAIRY STORIES
PP3
精霊が死んで、世界が生

Box: When a spirit dies, the world [...].

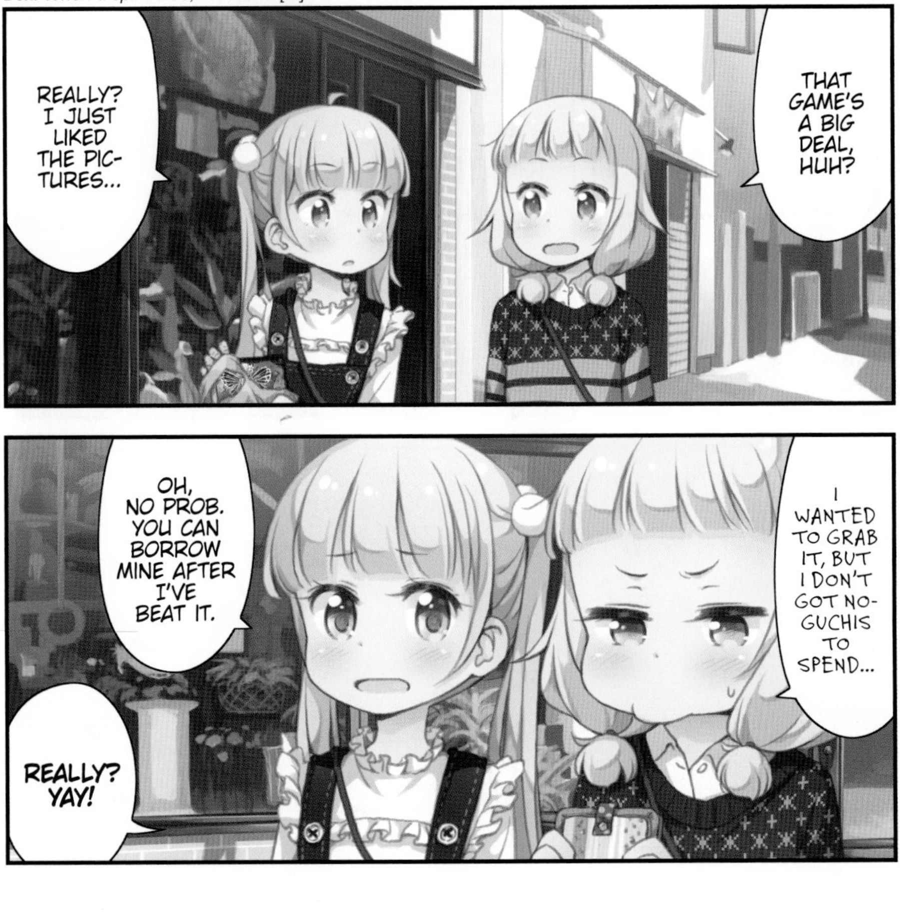
THAT GAME'S A BIG DEAL, HUH?
REALLY? I JUST LIKED THE PICTURES...
I WANTED TO GRAB IT, BUT I DON'T GOT NOGUCHIS TO SPEND...
OH, NO PROB. YOU CAN BORROW MINE AFTER I'VE BEAT IT.
REALLY? YAY!

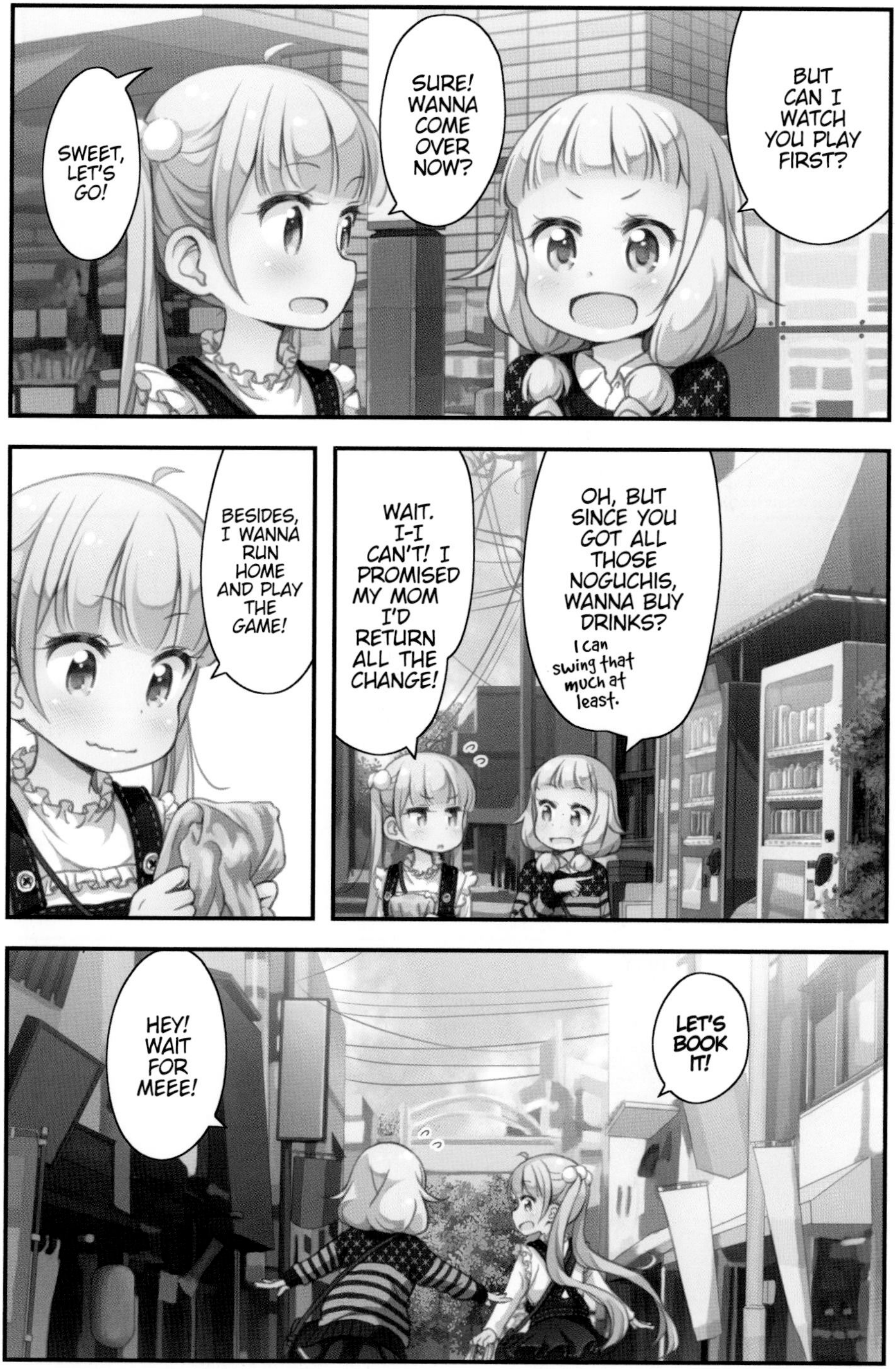
BUT CAN I WATCH YOU PLAY FIRST?
SURE! WANNA COME OVER NOW?
SWEET, LET'S GO!
OH, BUT SINCE YOU GOT ALL THOSE NOGUCHIS, WANNA BUY DRINKS?
I can swing that much at least.
WAIT. I-I CAN'T! I PROMISED MY MOM I'D RETURN ALL THE CHANGE!
BESIDES, I WANNA RUN HOME AND PLAY THE GAME!
LET'S BOOK IT!
HEY! WAIT FOR MEEE!

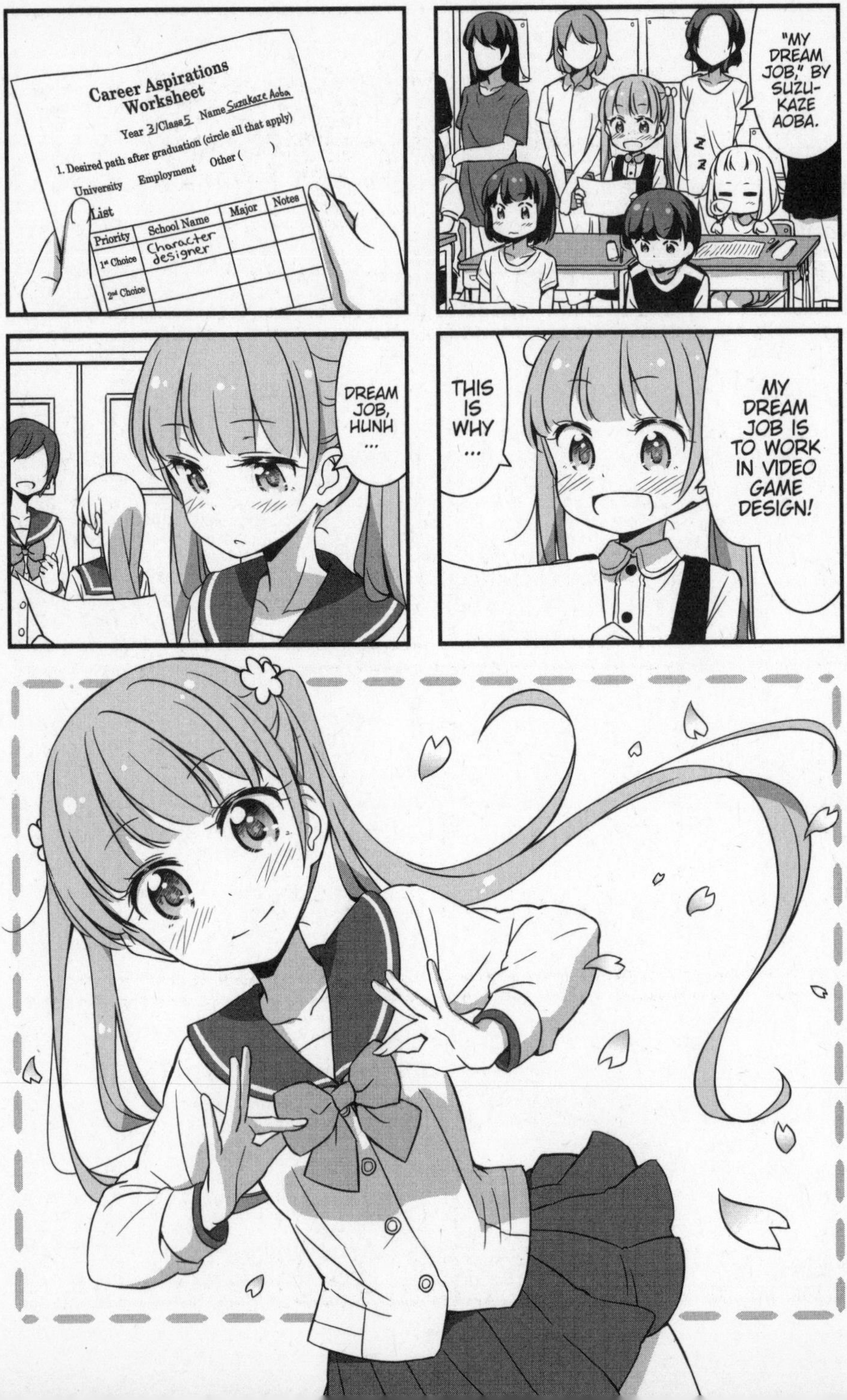
"MY DREAM JOB," BY SUZUKAZE AOBA.
Career Aspirations Worksheet
Year 3/Class 5 Name Suzukaze Aoba
1. Desired path after graduation (circle all that apply)
University Employment Other ( )
List
Priority
School Name
Major
Notes
1st Choice
Character designer
2nd Choice
MY DREAM JOB IS TO WORK IN VIDEO GAME DESIGN!
THIS IS WHY...
DREAM JOB, HUNH...

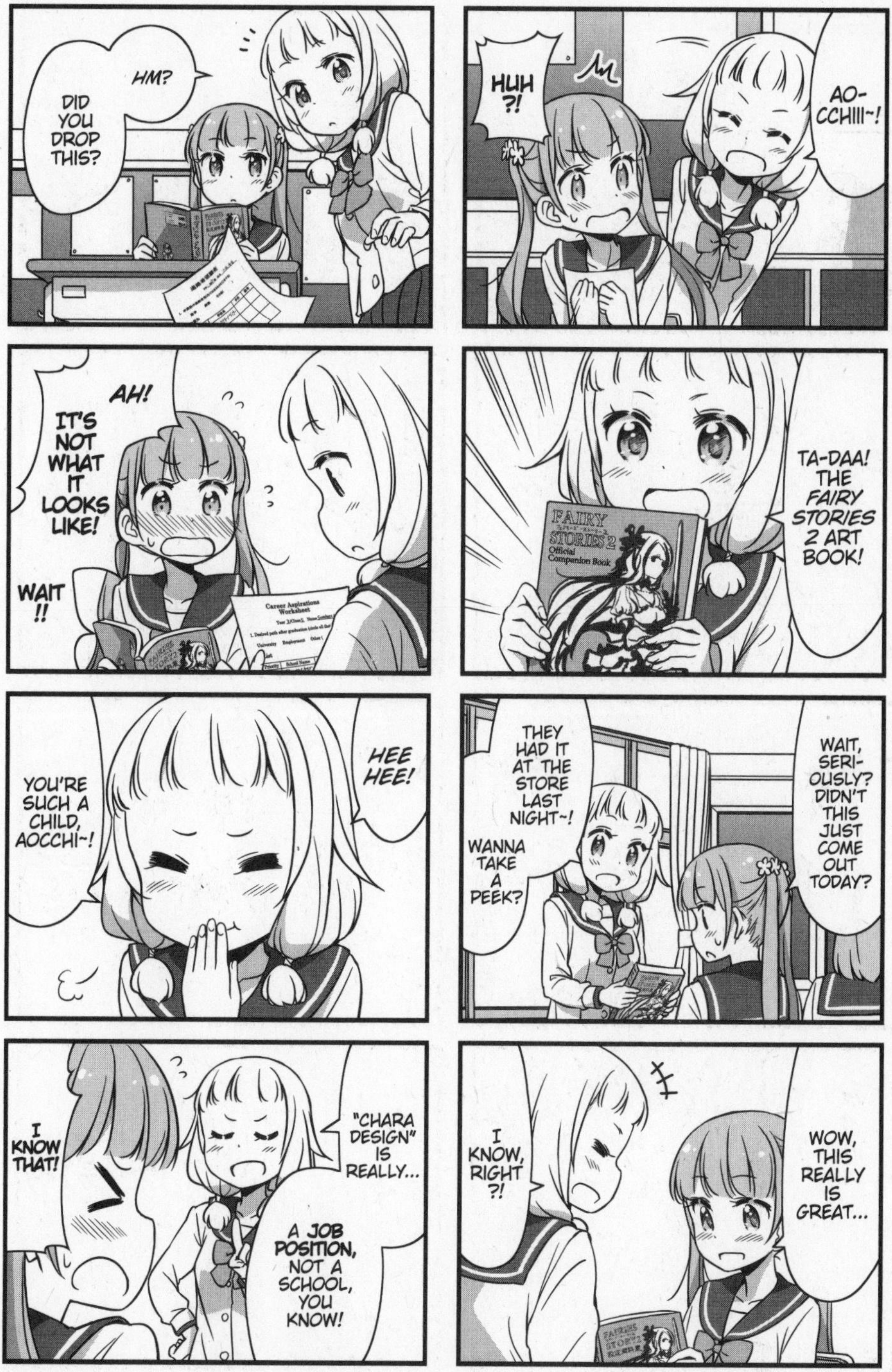

AO-CCHIII~!
HUH ?!
HM?
DID YOU DROP THIS?
TA-DAA! THE FAIRY STORIES 2 ART BOOK!
FAIRY STORIES 2 Official Companion Book
AH!
IT'S NOT WHAT IT LOOKS LIKE!
WAIT !!
Career Aspirations Worksheet
WAIT, SERIOUSLY? DIDN'T THIS JUST COME OUT TODAY?
THEY HAD IT AT THE STORE LAST NIGHT~!
WANNA TAKE A PEEK?
HEE HEE!
YOU'RE SUCH A CHILD, AOCCHI~!
WOW, THIS REALLY IS GREAT...
I KNOW, RIGHT ?!
"CHARA DESIGN" IS REALLY...
A JOB POSITION, NOT A SCHOOL, YOU KNOW!
I KNOW THAT!

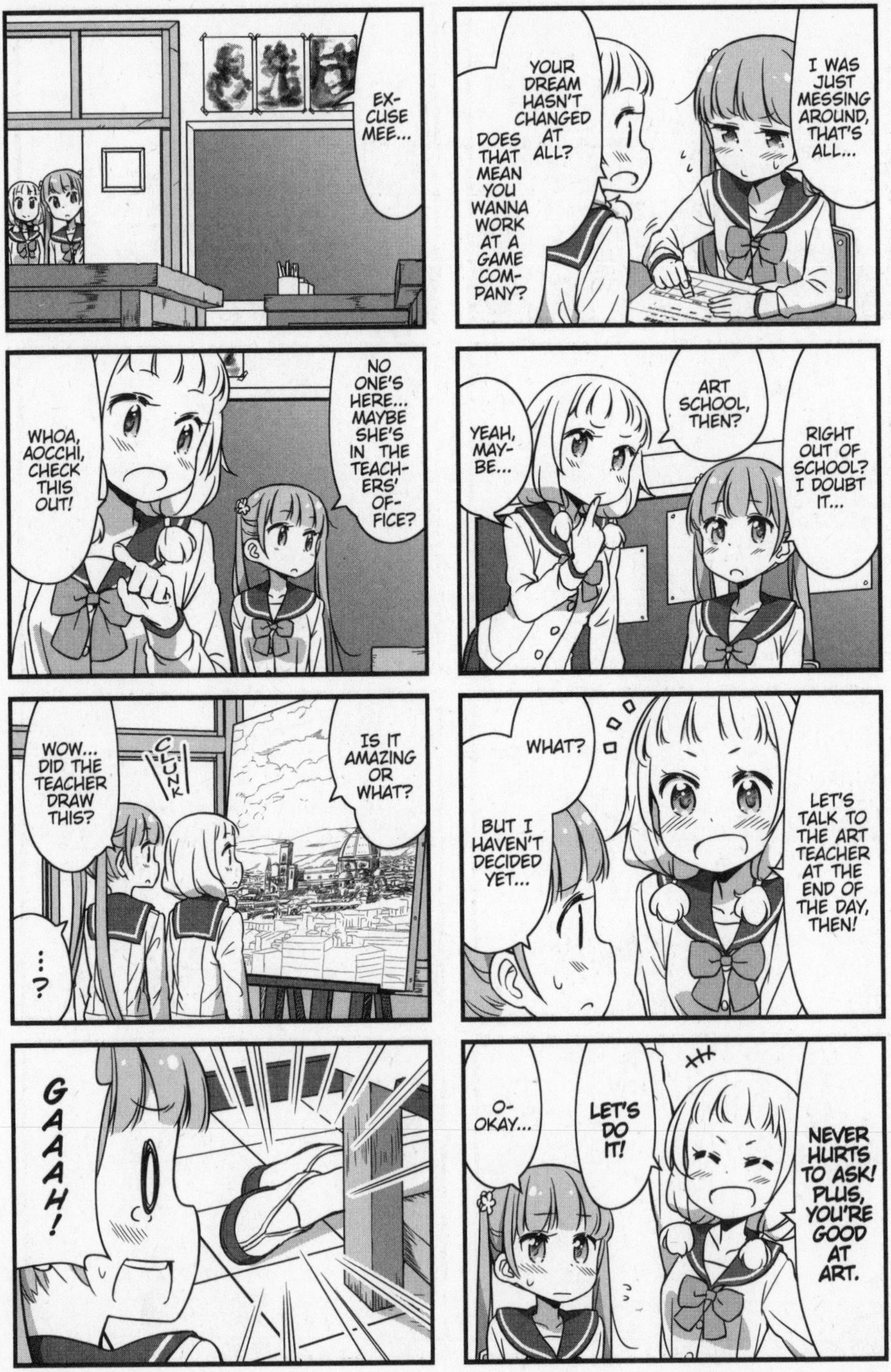
I WAS JUST MESSING AROUND, THAT'S ALL...
YOUR DREAM HASN'T CHANGED AT ALL?
DOES THAT MEAN YOU WANNA WORK AT A GAME COMPANY?
RIGHT OUT OF SCHOOL? I DOUBT IT...
ART SCHOOL, THEN?
YEAH, MAYBE...
LET'S TALK TO THE ART TEACHER AT THE END OF THE DAY, THEN!
WHAT?
BUT I HAVEN'T DECIDED YET...
NEVER HURTS TO ASK! PLUS, YOU'RE GOOD AT ART.
LET'S DO IT!
O-OKAY...
EX-CUSE MEE...
NO ONE'S HERE... MAYBE SHE'S IN THE TEACHERS' OFFICE?
WHOA, AOCCHI, CHECK THIS OUT!
IS IT AMAZING OR WHAT?
CLUNK
WOW... DID THE TEACHER DRAW THIS?
...?
GAAAH!

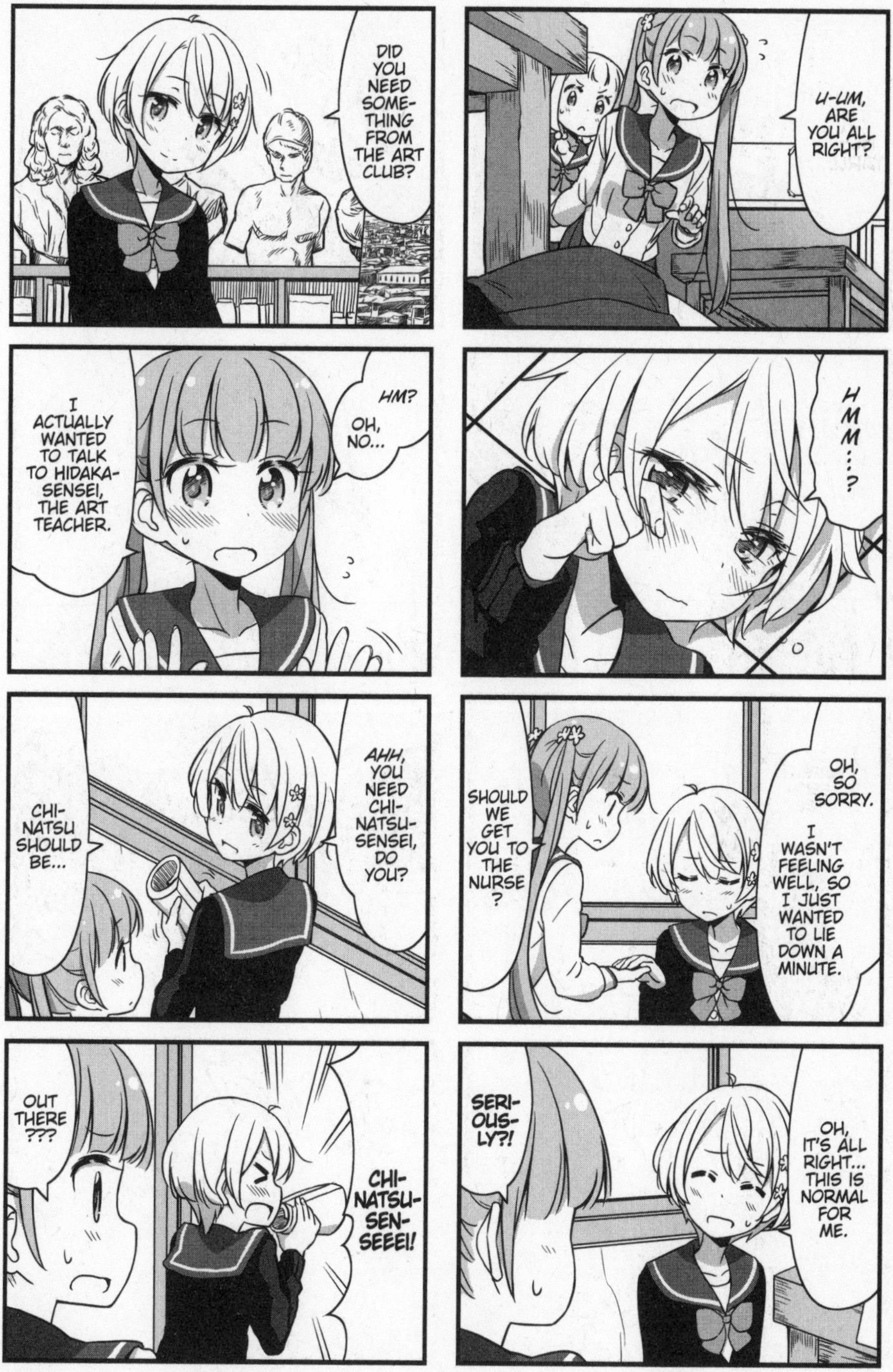
U-UM, ARE YOU ALL RIGHT?
DID YOU NEED SOMETHING FROM THE ART CLUB?
HMM...?
HM? OH, NO...
I ACTUALLY WANTED TO TALK TO HIDAKA-SENSEI, THE ART TEACHER.
OH, SO SORRY.
I WASN'T FEELING WELL, SO I JUST WANTED TO LIE DOWN A MINUTE.
SHOULD WE GET YOU TO THE NURSE?
AHH, YOU NEED CHINATSU-SENSEI, DO YOU?
CHINATSU SHOULD BE...
OH, IT'S ALL RIGHT... THIS IS NORMAL FOR ME.
SERIOUSLY?!
CHINATSU-SENSEEI!
OUT THERE???

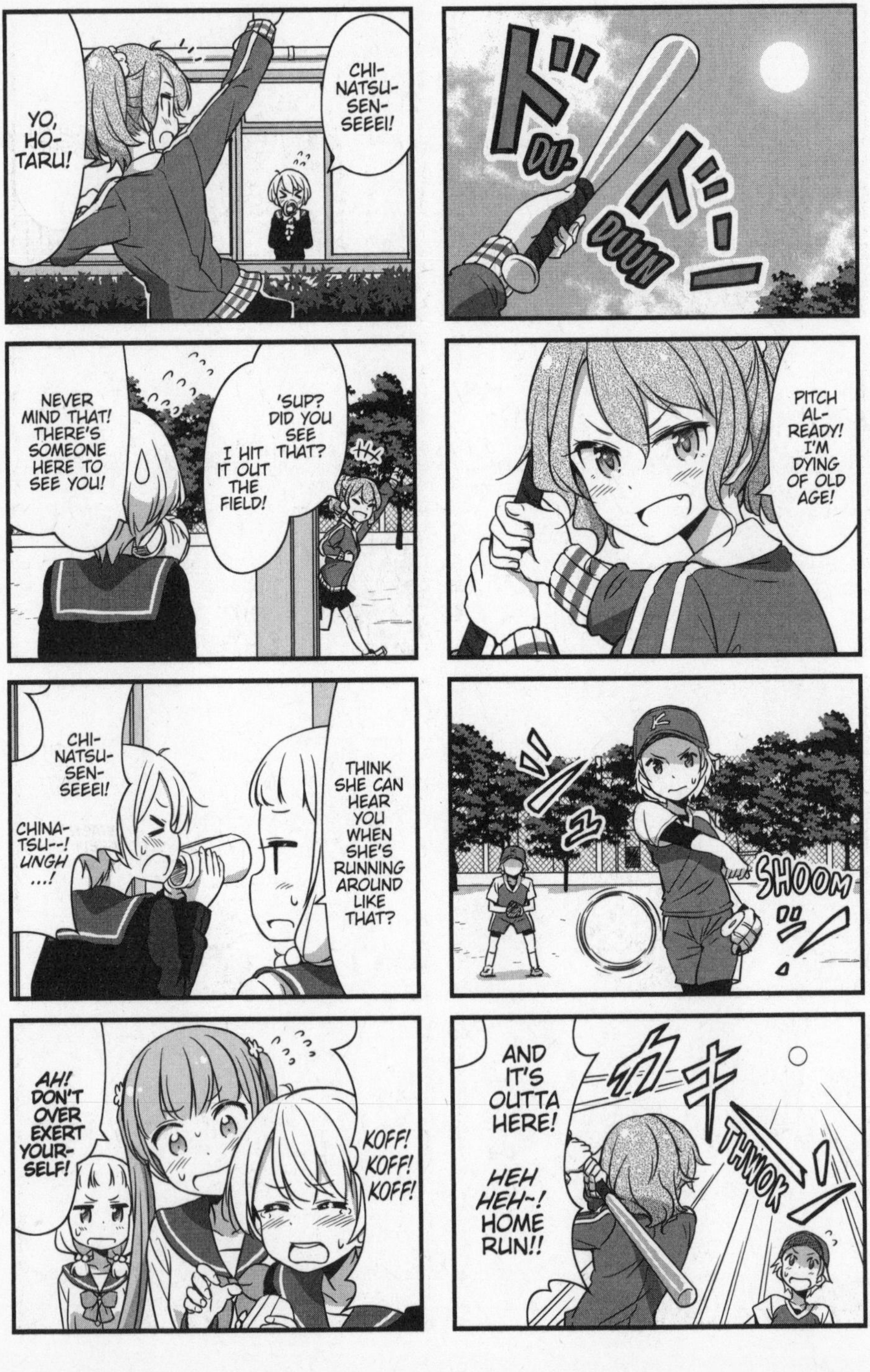

DU
DUUN
PITCH ALREADY! I'M DYING OF OLD AGE!
SHOOM
AND IT'S OUTTA HERE!
THWOK
HEH HEH~! HOME RUN!!
CHI-NATSU-SEN-SEEEI!
YO, HO-TARU!
'SUP? DID YOU SEE THAT?
I HIT IT OUT THE FIELD!
NEVER MIND THAT! THERE'S SOMEONE HERE TO SEE YOU!
THINK SHE CAN HEAR YOU WHEN SHE'S RUNNING AROUND LIKE THAT?
CHI-NATSU-SEN-SEEEI!
CHINA-TSU--! UNGH ...!
KOFF! KOFF! KOFF!
AH! DON'T OVER EXERT YOUR-SELF!

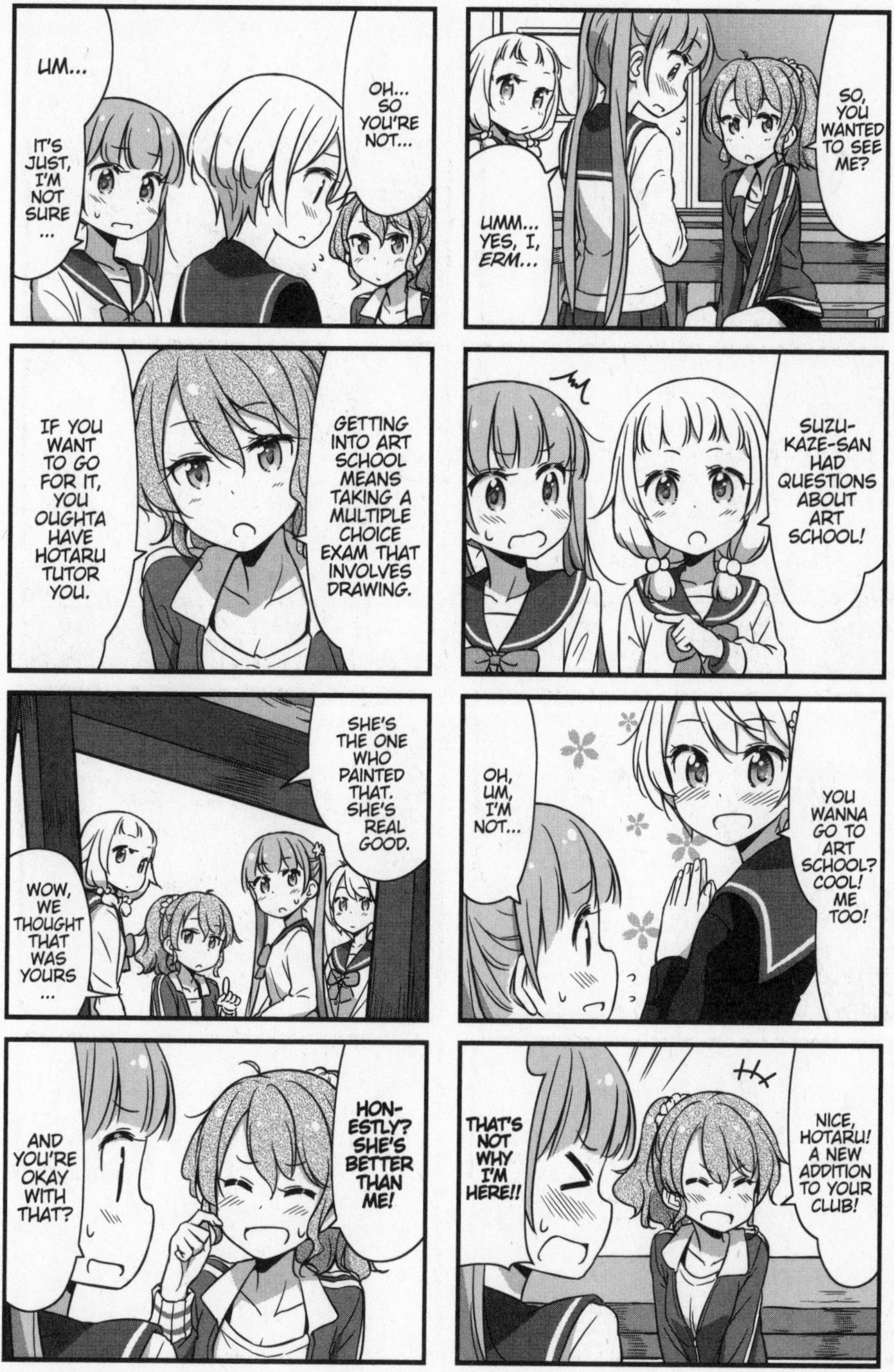
SO, YOU WANTED TO SEE ME?
UMM... YES, I, ERM...
OH... SO YOU'RE NOT...
UM...
IT'S JUST, I'M NOT SURE ...
SUZU-KAZE-SAN HAD QUESTIONS ABOUT ART SCHOOL!
GETTING INTO ART SCHOOL MEANS TAKING A MULTIPLE CHOICE EXAM THAT INVOLVES DRAWING.
IF YOU WANT TO GO FOR IT, YOU OUGHTA HAVE HOTARU TUTOR YOU.
YOU WANNA GO TO ART SCHOOL? COOL! ME TOO!
OH, UM, I'M NOT...
SHE'S THE ONE WHO PAINTED THAT. SHE'S REAL GOOD.
WOW, WE THOUGHT THAT WAS YOURS ...
NICE, HOTARU! A NEW ADDITION TO YOUR CLUB!
THAT'S NOT WHY I'M HERE!!
HON-ESTLY? SHE'S BETTER THAN ME!
AND YOU'RE OKAY WITH THAT?

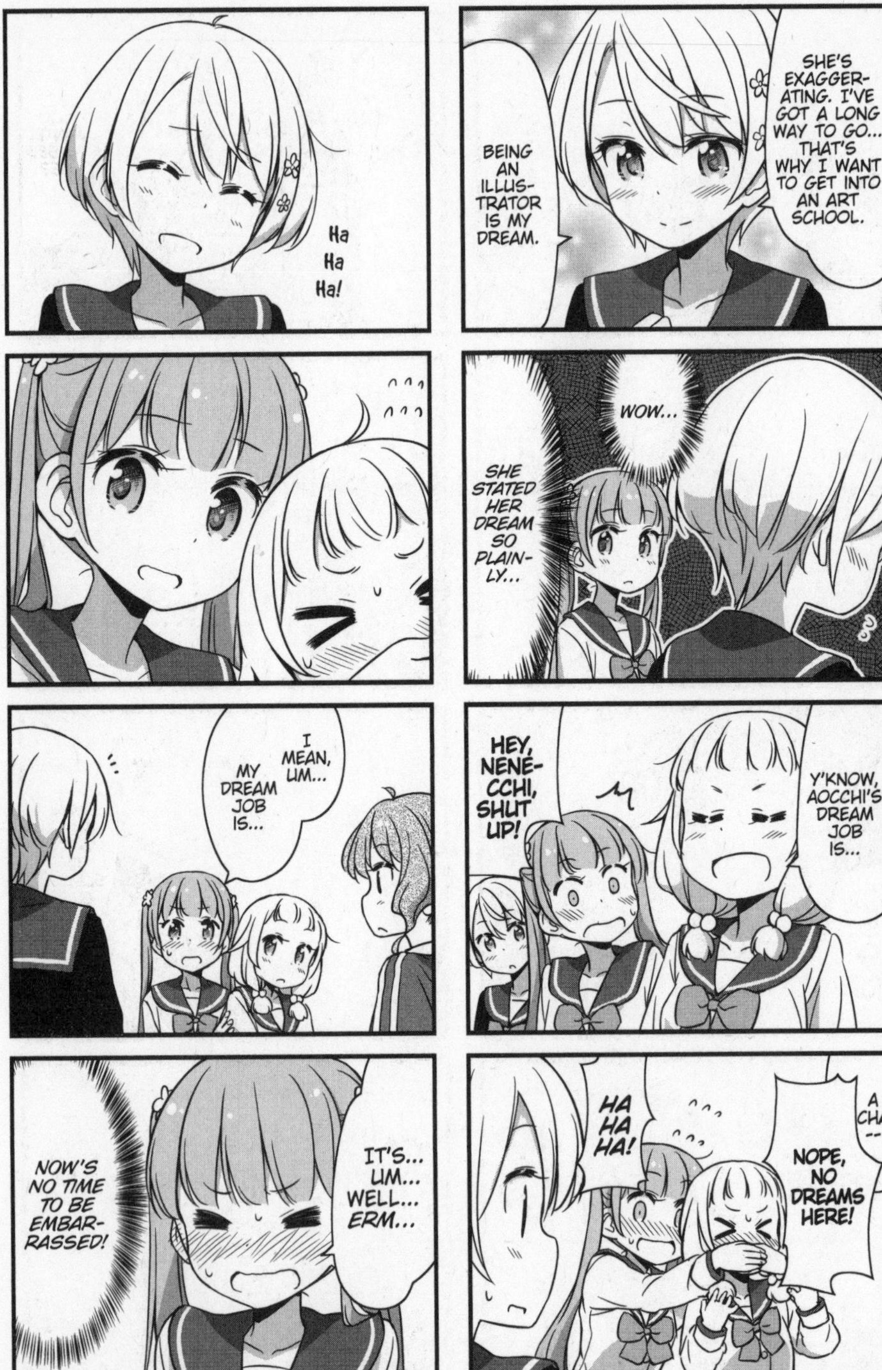
SHE'S EXAGGERATING. I'VE GOT A LONG WAY TO GO... THAT'S WHY I WANT TO GET INTO AN ART SCHOOL.
BEING AN ILLUSTRATOR IS MY DREAM.
Ha Ha Ha!
WOW...
SHE STATED HER DREAM SO PLAINLY...
Y'KNOW, AOCCHI'S DREAM JOB IS...
HEY, NENECCHI, SHUT UP!
I MEAN, UM...
MY DREAM JOB IS...
A CHA--
NOPE, NO DREAMS HERE!
HA HA HA!
IT'S... UM... WELL... ERM...
NOW'S NO TIME TO BE EMBARRASSED!

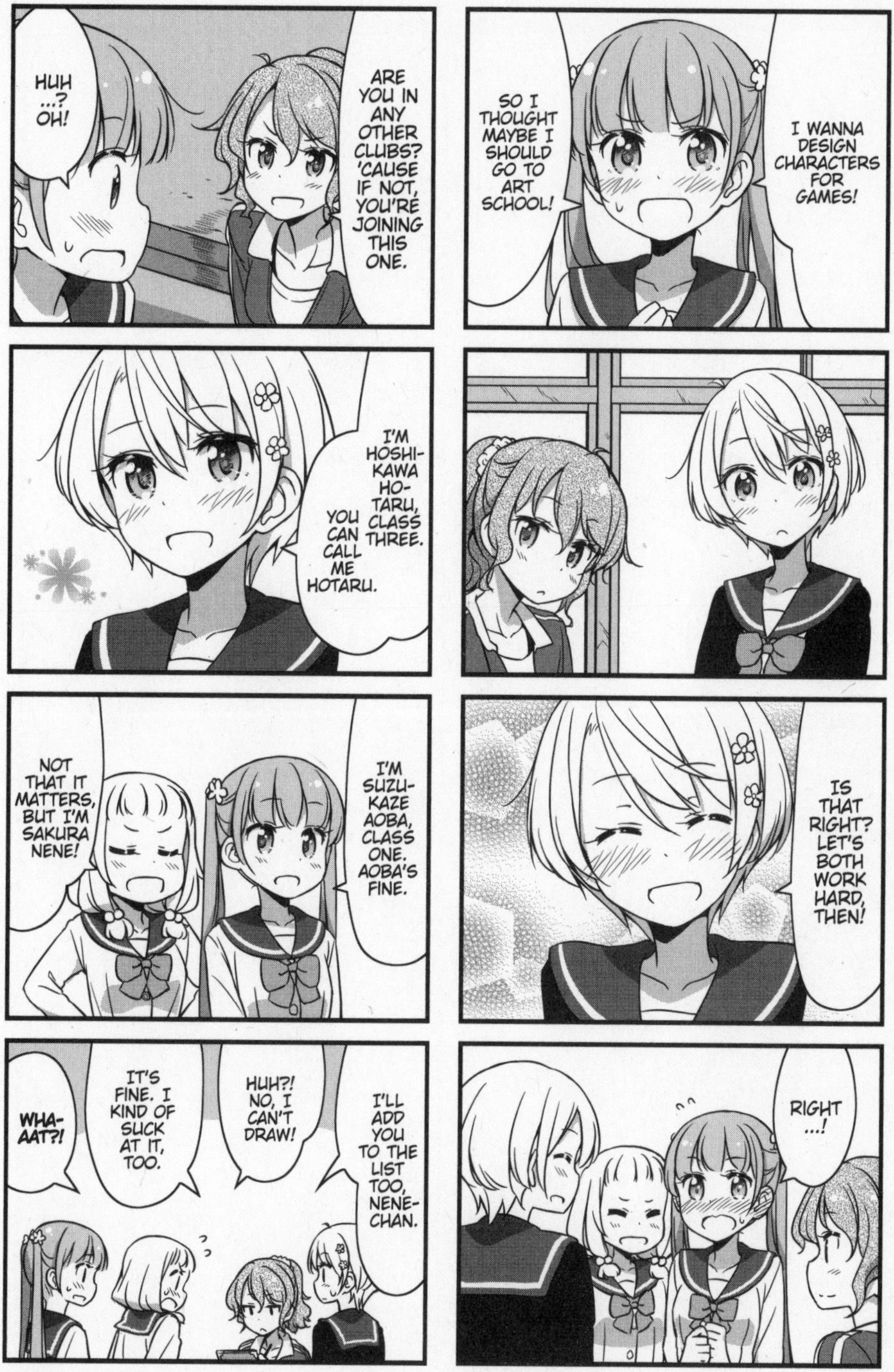
I WANNA DESIGN CHARACTERS FOR GAMES!
SO I THOUGHT MAYBE I SHOULD GO TO ART SCHOOL!
ARE YOU IN ANY OTHER CLUBS? 'CAUSE IF NOT, YOU'RE JOINING THIS ONE.
HUH ...? OH!
I'M HOSHIKAWA HOTARU, CLASS THREE.
YOU CAN CALL ME HOTARU.
IS THAT RIGHT? LET'S BOTH WORK HARD, THEN!
I'M SUZUKAZE AOBA, CLASS ONE. AOBA'S FINE.
NOT THAT IT MATTERS, BUT I'M SAKURA NENE!
RIGHT ...!
I'LL ADD YOU TO THE LIST TOO, NENE-CHAN.
HUH?! NO, I CAN'T DRAW!
IT'S FINE. I KIND OF SUCK AT IT, TOO.
WHA-AAT?!

NEW GAME!

NEW GAME!

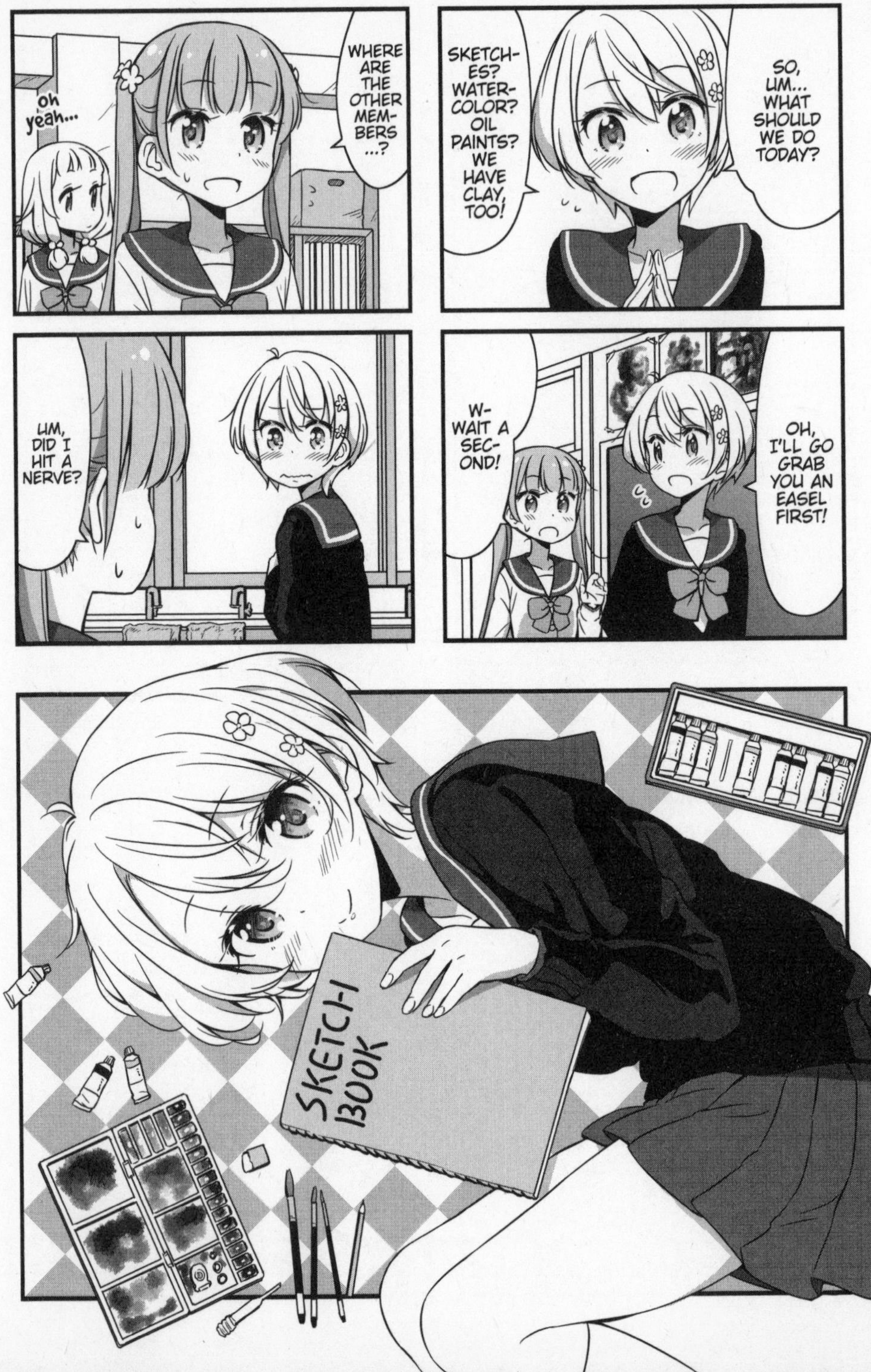
SO, UM... WHAT SHOULD WE DO TODAY?
SKETCHES? WATERCOLOR? OIL PAINTS? WE HAVE CLAY, TOO!
WHERE ARE THE OTHER MEMBERS...?
oh yeah...
OH, I'LL GO GRAB YOU AN EASEL FIRST!
W-WAIT A SECOND!
UM, DID I HIT A NERVE?
SKETCH BOOK

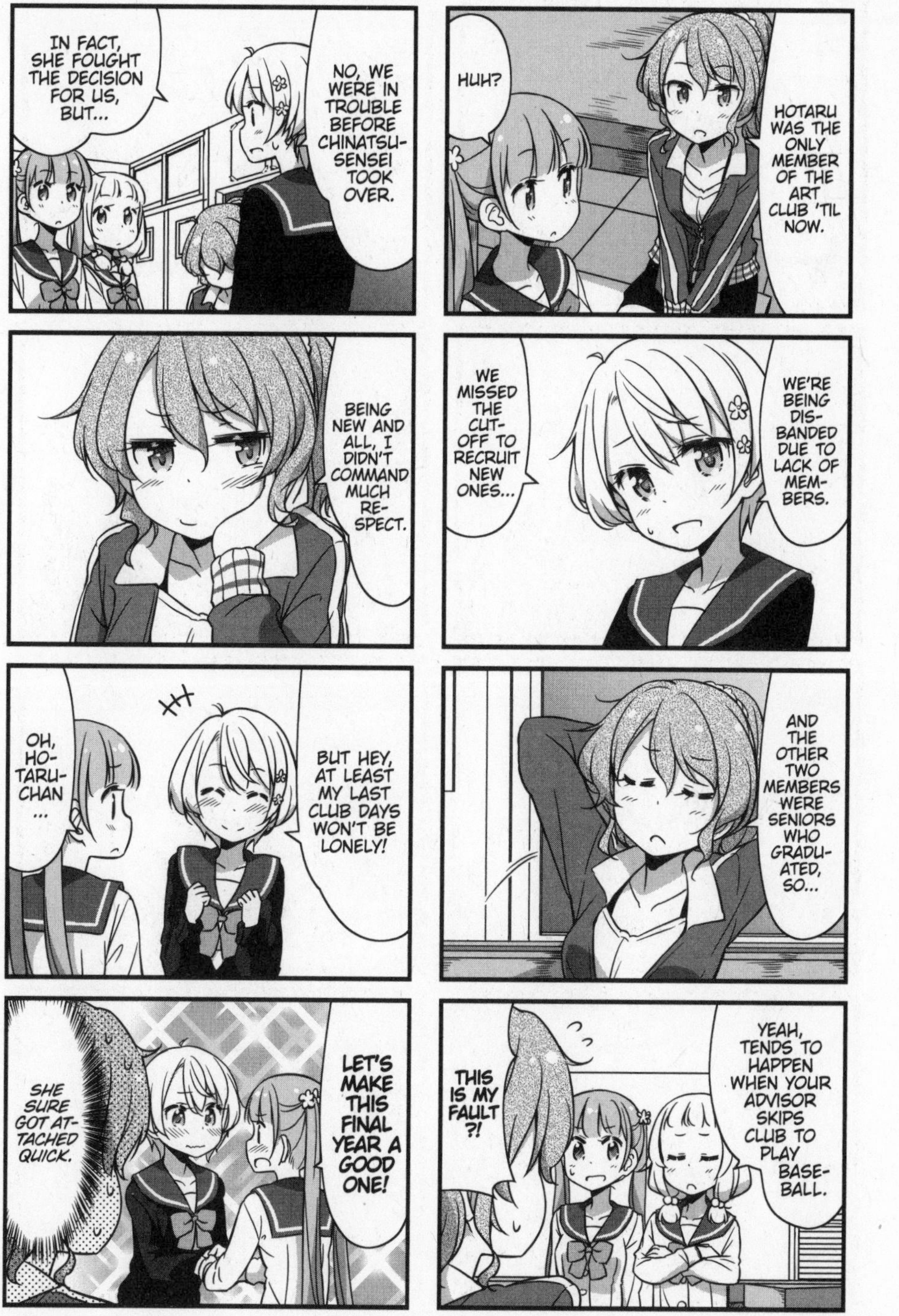
HUH?
HOTARU WAS THE ONLY MEMBER OF THE ART CLUB 'TIL NOW.
NO, WE WERE IN TROUBLE BEFORE CHINATSU-SENSEI TOOK OVER.
IN FACT, SHE FOUGHT THE DECISION FOR US, BUT...
WE'RE BEING DISBANDED DUE TO LACK OF MEMBERS.
WE MISSED THE CUT-OFF TO RECRUIT NEW ONES...
BEING NEW AND ALL, I DIDN'T COMMAND MUCH RESPECT.
AND THE OTHER TWO MEMBERS WERE SENIORS WHO GRADUATED, SO...
BUT HEY, AT LEAST MY LAST CLUB DAYS WON'T BE LONELY!
OH, HOTARU-CHAN...
YEAH, TENDS TO HAPPEN WHEN YOUR ADVISOR SKIPS CLUB TO PLAY BASEBALL.
THIS IS MY FAULT?!
LET'S MAKE THIS FINAL YEAR A GOOD ONE!
SHE SURE GOT ATTACHED QUICK.

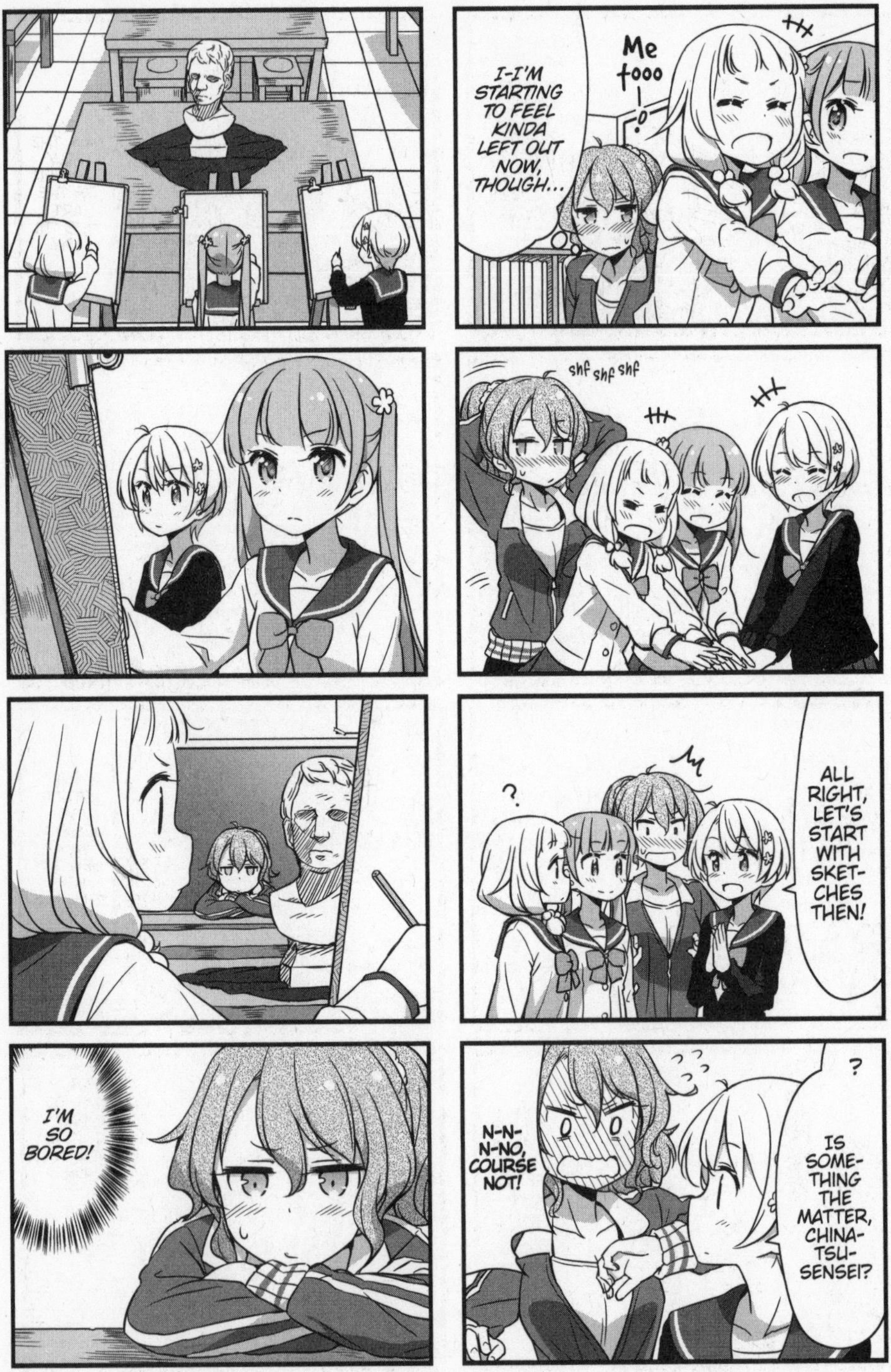
Me tooo!
I-I'M STARTING TO FEEL KINDA LEFT OUT NOW, THOUGH...
shf shf shf
ALL RIGHT, LET'S START WITH SKET-CHES THEN!
?
?
IS SOME-THING THE MATTER, CHINA-TSU-SENSEI?
N-N-N-NO, COURSE NOT!
I'M SO BORED!

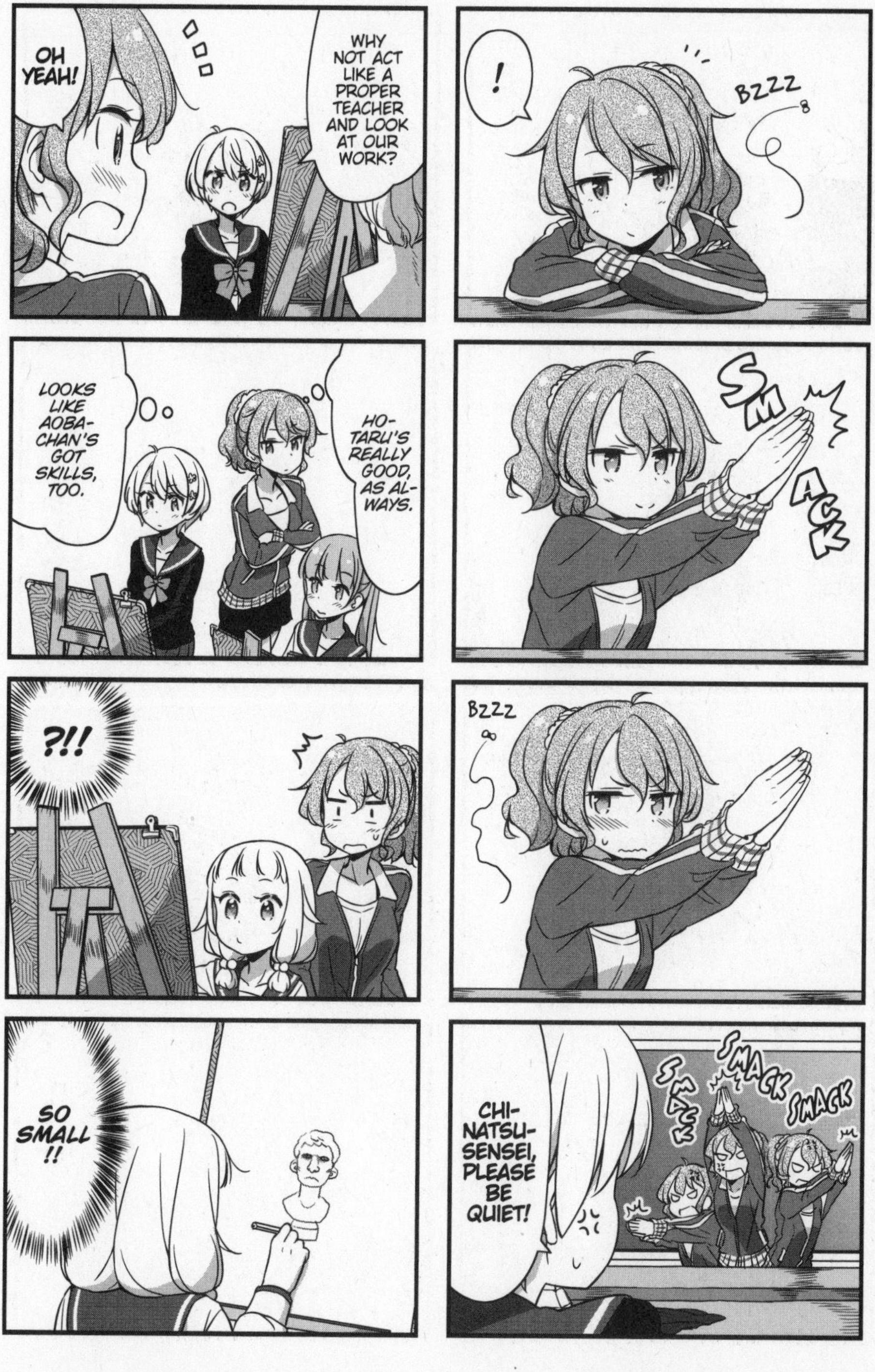
BZZZ
!
SMACK
BZZZ
SMACK
SMACK
SMACK
CHI-NATSU-SENSEI, PLEASE BE QUIET!
WHY NOT ACT LIKE A PROPER TEACHER AND LOOK AT OUR WORK?
OH YEAH!
HO-TARU'S REALLY GOOD, AS AL-WAYS.
LOOKS LIKE AOBA-CHAN'S GOT SKILLS, TOO.
?!!
SO SMALL !!

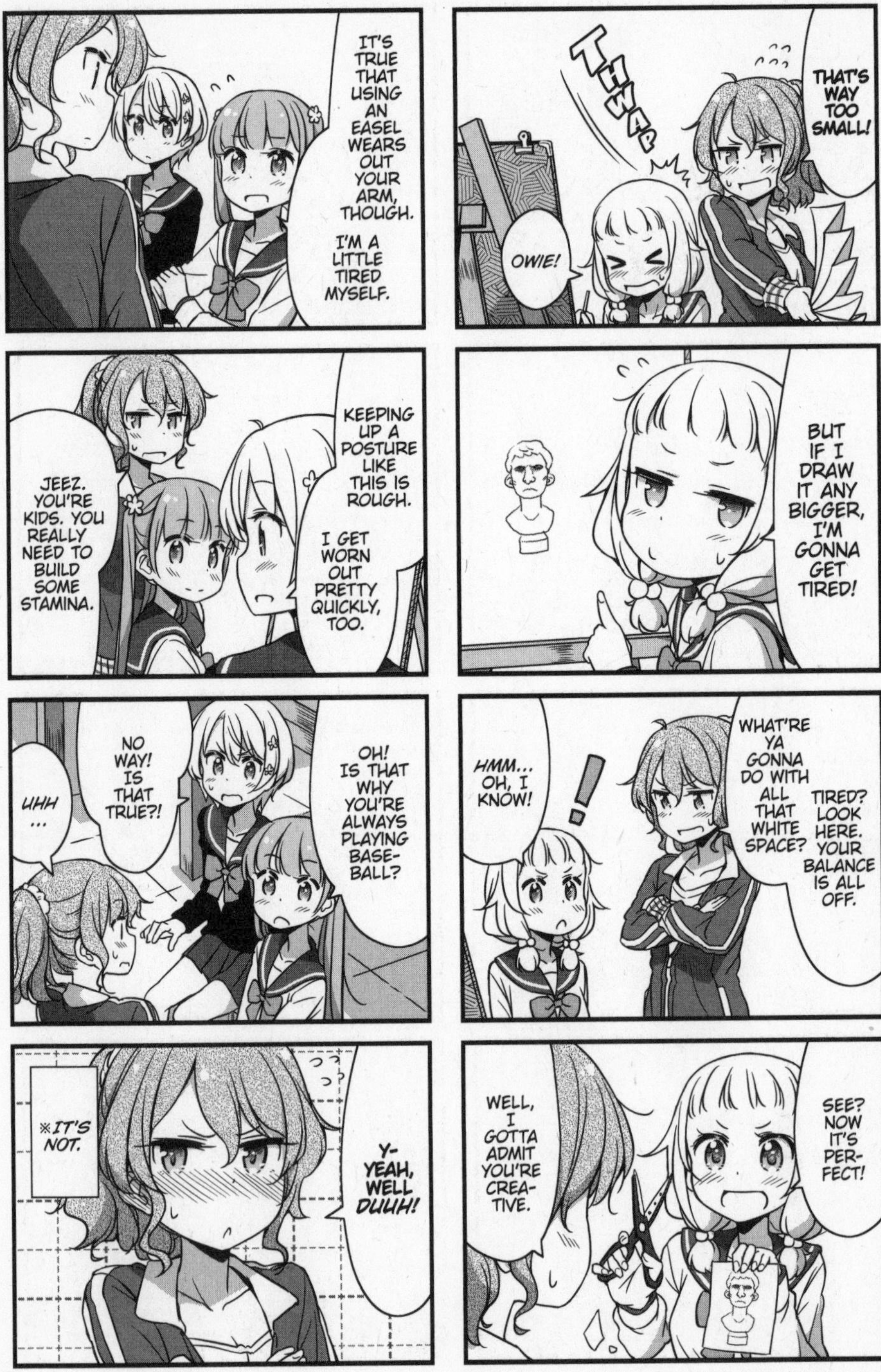
THAT'S WAY TOO SMALL!
THWAP
OWIE!
IT'S TRUE THAT USING AN EASEL WEARS OUT YOUR ARM, THOUGH.
I'M A LITTLE TIRED MYSELF.
BUT IF I DRAW IT ANY BIGGER, I'M GONNA GET TIRED!
KEEPING UP A POSTURE LIKE THIS IS ROUGH.
I GET WORN OUT PRETTY QUICKLY, TOO.
JEEZ. YOU'RE KIDS. YOU REALLY NEED TO BUILD SOME STAMINA.
TIRED? LOOK HERE. YOUR BALANCE IS ALL OFF.
WHAT'RE YA GONNA DO WITH ALL THAT WHITE SPACE?
HMM... OH, I KNOW!
!
OH! IS THAT WHY YOU'RE ALWAYS PLAYING BASEBALL?
NO WAY! IS THAT TRUE?!
UHH...
SEE? NOW IT'S PERFECT!
WELL, I GOTTA ADMIT YOU'RE CREATIVE.
Y-YEAH, WELL DUUH!
※IT'S NOT.

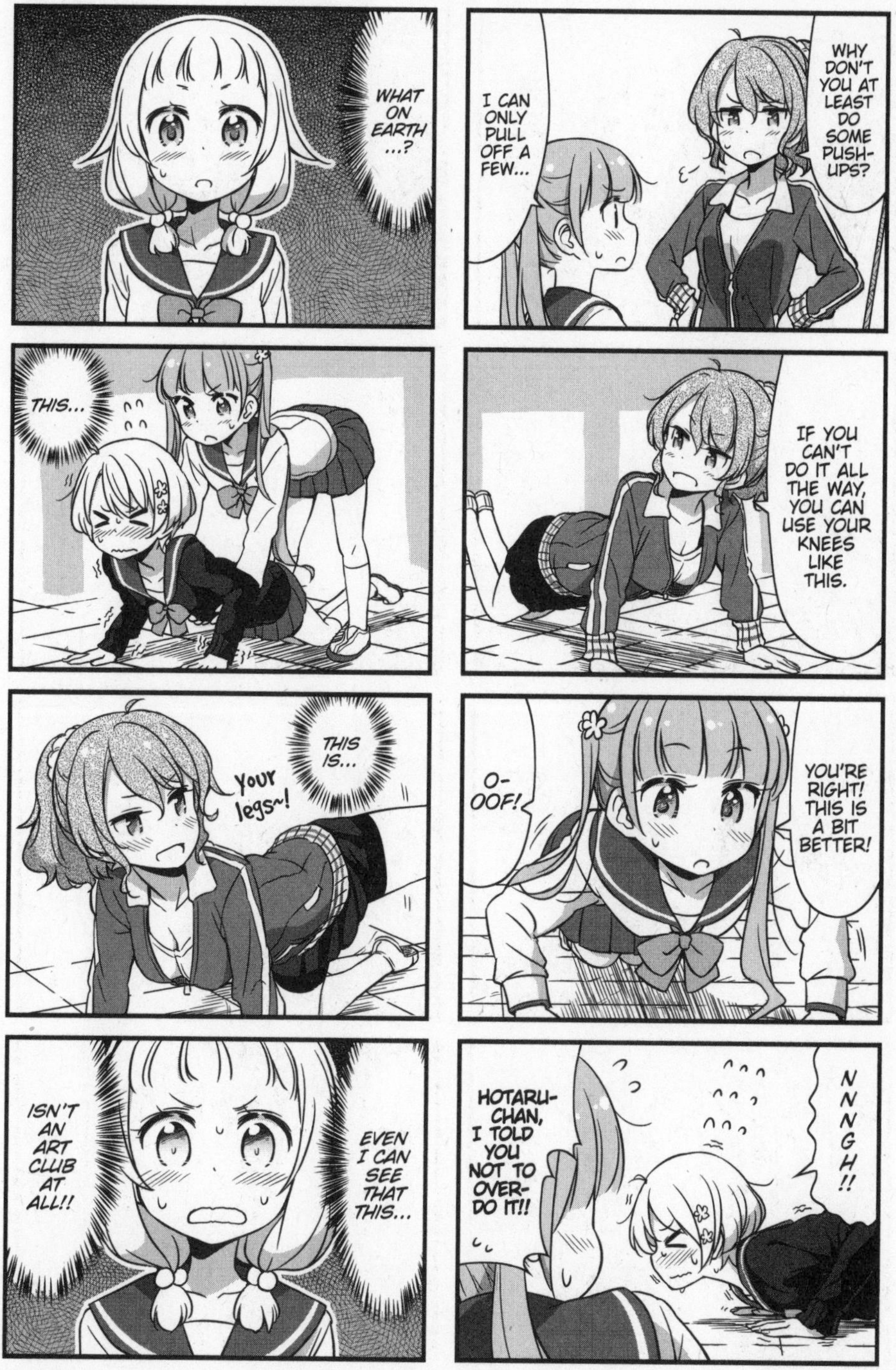
WHY DON'T YOU AT LEAST DO SOME PUSH-UPS?
I CAN ONLY PULL OFF A FEW...
WHAT ON EARTH ...?
IF YOU CAN'T DO IT ALL THE WAY, YOU CAN USE YOUR KNEES LIKE THIS.
THIS...
YOU'RE RIGHT! THIS IS A BIT BETTER!
O-OOF!
THIS IS...
Your legs~!
NNNGH!!
HOTARU-CHAN, I TOLD YOU NOT TO OVER-DO IT!!
EVEN I CAN SEE THAT THIS...
ISN'T AN ART CLUB AT ALL!!

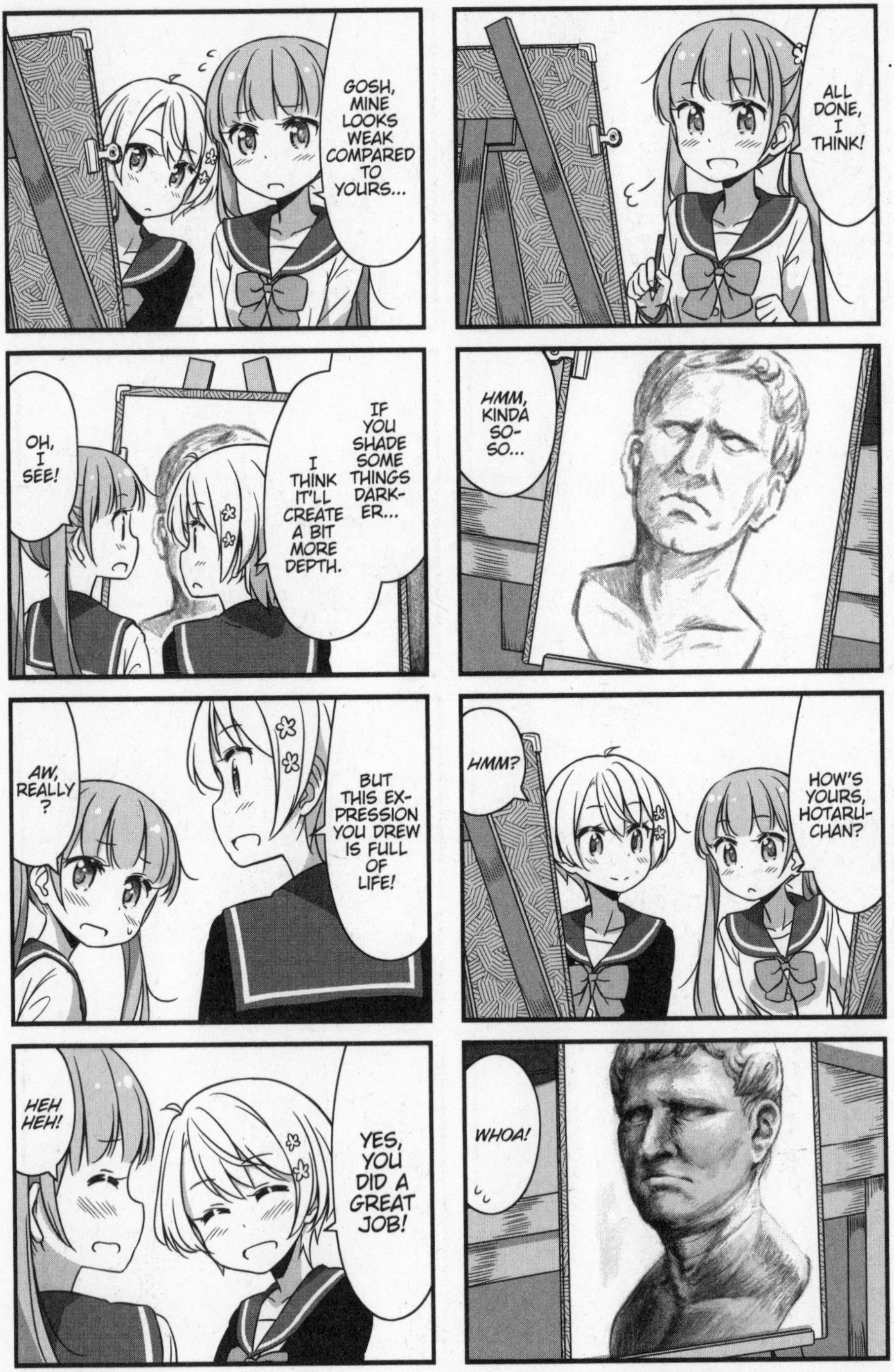
ALL DONE, I THINK!
HMM, KINDA SO-SO...
HOW'S YOURS, HOTARU-CHAN?
HMM?
WHOA!
GOSH, MINE LOOKS WEAK COMPARED TO YOURS...
IF YOU SHADE SOME THINGS DARKER...
I THINK IT'LL CREATE A BIT MORE DEPTH.
OH, I SEE!
BUT THIS EXPRESSION YOU DREW IS FULL OF LIFE!
AW, REALLY?
YES, YOU DID A GREAT JOB!
HEH HEH!

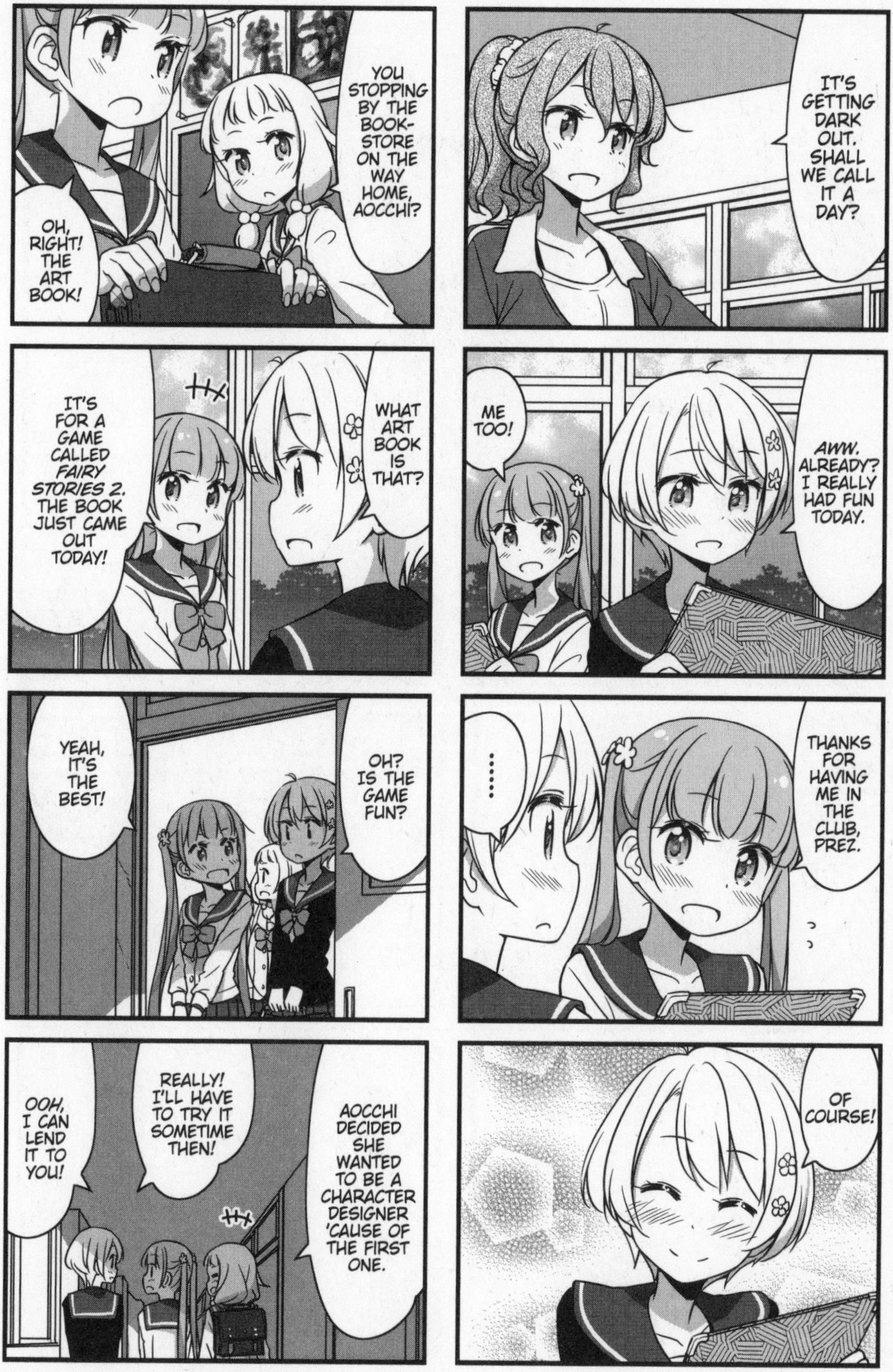
IT'S GETTING DARK OUT. SHALL WE CALL IT A DAY?
YOU STOPPING BY THE BOOK-STORE ON THE WAY HOME, AOCCHI?
OH, RIGHT! THE ART BOOK!
AWW. ALREADY? I REALLY HAD FUN TODAY.
ME TOO!
WHAT ART BOOK IS THAT?
IT'S FOR A GAME CALLED *FAIRY STORIES 2*. THE BOOK JUST CAME OUT TODAY!
THANKS FOR HAVING ME IN THE CLUB, PREZ.
......
OH? IS THE GAME FUN?
YEAH, IT'S THE BEST!
OF COURSE!
AOCCHI DECIDED SHE WANTED TO BE A CHARACTER DESIGNER 'CAUSE OF THE FIRST ONE.
REALLY! I'LL HAVE TO TRY IT SOMETIME THEN!
OOH, I CAN LEND IT TO YOU!

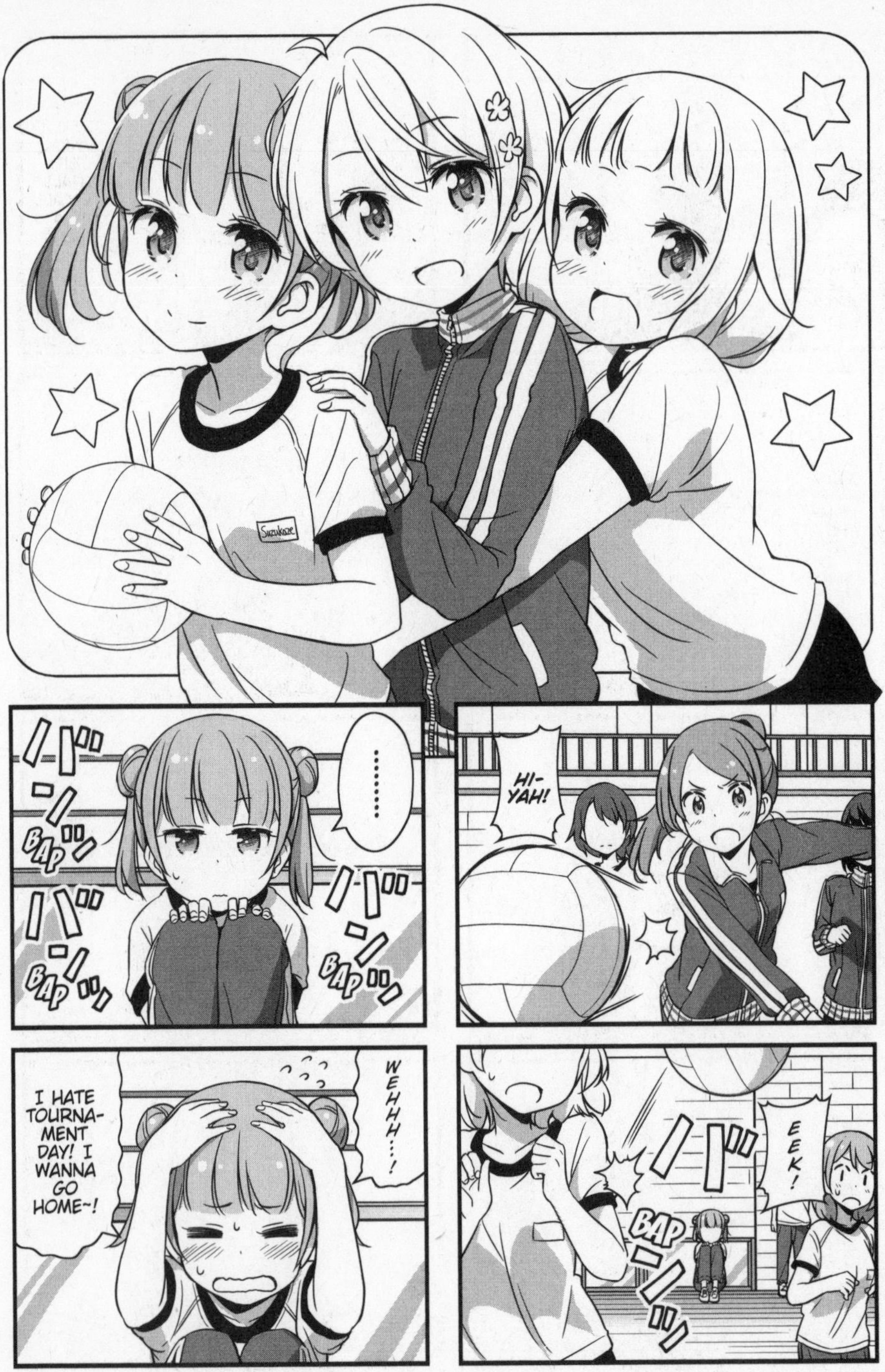
Suzukaze
HI-YAH!
....
BAP
BAP
BAP
EEK!
BAP
WEHHH...!
I HATE TOURNAMENT DAY! I WANNA GO HOME~!

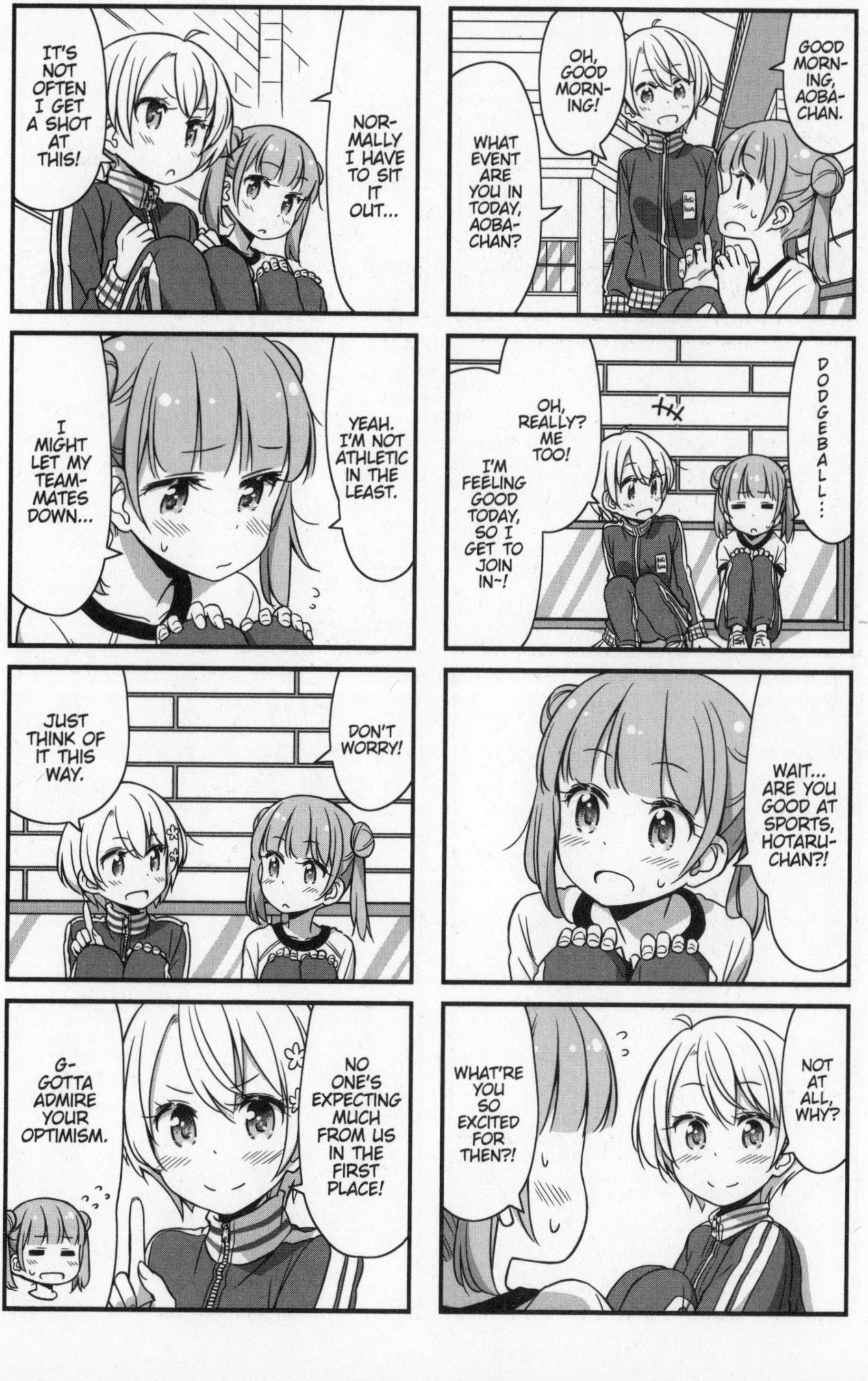
GOOD MORNING, AOBA-CHAN.
OH, GOOD MORNING!
WHAT EVENT ARE YOU IN TODAY, AOBA-CHAN?
DODGEBALL...
OH, REALLY? ME TOO!
I'M FEELING GOOD TODAY, SO I GET TO JOIN IN~!
WAIT... ARE YOU GOOD AT SPORTS, HOTARU-CHAN?!
NOT AT ALL, WHY?
WHAT'RE YOU SO EXCITED FOR THEN?!
NORMALLY I HAVE TO SIT IT OUT...
IT'S NOT OFTEN I GET A SHOT AT THIS!
YEAH. I'M NOT ATHLETIC IN THE LEAST.
I MIGHT LET MY TEAMMATES DOWN...
DON'T WORRY!
JUST THINK OF IT THIS WAY.
NO ONE'S EXPECTING MUCH FROM US IN THE FIRST PLACE!
G-GOTTA ADMIRE YOUR OPTIMISM.

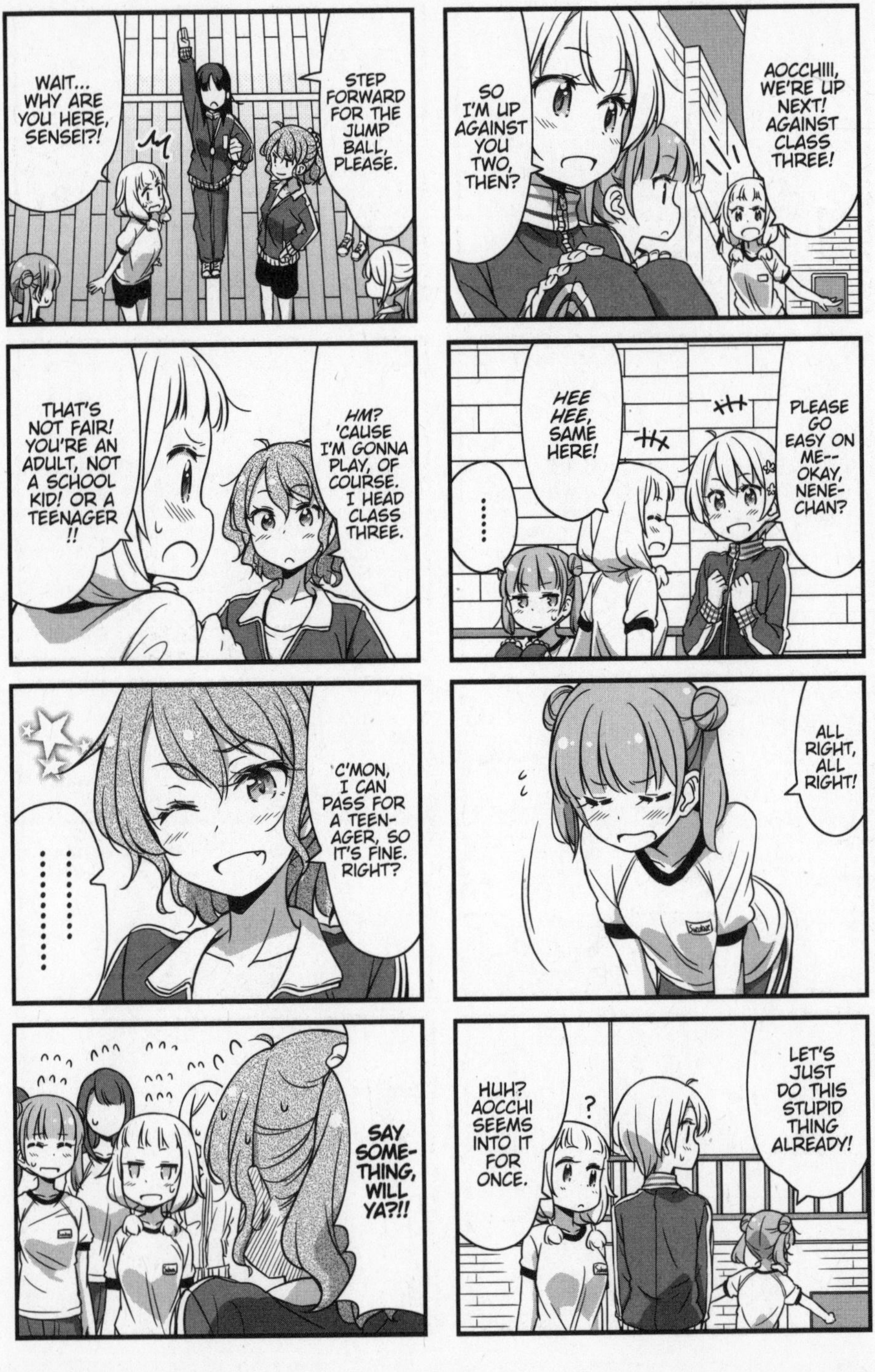
AOCCHIII, WE'RE UP NEXT! AGAINST CLASS THREE!
SO I'M UP AGAINST YOU TWO, THEN?
PLEASE GO EASY ON ME--OKAY, NENE-CHAN?
HEE HEE, SAME HERE!
......
ALL RIGHT, ALL RIGHT!
LET'S JUST DO THIS STUPID THING ALREADY!
?
HUH? AOCCHI SEEMS INTO IT FOR ONCE.
STEP FORWARD FOR THE JUMP BALL, PLEASE.
WAIT... WHY ARE YOU HERE, SENSEI?!
HM? 'CAUSE I'M GONNA PLAY, OF COURSE. I HEAD CLASS THREE.
THAT'S NOT FAIR! YOU'RE AN ADULT, NOT A SCHOOL KID! OR A TEENAGER!!
C'MON, I CAN PASS FOR A TEENAGER, SO IT'S FINE. RIGHT?
....
SAY SOMETHING, WILL YA?!!

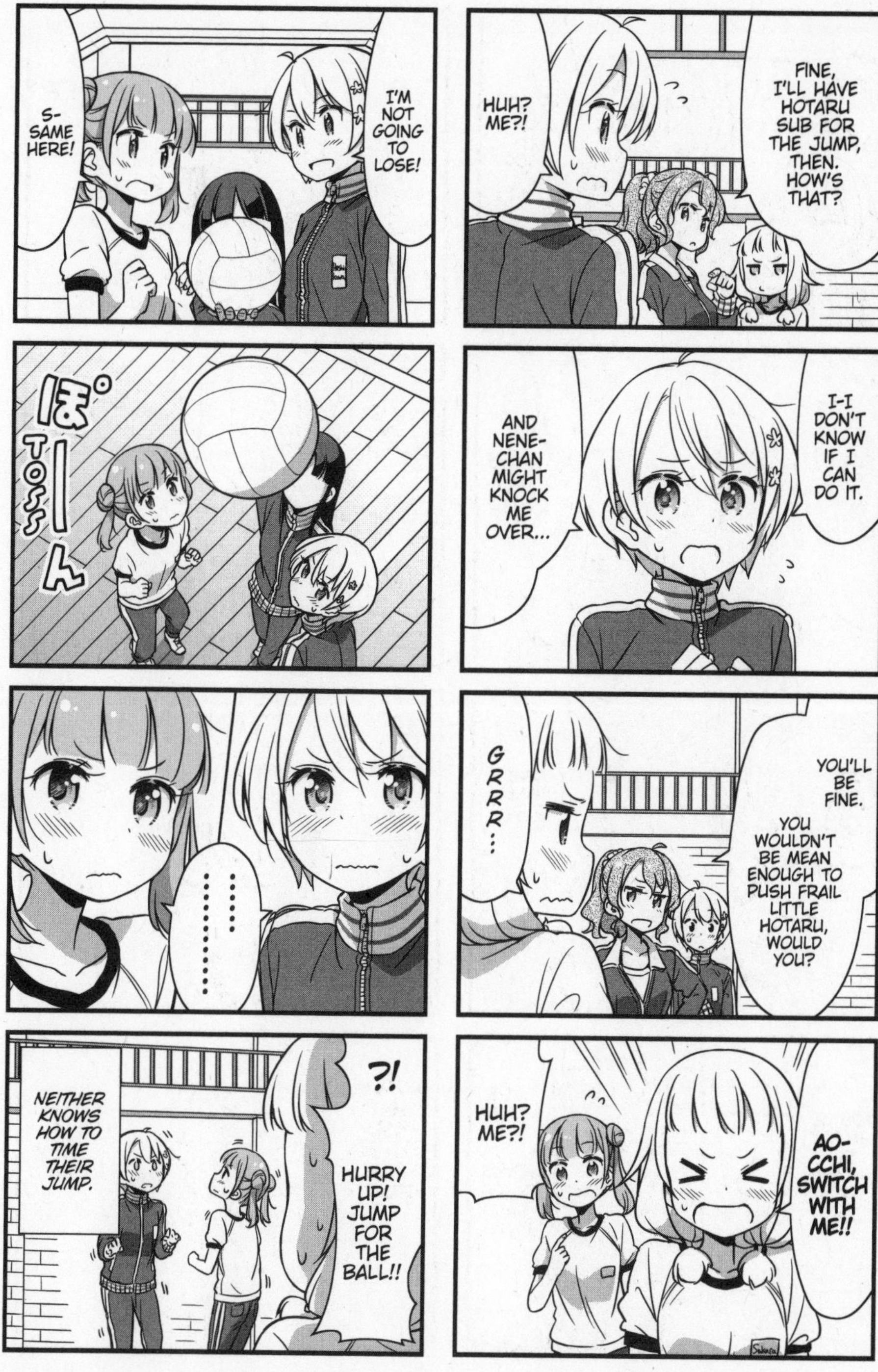
FINE, I'LL HAVE HOTARU SUB FOR THE JUMP, THEN. HOW'S THAT?
HUH? ME?!
I'M NOT GOING TO LOSE!
S-SAME HERE!
I-I DON'T KNOW IF I CAN DO IT.
AND NENE-CHAN MIGHT KNOCK ME OVER...
ぽーん
TOSS
YOU'LL BE FINE.
YOU WOULDN'T BE MEAN ENOUGH TO PUSH FRAIL LITTLE HOTARU, WOULD YOU?
GRRR...
......
AO-CCHI, SWITCH WITH ME!!
HUH? ME?!
?!
HURRY UP! JUMP FOR THE BALL!!
NEITHER KNOWS HOW TO TIME THEIR JUMP.

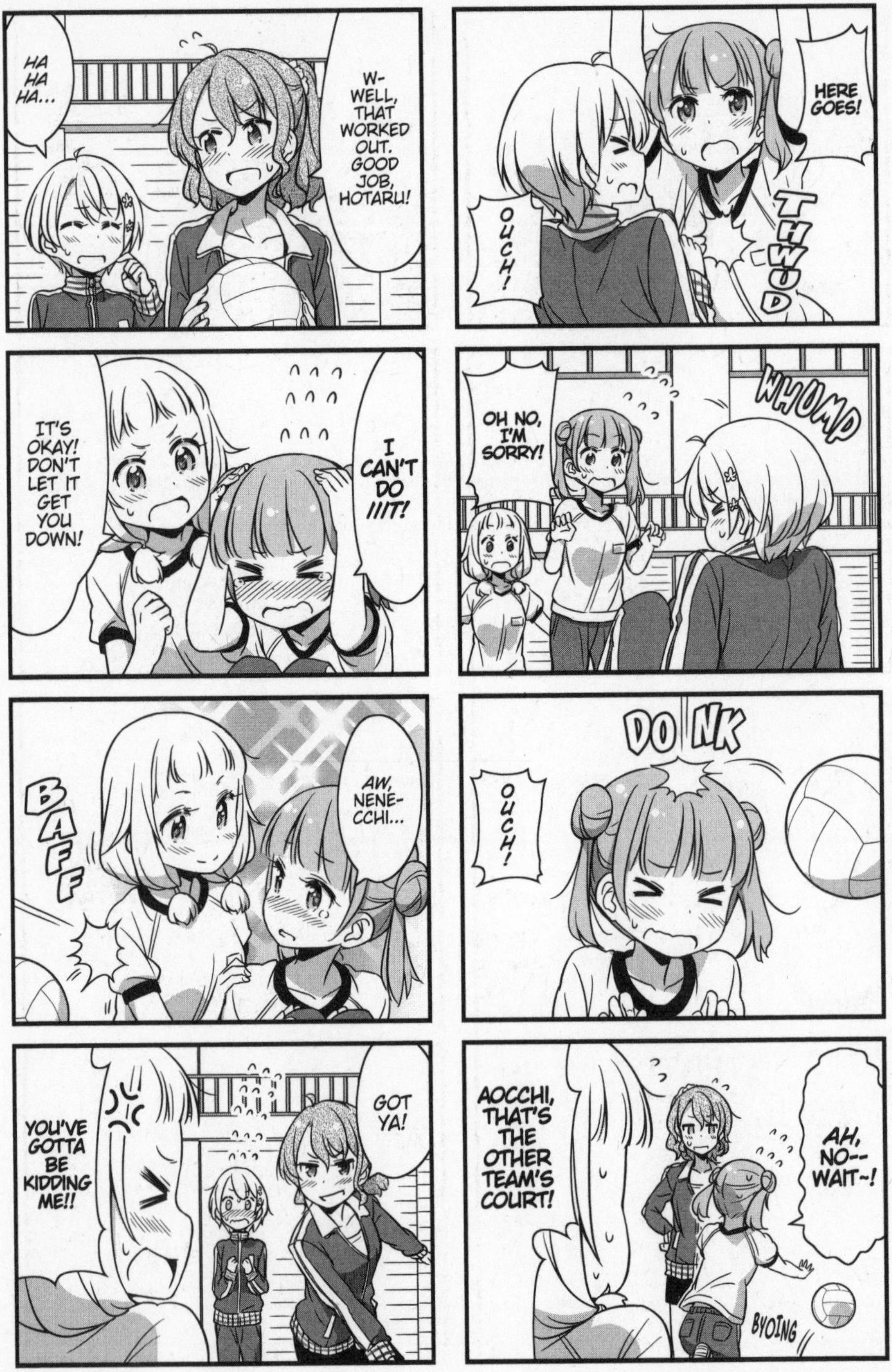
HERE GOES!
OUCH!
THWUD
W-WELL, THAT WORKED OUT. GOOD JOB, HOTARU!
HA HA HA...
WHUMP
OH NO, I'M SORRY!
I CAN'T DO IIIIT!
IT'S OKAY! DON'T LET IT GET YOU DOWN!
DONK
OUCH!
AW, NENE-CCHI...
BAFF
AH, NO-- WAIT~!
AOCCHI, THAT'S THE OTHER TEAM'S COURT!
BYOING
GOT YA!
YOU'VE GOTTA BE KIDDING ME!!

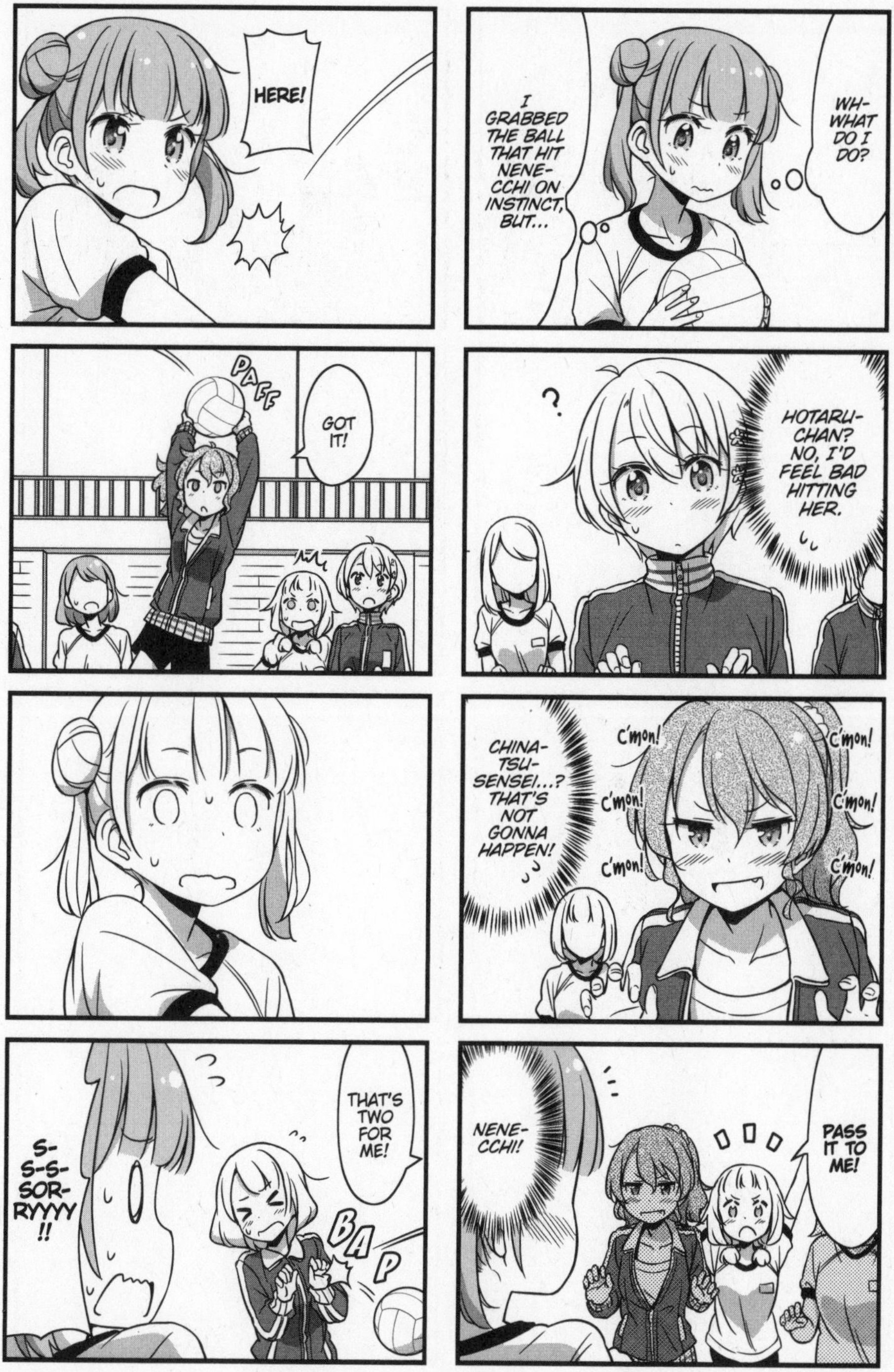
WH-WHAT DO I DO?
I GRABBED THE BALL THAT HIT NENE-CCHI ON INSTINCT, BUT...
HERE!
?
HOTARU-CHAN? NO, I'D FEEL BAD HITTING HER.
GOT IT!
PAFF
C'mon!
C'mon!
C'mon!
C'mon!
C'mon!
C'mon!
CHINA-TSU-SENSEI...? THAT'S NOT GONNA HAPPEN!
PASS IT TO ME!
NENE-CCHI!
THAT'S TWO FOR ME!
BAP
S-S-S-SOR-RYYYY!!

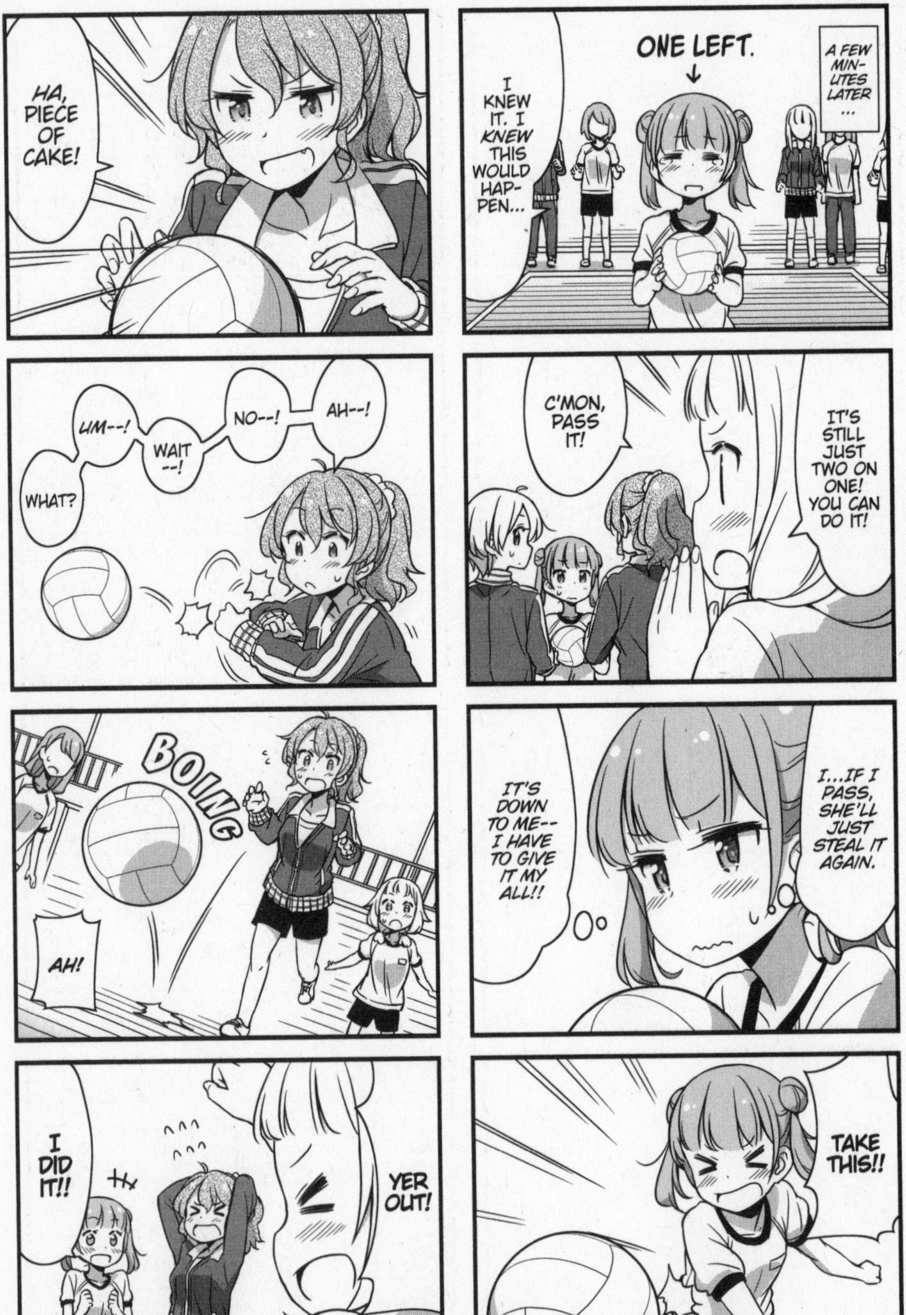
A FEW MIN-UTES LATER...
ONE LEFT. ↓
I KNEW IT. I KNEW THIS WOULD HAP-PEN...
HA, PIECE OF CAKE!
IT'S STILL JUST TWO ON ONE! YOU CAN DO IT!
C'MON, PASS IT!
AH--!
NO--!
WAIT --!
UM--!
WHAT?
I...IF I PASS, SHE'LL JUST STEAL IT AGAIN.
IT'S DOWN TO ME-- I HAVE TO GIVE IT MY ALL!!
BOING
AH!
TAKE THIS!!
YER OUT!
I DID IT!!

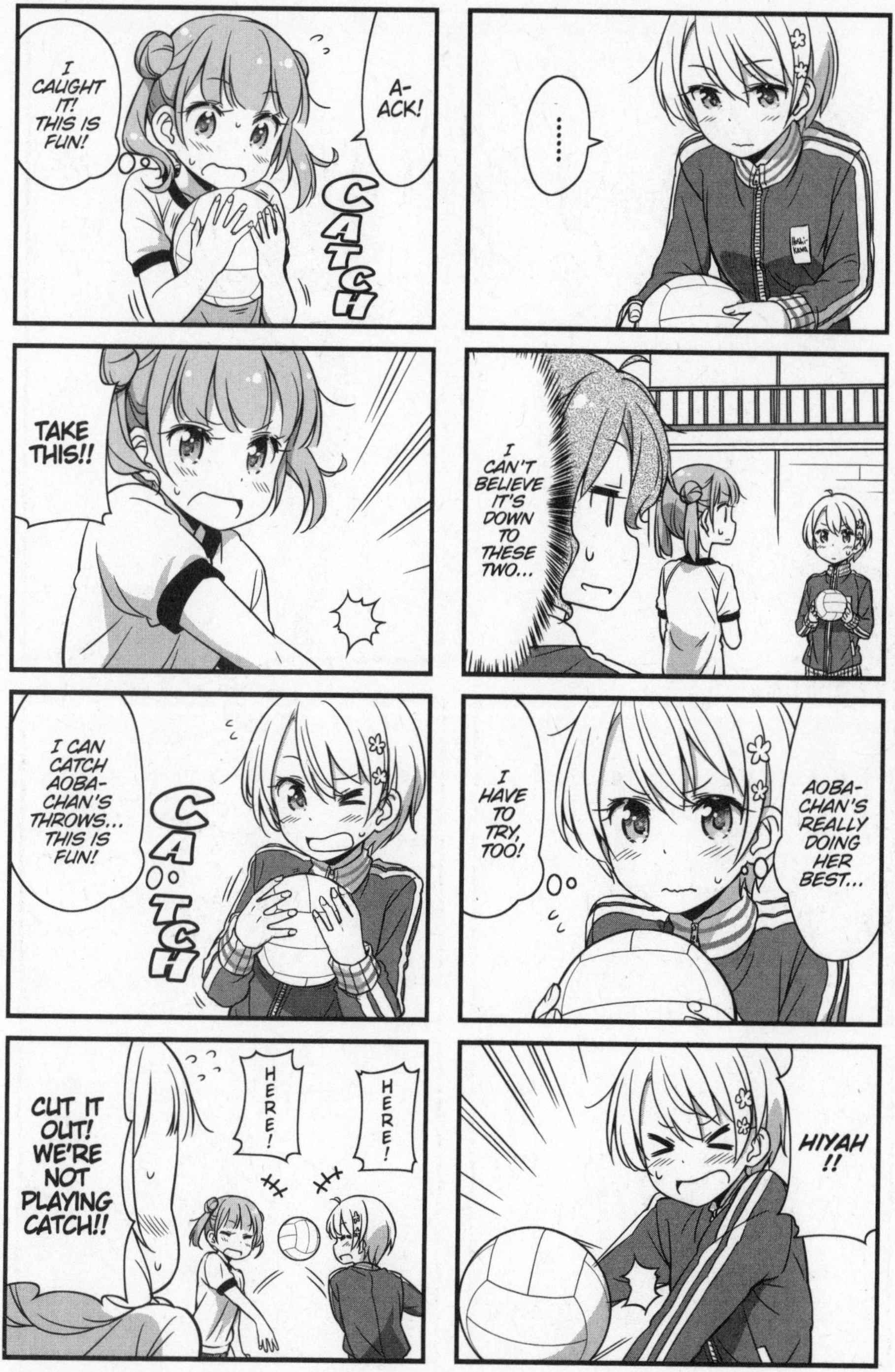
……
A-ACK!
I CAUGHT IT! THIS IS FUN!
CATCH
I CAN'T BELIEVE IT'S DOWN TO THESE TWO…
TAKE THIS!!
AOBA-CHAN'S REALLY DOING HER BEST…
I HAVE TO TRY, TOO!
CATCH
I CAN CATCH AOBA-CHAN'S THROWS… THIS IS FUN!
HIYAH!!
HERE!
HERE!
CUT IT OUT! WE'RE NOT PLAYING CATCH!!

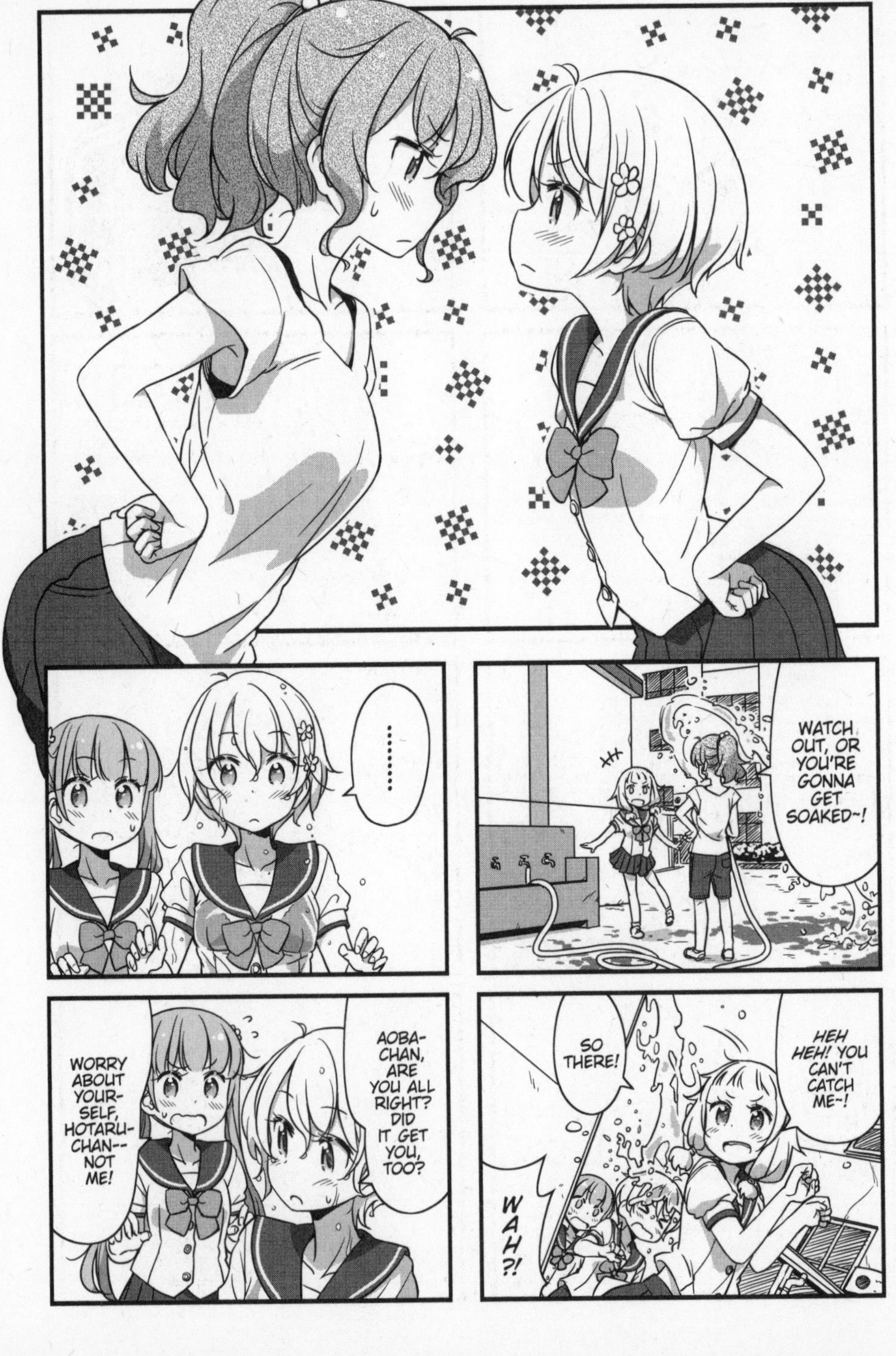
WATCH OUT, OR YOU'RE GONNA GET SOAKED~!
......
HEH HEH! YOU CAN'T CATCH ME~!
SO THERE!
WAH?!
AOBA-CHAN, ARE YOU ALL RIGHT? DID IT GET YOU, TOO?
WORRY ABOUT YOURSELF, HOTARU-CHAN--NOT ME!

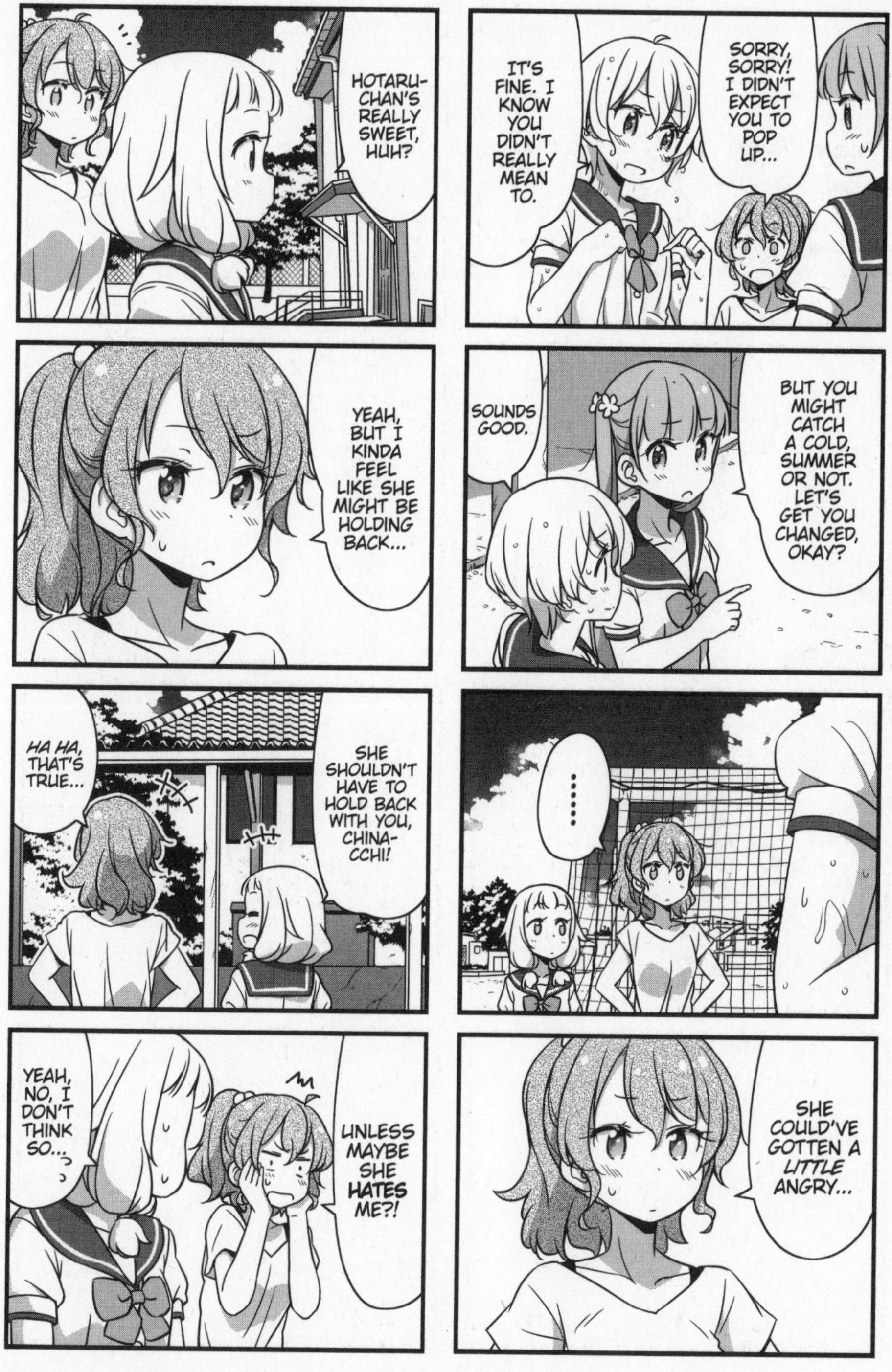
SORRY, SORRY! I DIDN'T EXPECT YOU TO POP UP...
IT'S FINE. I KNOW YOU DIDN'T REALLY MEAN TO.
BUT YOU MIGHT CATCH A COLD, SUMMER OR NOT. LET'S GET YOU CHANGED, OKAY?
SOUNDS GOOD.
......
SHE COULD'VE GOTTEN A *LITTLE* ANGRY...
HOTARU-CHAN'S REALLY SWEET, HUH?
YEAH, BUT I KINDA FEEL LIKE SHE MIGHT BE HOLDING BACK...
SHE SHOULDN'T HAVE TO HOLD BACK WITH YOU, CHINA-CCHI!
HA HA, THAT'S TRUE...
UNLESS MAYBE SHE **HATES** ME?!
YEAH, NO, I DON'T THINK SO...

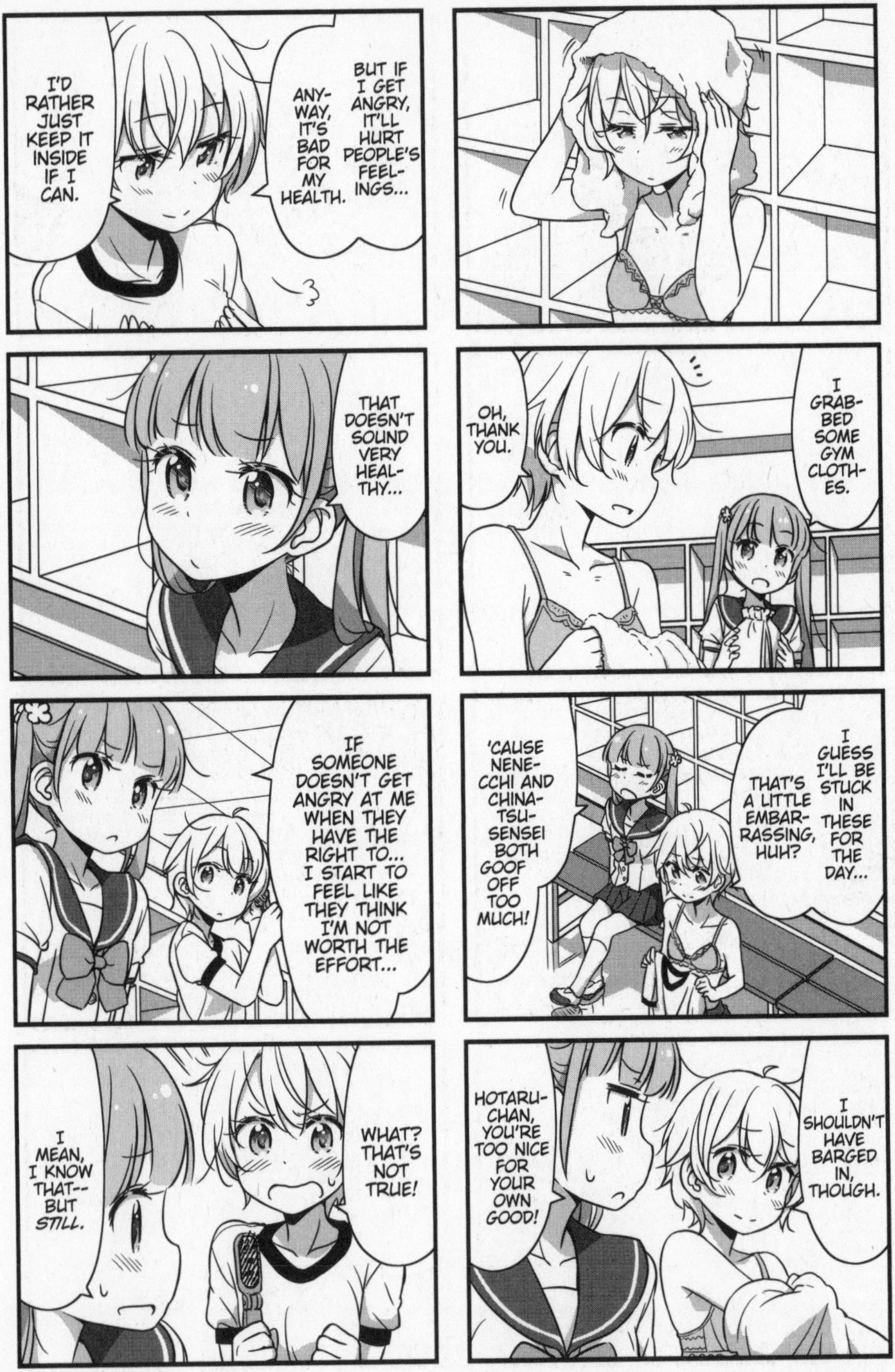
BUT IF I GET ANGRY, IT'LL HURT PEOPLE'S FEELINGS...
ANYWAY, IT'S BAD FOR MY HEALTH.
I'D RATHER JUST KEEP IT INSIDE IF I CAN.
I GRABBED SOME GYM CLOTHES.
OH, THANK YOU.
THAT DOESN'T SOUND VERY HEALTHY...
I GUESS I'LL BE STUCK IN THESE FOR THE DAY...
THAT'S A LITTLE EMBARRASSING, HUH?
'CAUSE NENECCHI AND CHINATSU-SENSEI BOTH GOOF OFF TOO MUCH!
IF SOMEONE DOESN'T GET ANGRY AT ME WHEN THEY HAVE THE RIGHT TO... I START TO FEEL LIKE THEY THINK I'M NOT WORTH THE EFFORT...
I SHOULDN'T HAVE BARGED IN, THOUGH.
HOTARU-CHAN, YOU'RE TOO NICE FOR YOUR OWN GOOD!
WHAT? THAT'S NOT TRUE!
I MEAN, I KNOW THAT-- BUT *STILL*.

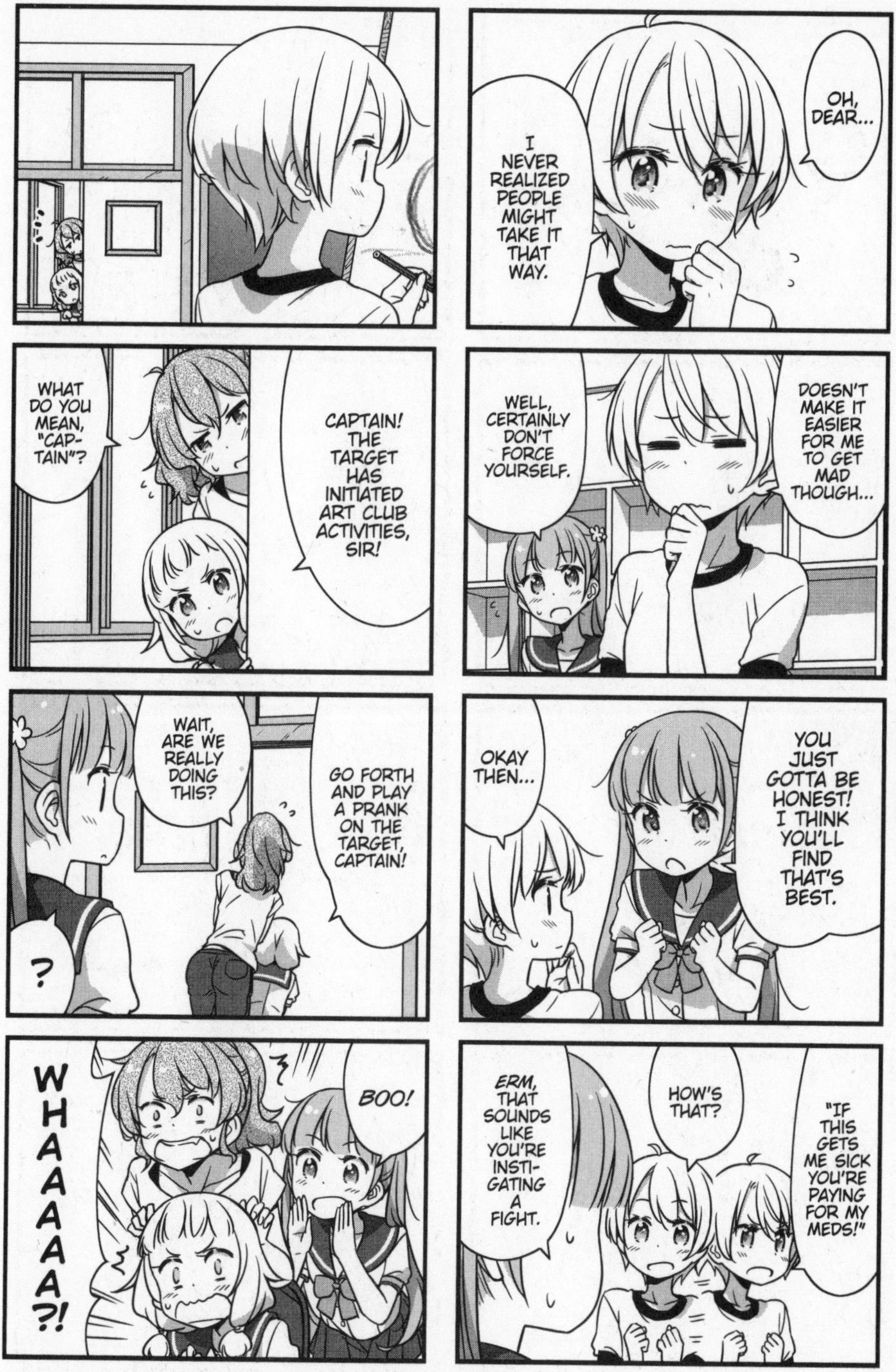
OH, DEAR...
I NEVER REALIZED PEOPLE MIGHT TAKE IT THAT WAY.
DOESN'T MAKE IT EASIER FOR ME TO GET MAD THOUGH...
WELL, CERTAINLY DON'T FORCE YOURSELF.
CAPTAIN! THE TARGET HAS INITIATED ART CLUB ACTIVITIES, SIR!
WHAT DO YOU MEAN, "CAP-TAIN"?
YOU JUST GOTTA BE HONEST! I THINK YOU'LL FIND THAT'S BEST.
OKAY THEN...
GO FORTH AND PLAY A PRANK ON THE TARGET, CAPTAIN!
WAIT, ARE WE REALLY DOING THIS?
?
"IF THIS GETS ME SICK YOU'RE PAYING FOR MY MEDS!"
HOW'S THAT?
ERM, THAT SOUNDS LIKE YOU'RE INSTI-GATING A FIGHT.
BOO!
WHAAAAA?!

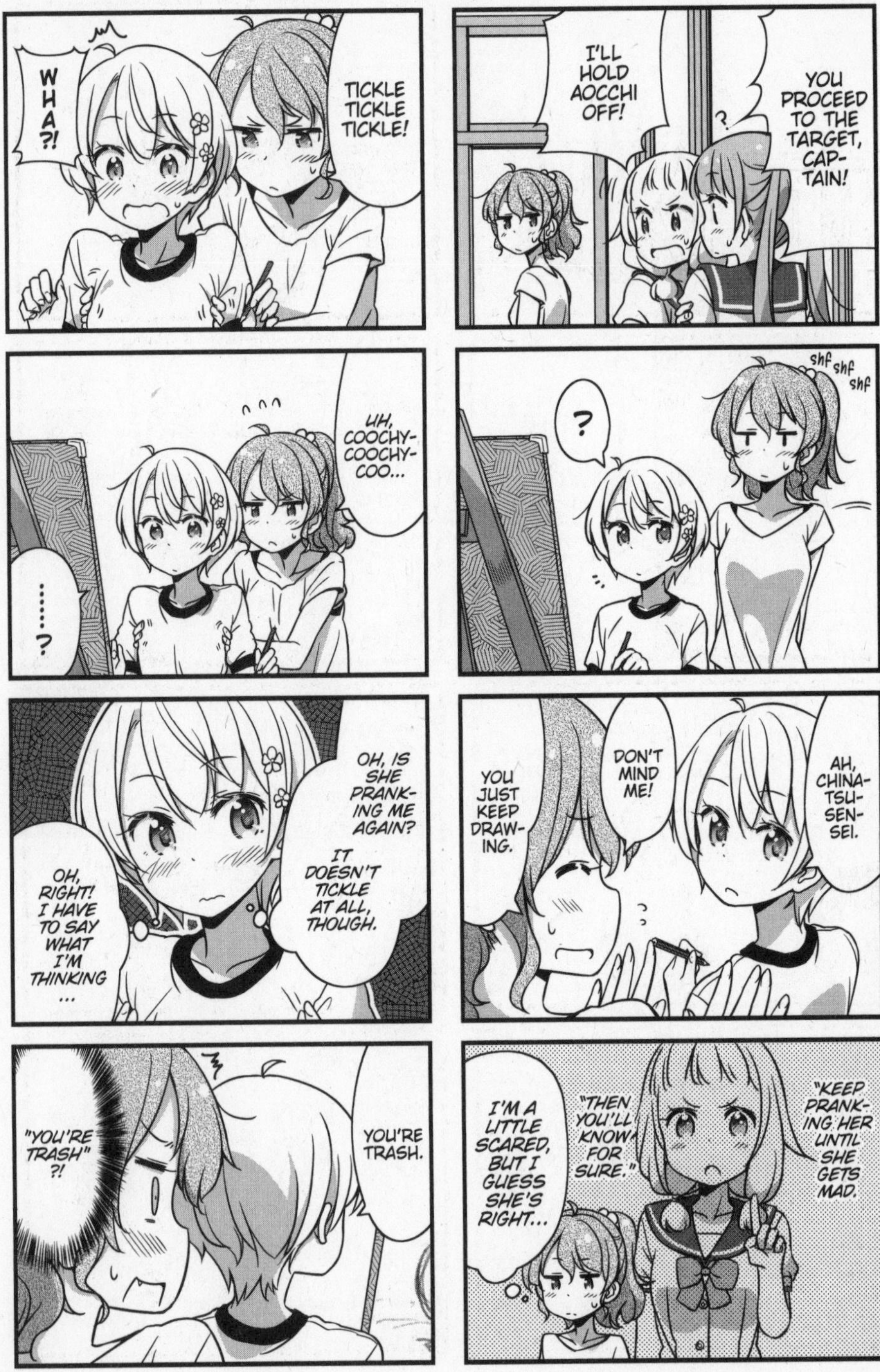
YOU PROCEED TO THE TARGET, CAP-TAIN!
?
I'LL HOLD AOCCHI OFF!
TICKLE TICKLE TICKLE!
WHA?!
shf shf shf
?
UH, COOCHY-COOCHY-COO...
......?
AH, CHINA-TSU-SEN-SEI.
DON'T MIND ME!
YOU JUST KEEP DRAW-ING.
OH, IS SHE PRANK-ING ME AGAIN?
IT DOESN'T TICKLE AT ALL, THOUGH.
OH, RIGHT! I HAVE TO SAY WHAT I'M THINKING ...
"KEEP PRANK-ING HER UNTIL SHE GETS MAD.
"THEN YOU'LL KNOW FOR SURE."
I'M A LITTLE SCARED, BUT I GUESS SHE'S RIGHT...
YOU'RE TRASH.
"YOU'RE TRASH" ?!

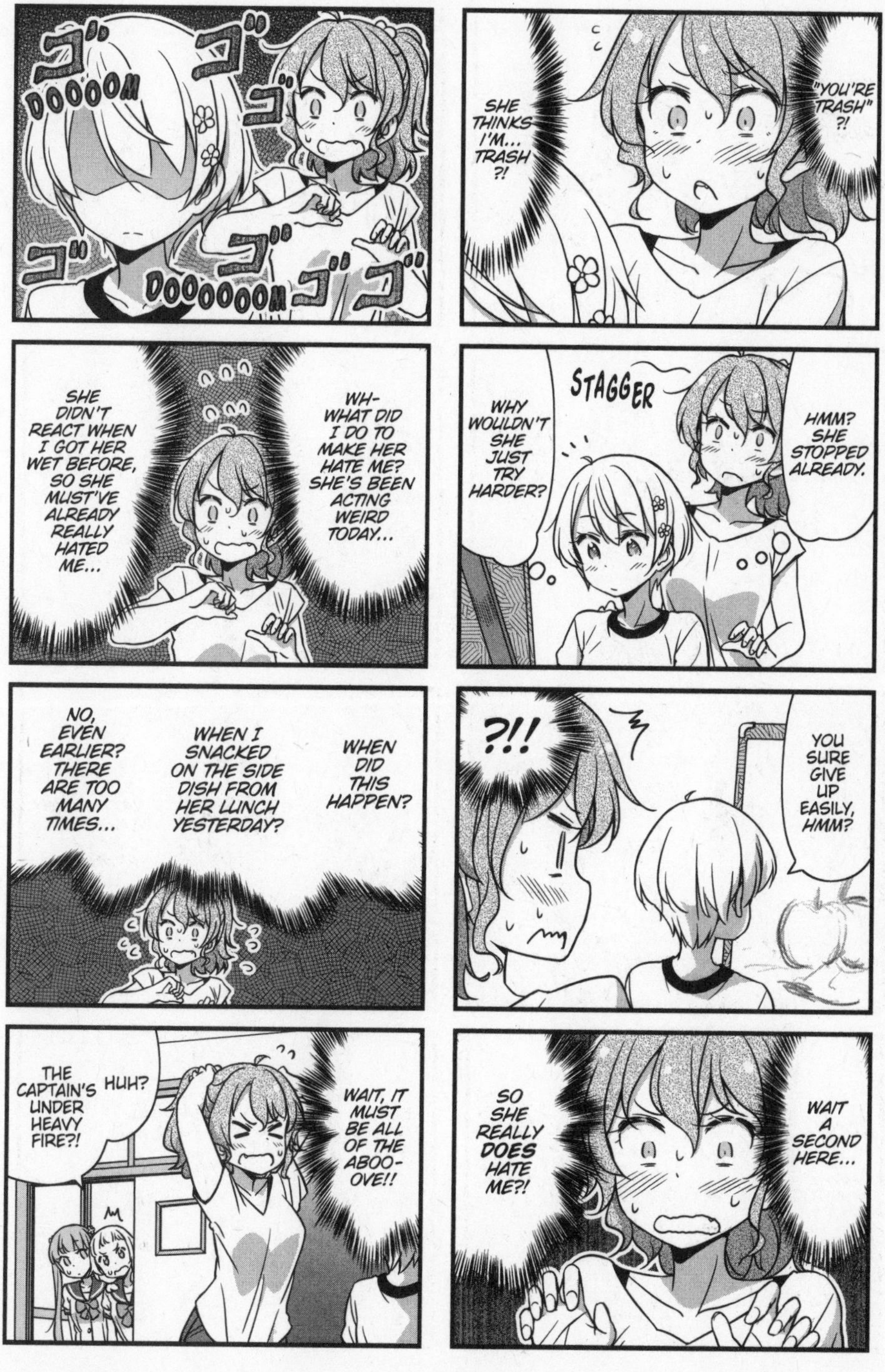
"YOU'RE TRASH" ?!
SHE THINKS I'M... TRASH ?!
DOOOOOM
DOOOOOOOM
HMM? SHE STOPPED ALREADY.
STAGGER
WHY WOULDN'T SHE JUST TRY HARDER?
WH- WHAT DID I DO TO MAKE HER HATE ME? SHE'S BEEN ACTING WEIRD TODAY...
SHE DIDN'T REACT WHEN I GOT HER WET BEFORE, SO SHE MUST'VE ALREADY REALLY HATED ME...
YOU SURE GIVE UP EASILY, HMM?
?!!
WHEN DID THIS HAPPEN?
WHEN I SNACKED ON THE SIDE DISH FROM HER LUNCH YESTERDAY?
NO, EVEN EARLIER? THERE ARE TOO MANY TIMES...
WAIT A SECOND HERE...
SO SHE REALLY DOES HATE ME?!
WAIT, IT MUST BE ALL OF THE ABOO-OVE!!
HUH?
THE CAPTAIN'S UNDER HEAVY FIRE?!

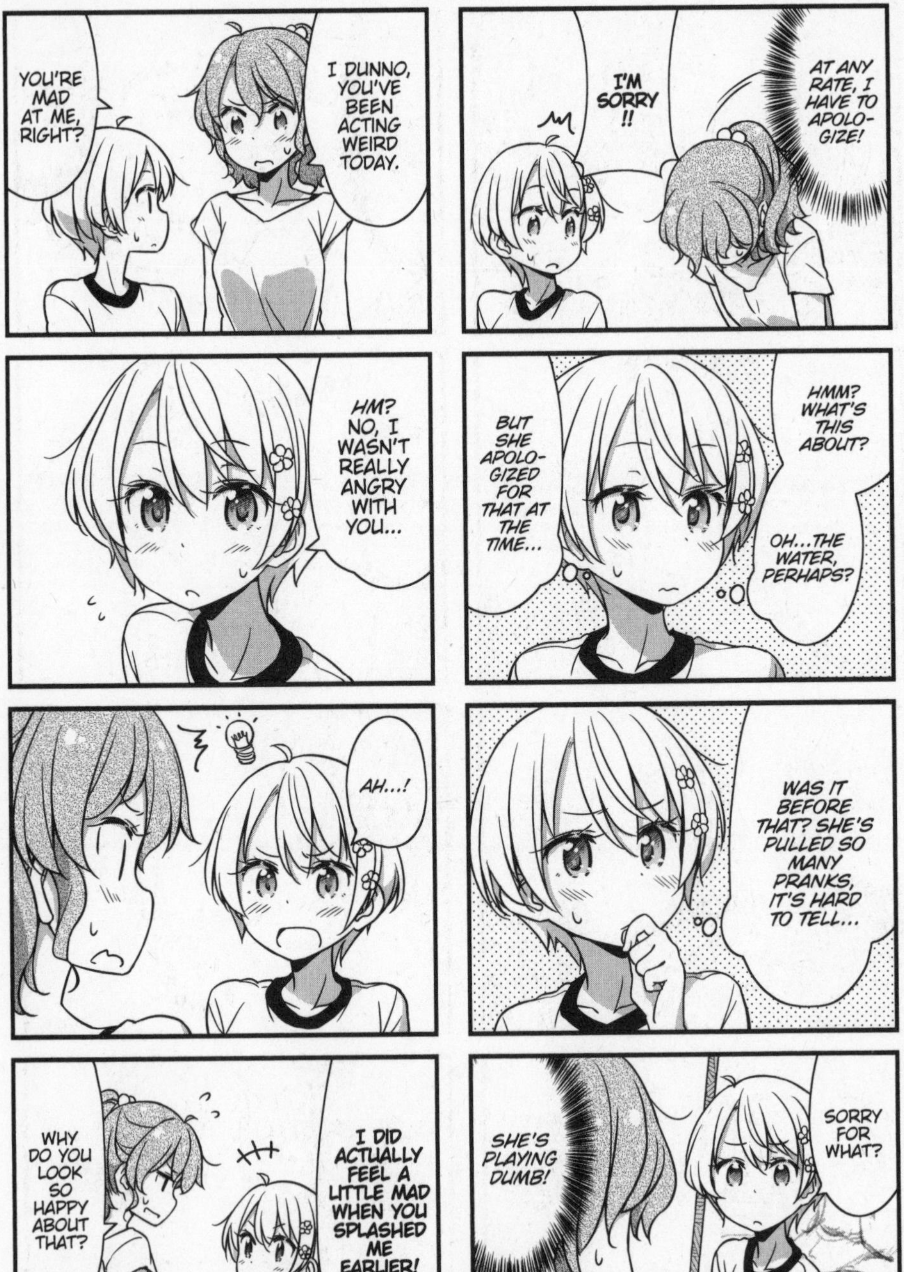
AT ANY RATE, I HAVE TO APOLOGIZE!
I'M SORRY!!
I DUNNO, YOU'VE BEEN ACTING WEIRD TODAY.
YOU'RE MAD AT ME, RIGHT?
HMM? WHAT'S THIS ABOUT?
OH...THE WATER, PERHAPS?
BUT SHE APOLOGIZED FOR THAT AT THE TIME...
HM? NO, I WASN'T REALLY ANGRY WITH YOU...
WAS IT BEFORE THAT? SHE'S PULLED SO MANY PRANKS, IT'S HARD TO TELL...
AH...!
SORRY FOR WHAT?
SHE'S PLAYING DUMB!
I DID ACTUALLY FEEL A LITTLE MAD WHEN YOU SPLASHED ME EARLIER!
WHY DO YOU LOOK SO HAPPY ABOUT THAT?

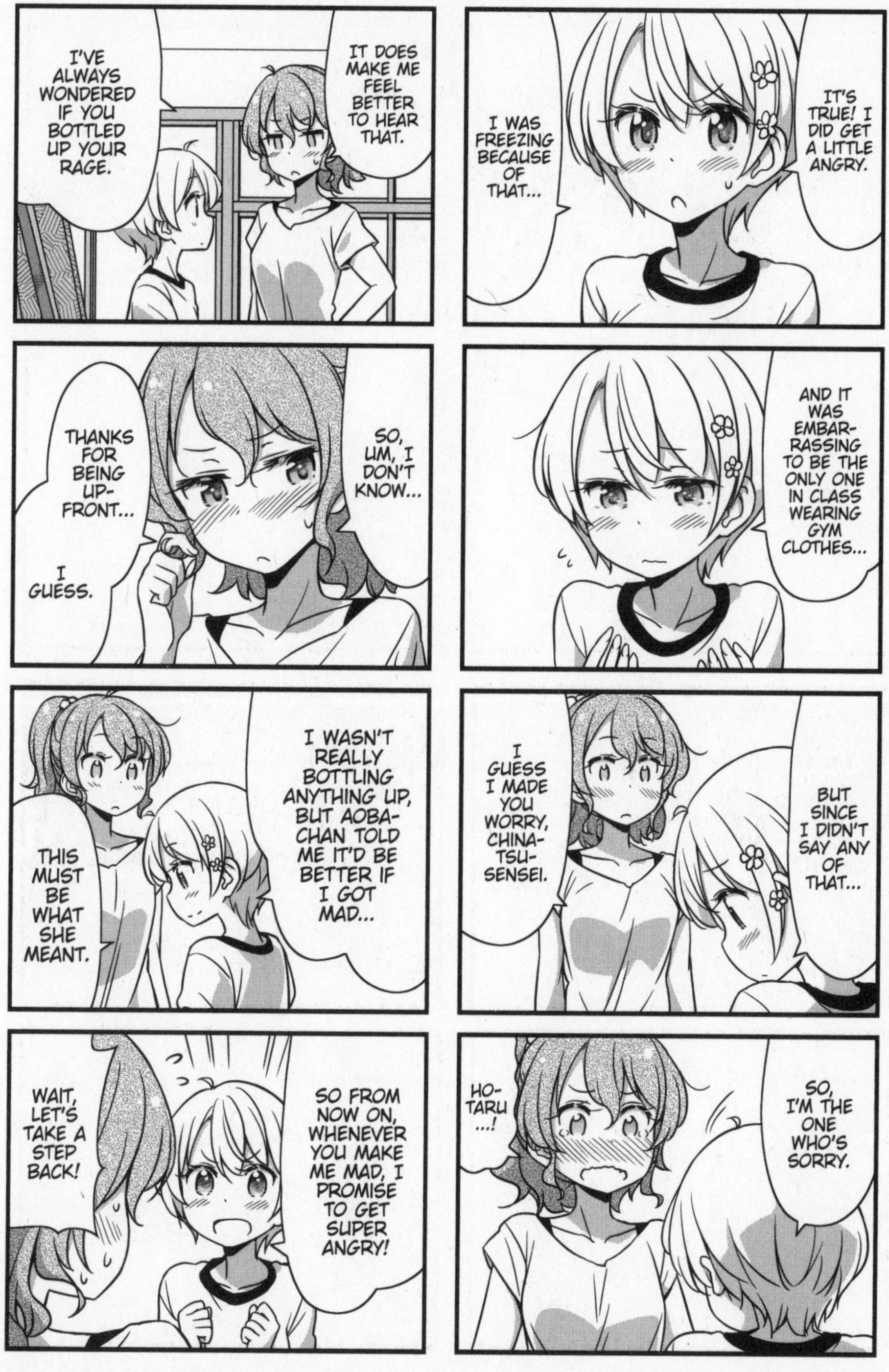
IT'S TRUE! I DID GET A LITTLE ANGRY.
I WAS FREEZING BECAUSE OF THAT...
IT DOES MAKE ME FEEL BETTER TO HEAR THAT.
I'VE ALWAYS WONDERED IF YOU BOTTLED UP YOUR RAGE.
AND IT WAS EMBARRASSING TO BE THE ONLY ONE IN CLASS WEARING GYM CLOTHES...
SO, UM, I DON'T KNOW...
THANKS FOR BEING UP-FRONT...
I GUESS.
BUT SINCE I DIDN'T SAY ANY OF THAT...
I GUESS I MADE YOU WORRY, CHINATSU-SENSEI.
I WASN'T REALLY BOTTLING ANYTHING UP, BUT AOBA-CHAN TOLD ME IT'D BE BETTER IF I GOT MAD...
THIS MUST BE WHAT SHE MEANT.
SO, I'M THE ONE WHO'S SORRY.
HOTARU...!
SO FROM NOW ON, WHENEVER YOU MAKE ME MAD, I PROMISE TO GET SUPER ANGRY!
WAIT, LET'S TAKE A STEP BACK!

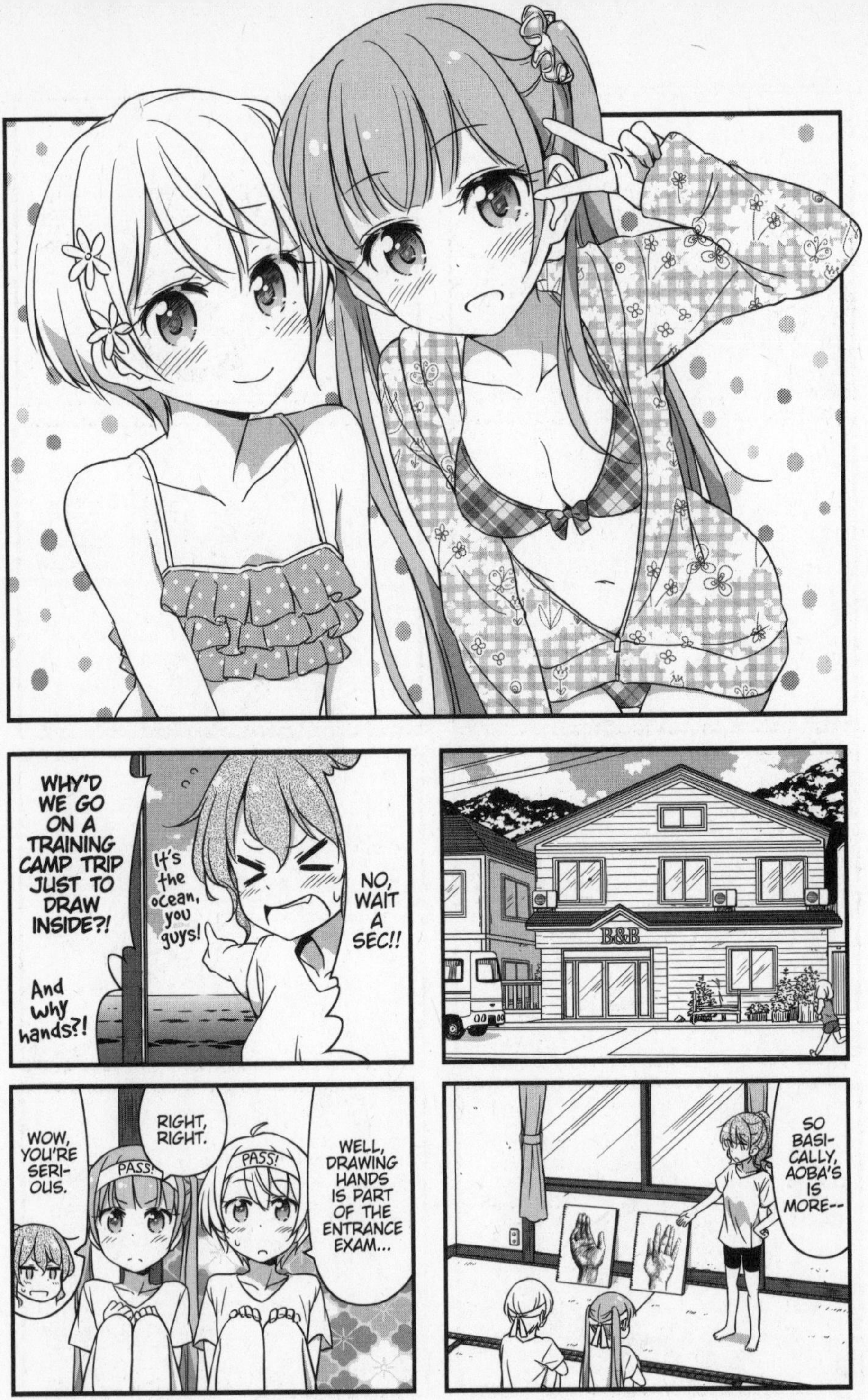
B&B
NO, WAIT A SEC!!
It's the ocean, you guys!
WHY'D WE GO ON A TRAINING CAMP TRIP JUST TO DRAW INSIDE?!
And why hands?!
SO BASICALLY, AOBA'S IS MORE--
WELL, DRAWING HANDS IS PART OF THE ENTRANCE EXAM...
RIGHT, RIGHT.
PASS!
PASS!
WOW, YOU'RE SERIOUS.

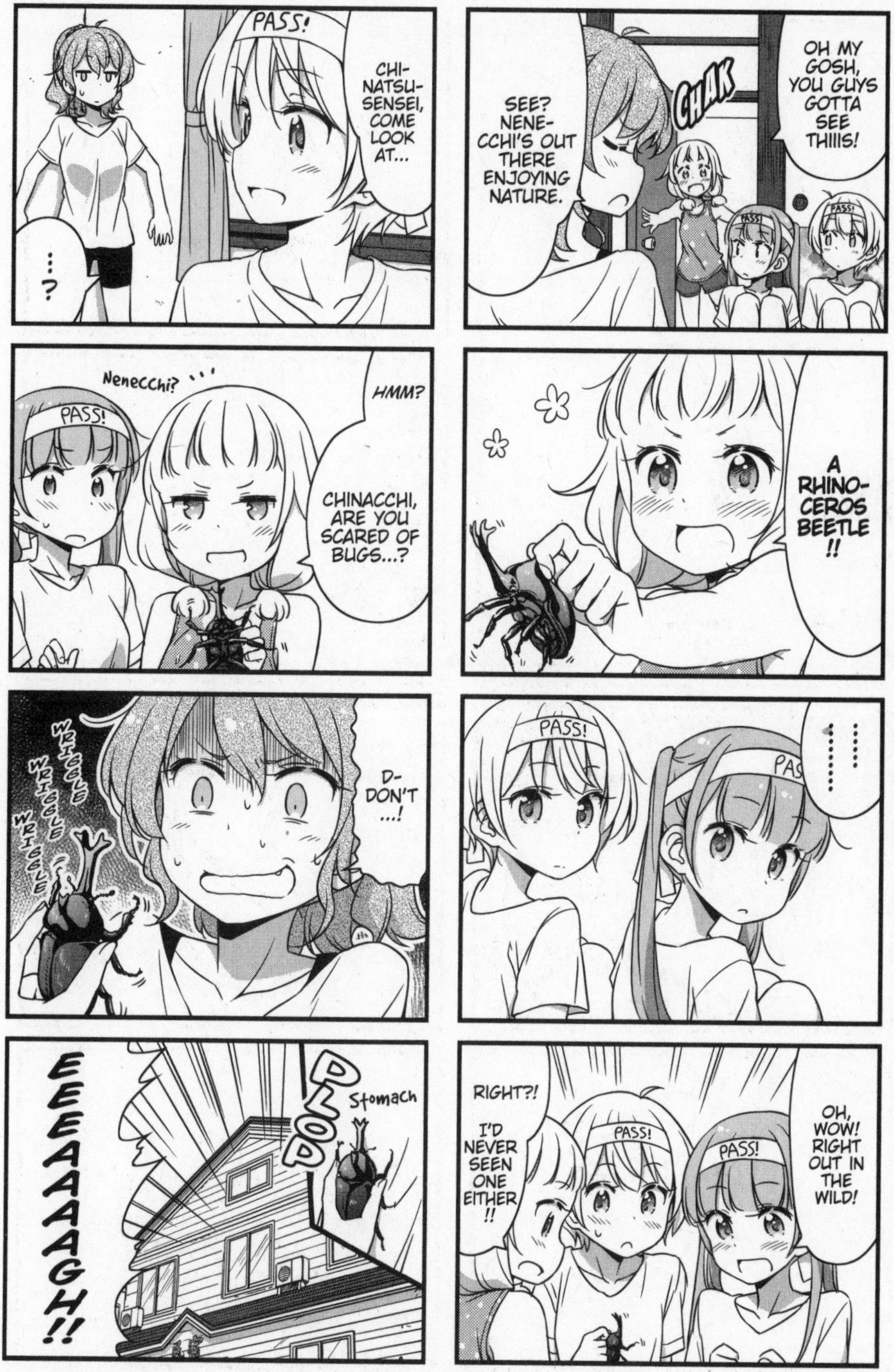
OH MY GOSH, YOU GUYS GOTTA SEE THIIIS!
CHAK
SEE? NENECCHI'S OUT THERE ENJOYING NATURE.
CHI-NATSU-SENSEI, COME LOOK AT...
...?
A RHINOCEROS BEETLE!!
HMM?
CHINACCHI, ARE YOU SCARED OF BUGS...?
Nenecchi? ...
!!......
D-DON'T...!
WRIGGLE WRIGGLE WRIGGLE
OH, WOW! RIGHT OUT IN THE WILD!
RIGHT?!
I'D NEVER SEEN ONE EITHER!!
Stomach
PLOP
EEEAAAAAGH!!

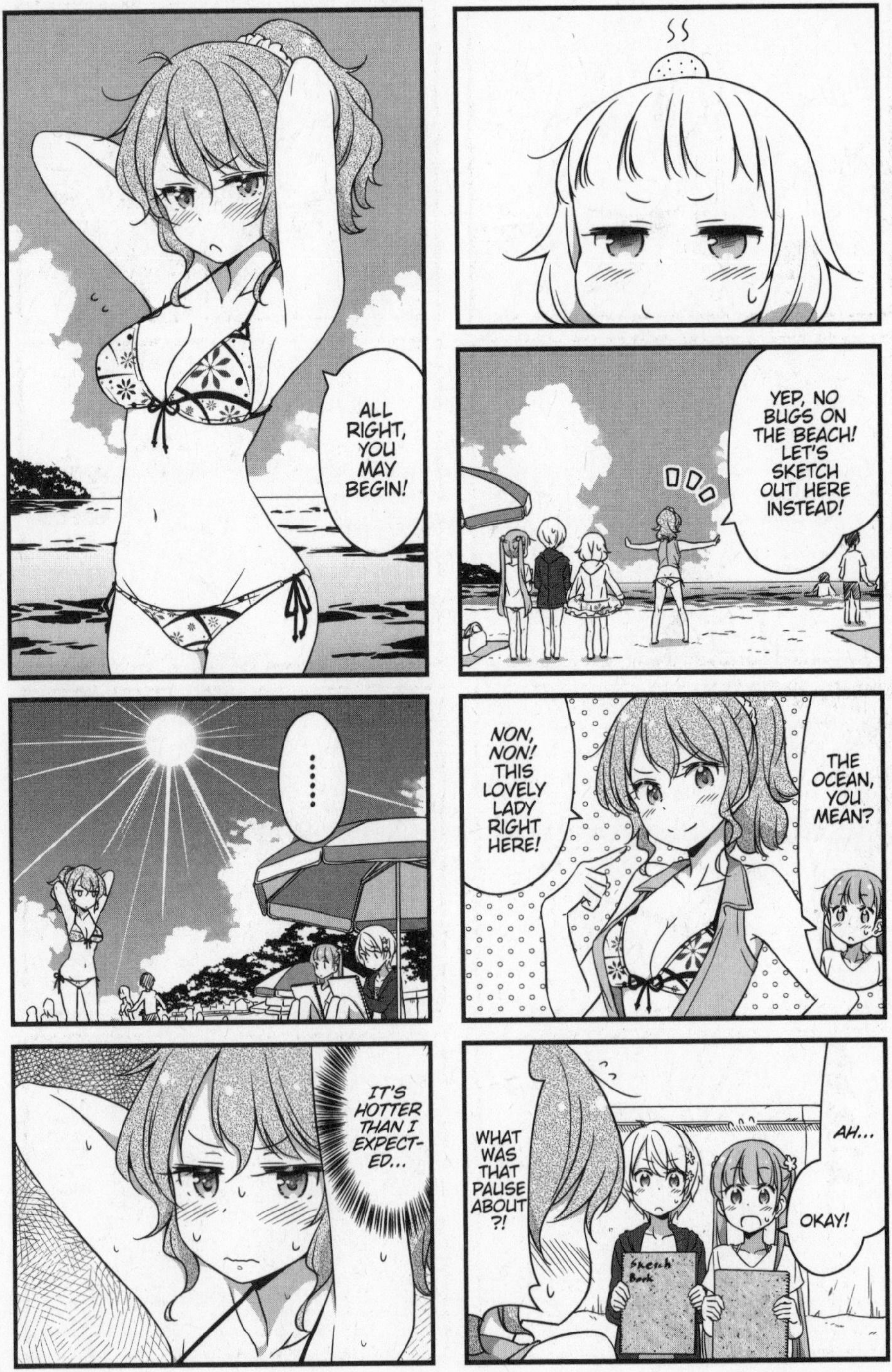
YEP, NO BUGS ON THE BEACH! LET'S SKETCH OUT HERE INSTEAD!
ALL RIGHT, YOU MAY BEGIN!
THE OCEAN, YOU MEAN?
NON, NON! THIS LOVELY LADY RIGHT HERE!
......
AH...
OKAY!
WHAT WAS THAT PAUSE ABOUT?!
IT'S HOTTER THAN I EXPECTED...

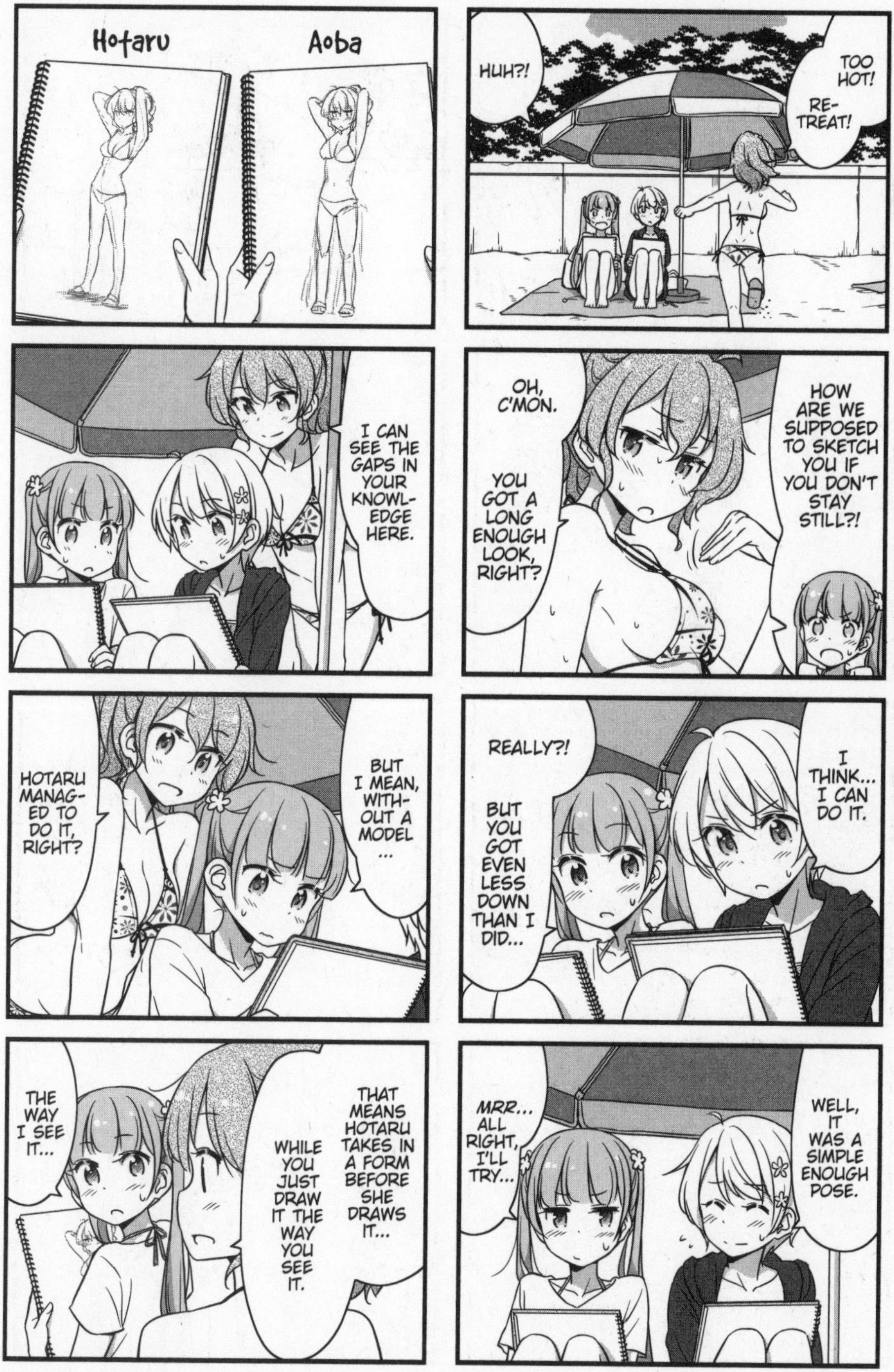
TOO HOT! RE-TREAT!
HUH?!
Aoba
Hotaru
HOW ARE WE SUPPOSED TO SKETCH YOU IF YOU DON'T STAY STILL?!
OH, C'MON.
YOU GOT A LONG ENOUGH LOOK, RIGHT?
I CAN SEE THE GAPS IN YOUR KNOWL-EDGE HERE.
I THINK... I CAN DO IT.
REALLY?!
BUT YOU GOT EVEN LESS DOWN THAN I DID...
BUT I MEAN, WITH-OUT A MODEL ...
HOTARU MANAG-ED TO DO IT, RIGHT?
WELL, IT WAS A SIMPLE ENOUGH POSE.
MRR... ALL RIGHT, I'LL TRY...
THAT MEANS HOTARU TAKES IN A FORM BEFORE SHE DRAWS IT...
WHILE YOU JUST DRAW IT THE WAY YOU SEE IT.
THE WAY I SEE IT...

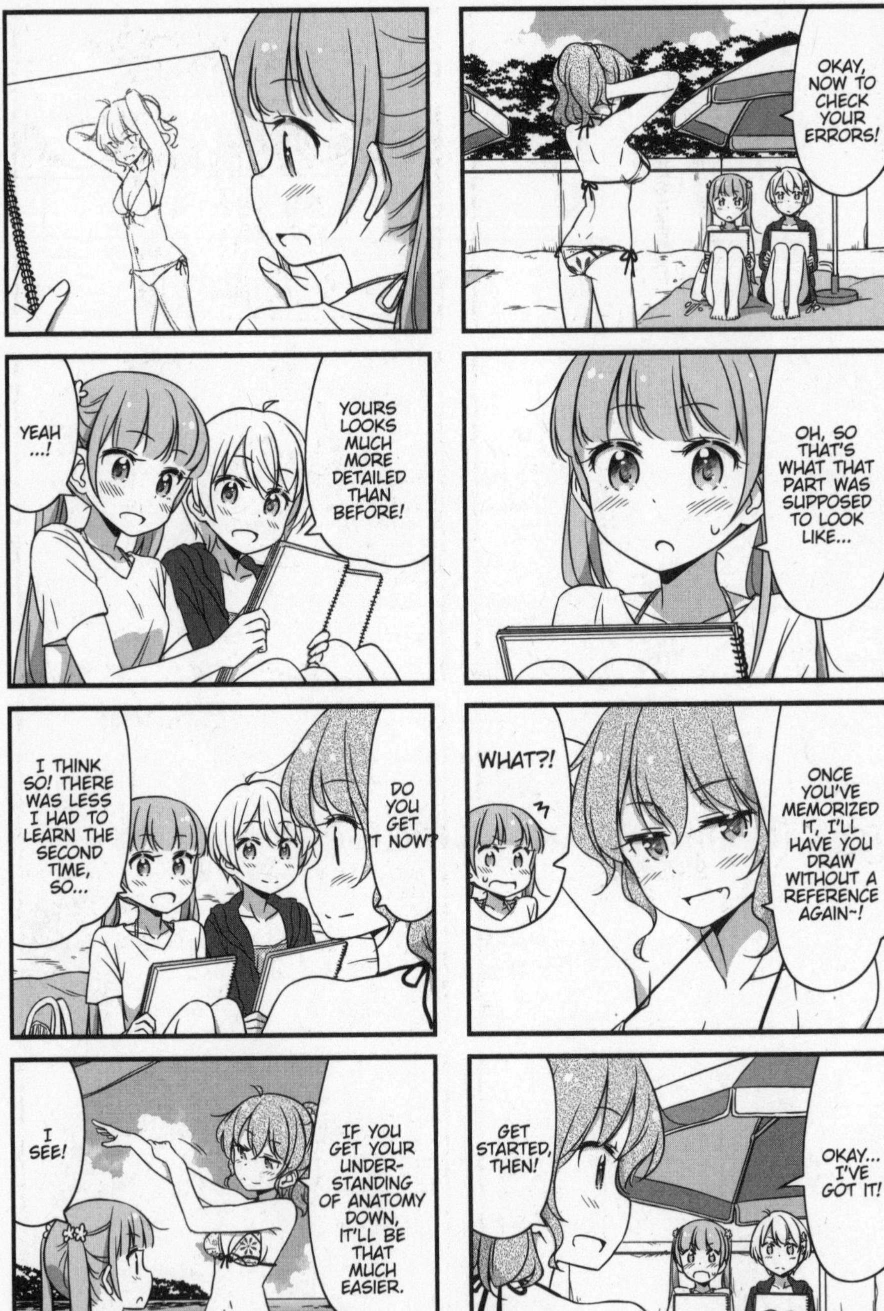
OKAY, NOW TO CHECK YOUR ERRORS!
OH, SO THAT'S WHAT THAT PART WAS SUPPOSED TO LOOK LIKE...
YOURS LOOKS MUCH MORE DETAILED THAN BEFORE!
YEAH ...!
ONCE YOU'VE MEMORIZED IT, I'LL HAVE YOU DRAW WITHOUT A REFERENCE AGAIN~!
WHAT?!
DO YOU GET T NOW?
I THINK SO! THERE WAS LESS I HAD TO LEARN THE SECOND TIME, SO...
OKAY... I'VE GOT IT!
GET STARTED, THEN!
IF YOU GET YOUR UNDER-STANDING OF ANATOMY DOWN, IT'LL BE THAT MUCH EASIER.
I SEE!

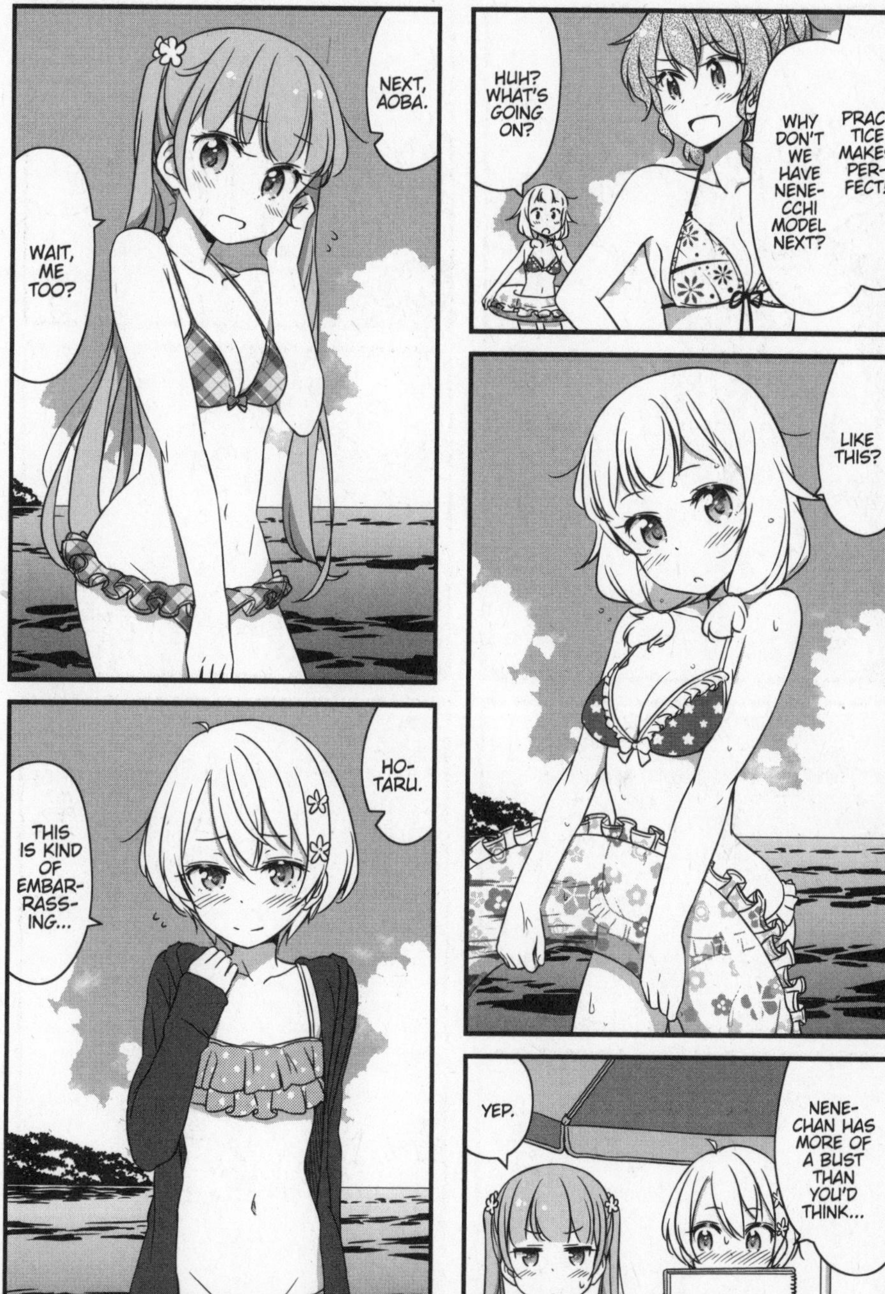
PRAC-TICE MAKES PER-FECT!
WHY DON'T WE HAVE NENE-CCHI MODEL NEXT?
HUH? WHAT'S GOING ON?
LIKE THIS?
NEXT, AOBA.
WAIT, ME TOO?
NENE-CHAN HAS MORE OF A BUST THAN YOU'D THINK...
YEP.
HO-TARU.
THIS IS KIND OF EMBAR-RASS-ING...

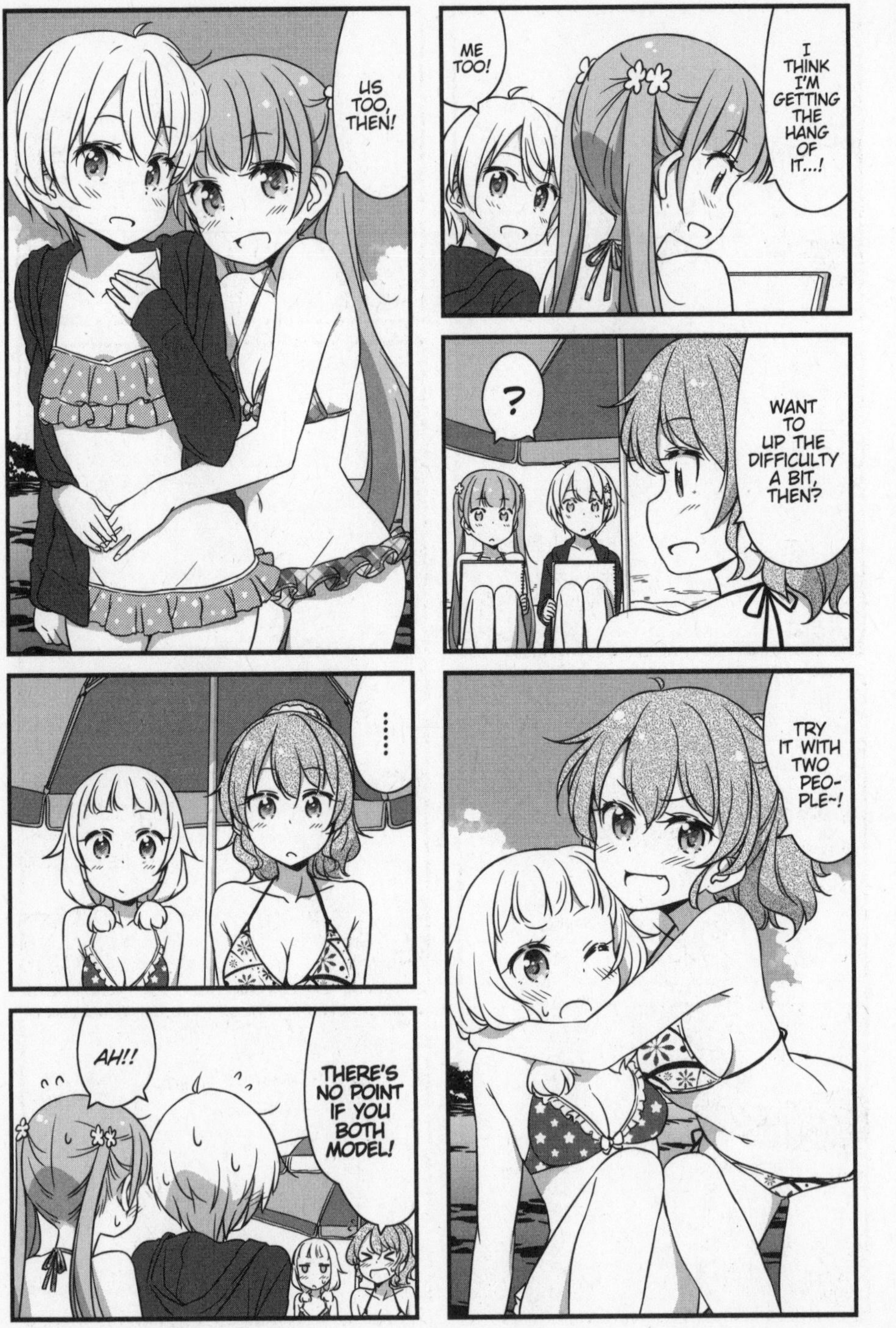
I THINK I'M GETTING THE HANG OF IT...!
ME TOO!
WANT TO UP THE DIFFICULTY A BIT, THEN?
?
US TOO, THEN!
TRY IT WITH TWO PEO-PLE~!
......
THERE'S NO POINT IF YOU BOTH MODEL!
AH!!

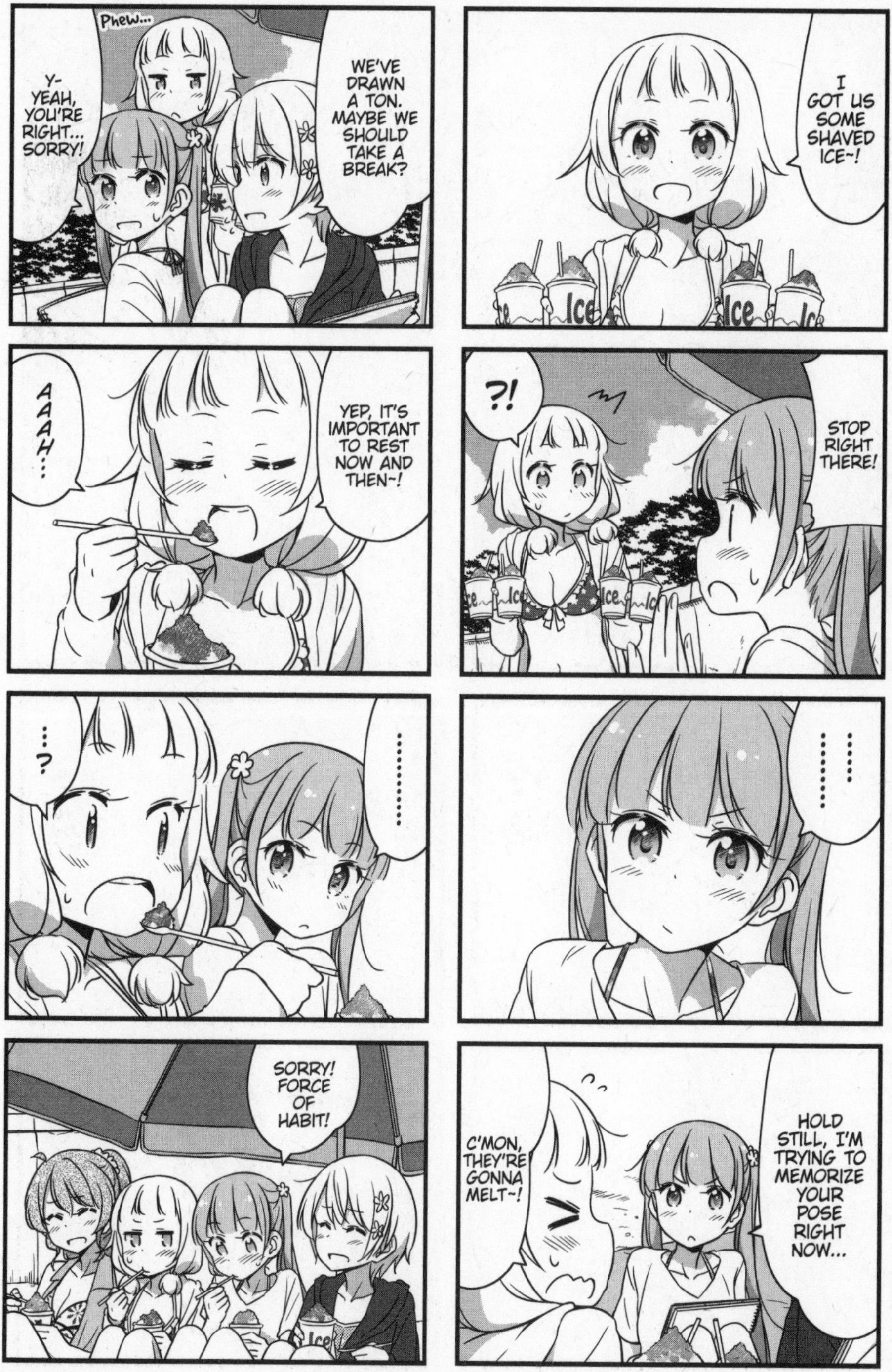
I GOT US SOME SHAVED ICE~!
Ice
STOP RIGHT THERE!
?!
......
HOLD STILL, I'M TRYING TO MEMORIZE YOUR POSE RIGHT NOW...
C'MON, THEY'RE GONNA MELT~!
WE'VE DRAWN A TON. MAYBE WE SHOULD TAKE A BREAK?
Phew...
Y-YEAH, YOU'RE RIGHT... SORRY!
YEP, IT'S IMPORTANT TO REST NOW AND THEN~!
AAAH...
....
...?
SORRY! FORCE OF HABIT!

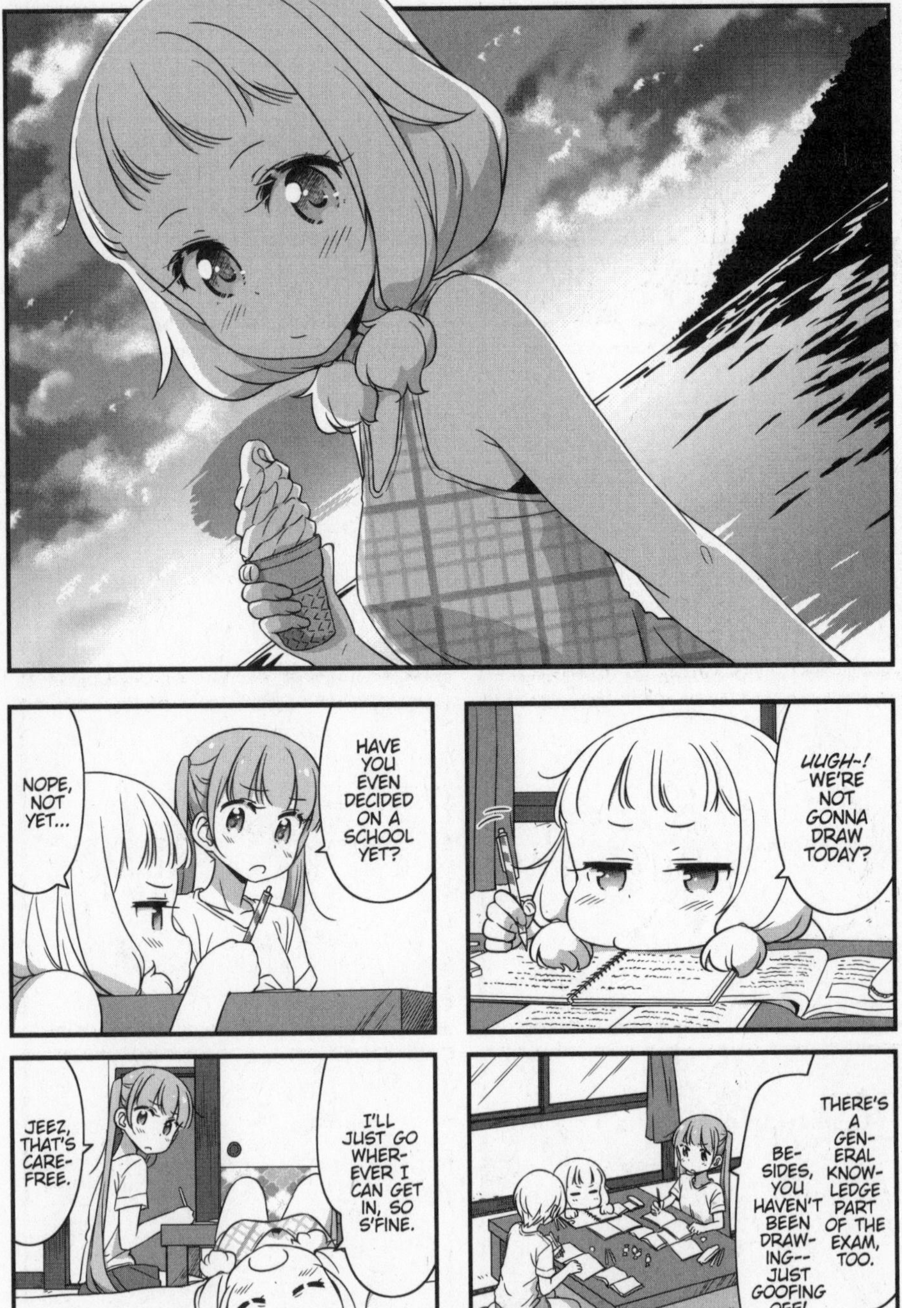
UUGH--! WE'RE NOT GONNA DRAW TODAY?
HAVE YOU EVEN DECIDED ON A SCHOOL YET?
NOPE, NOT YET...
THERE'S A GENERAL KNOWLEDGE PART OF THE EXAM, TOO.
BESIDES, YOU HAVEN'T BEEN DRAWING-- JUST GOOFING OFF!
I'LL JUST GO WHEREVER I CAN GET IN, SO S'FINE.
JEEZ, THAT'S CAREFREE.

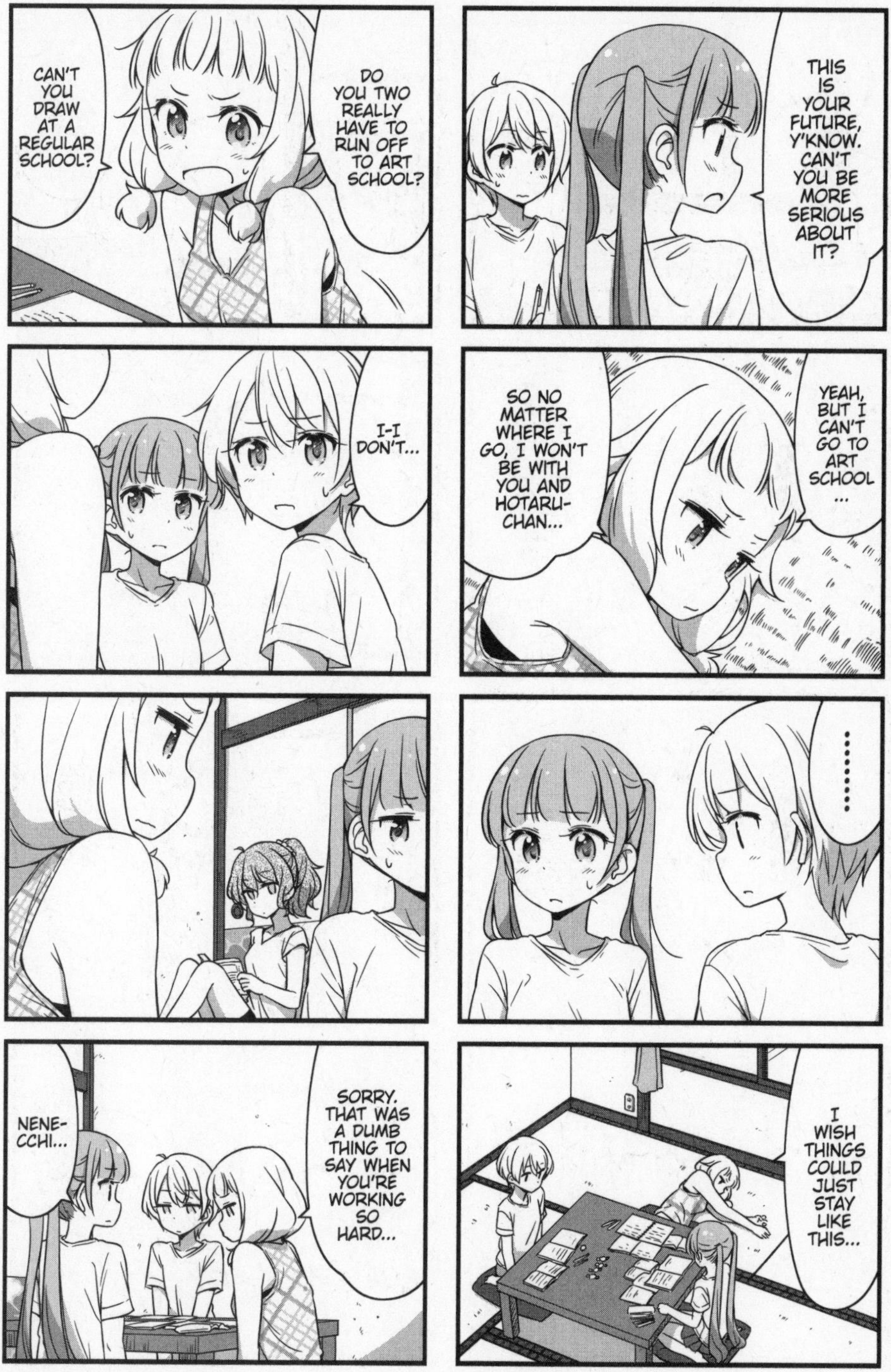
THIS IS YOUR FUTURE, Y'KNOW. CAN'T YOU BE MORE SERIOUS ABOUT IT?
YEAH, BUT I CAN'T GO TO ART SCHOOL...
SO NO MATTER WHERE I GO, I WON'T BE WITH YOU AND HOTARU-CHAN...
....
I WISH THINGS COULD JUST STAY LIKE THIS...
DO YOU TWO REALLY HAVE TO RUN OFF TO ART SCHOOL?
CAN'T YOU DRAW AT A REGULAR SCHOOL?
I-I DON'T...
SORRY. THAT WAS A DUMB THING TO SAY WHEN YOU'RE WORKING SO HARD...
NENE-CCHI...

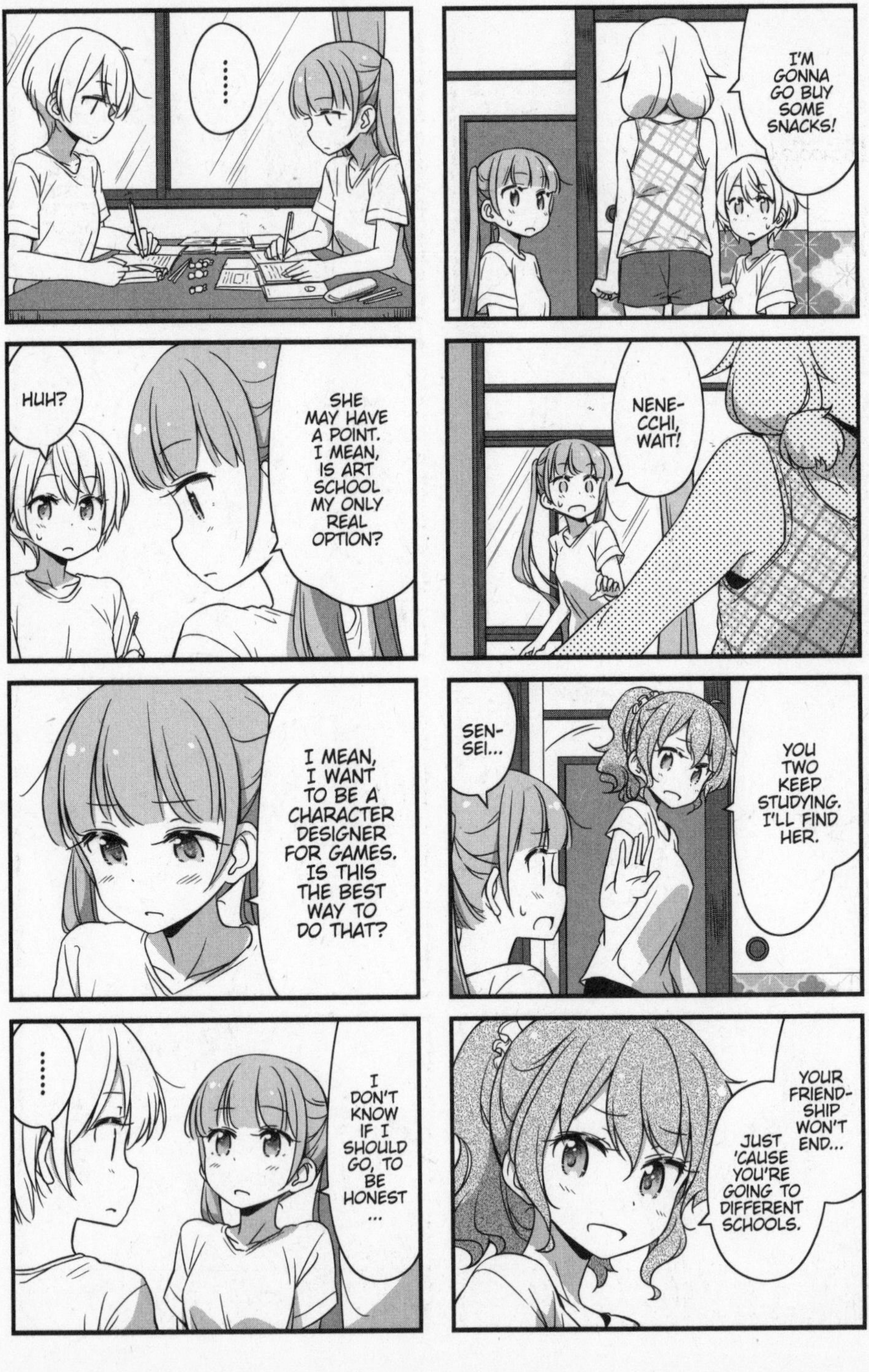
I'M GONNA GO BUY SOME SNACKS!
......
NENE-CCHI, WAIT!
SHE MAY HAVE A POINT. I MEAN, IS ART SCHOOL MY ONLY REAL OPTION?
HUH?
YOU TWO KEEP STUDYING. I'LL FIND HER.
SEN-SEI...
I MEAN, I WANT TO BE A CHARACTER DESIGNER FOR GAMES. IS THIS THE BEST WAY TO DO THAT?
YOUR FRIEND-SHIP WON'T END...
JUST 'CAUSE YOU'RE GOING TO DIFFERENT SCHOOLS.
I DON'T KNOW IF I SHOULD GO, TO BE HONEST ...
......

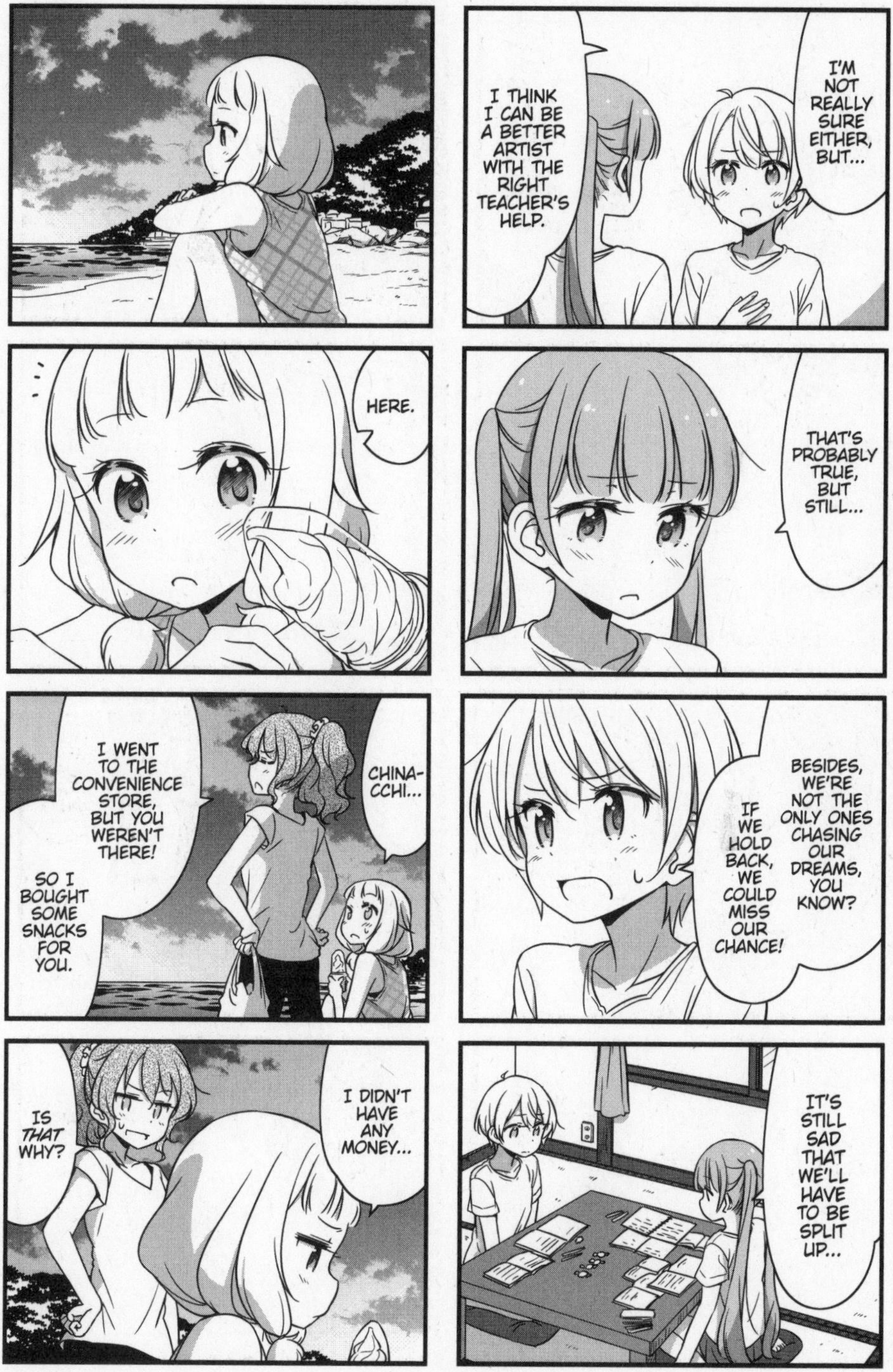
I'M NOT REALLY SURE EITHER, BUT...
I THINK I CAN BE A BETTER ARTIST WITH THE RIGHT TEACHER'S HELP.
THAT'S PROBABLY TRUE, BUT STILL...
BESIDES, WE'RE NOT THE ONLY ONES CHASING OUR DREAMS, YOU KNOW?
IF WE HOLD BACK, WE COULD MISS OUR CHANCE!
IT'S STILL SAD THAT WE'LL HAVE TO BE SPLIT UP...
HERE.
CHINA-CCHI...
I WENT TO THE CONVENIENCE STORE, BUT YOU WEREN'T THERE!
SO I BOUGHT SOME SNACKS FOR YOU.
I DIDN'T HAVE ANY MONEY...
IS *THAT* WHY?

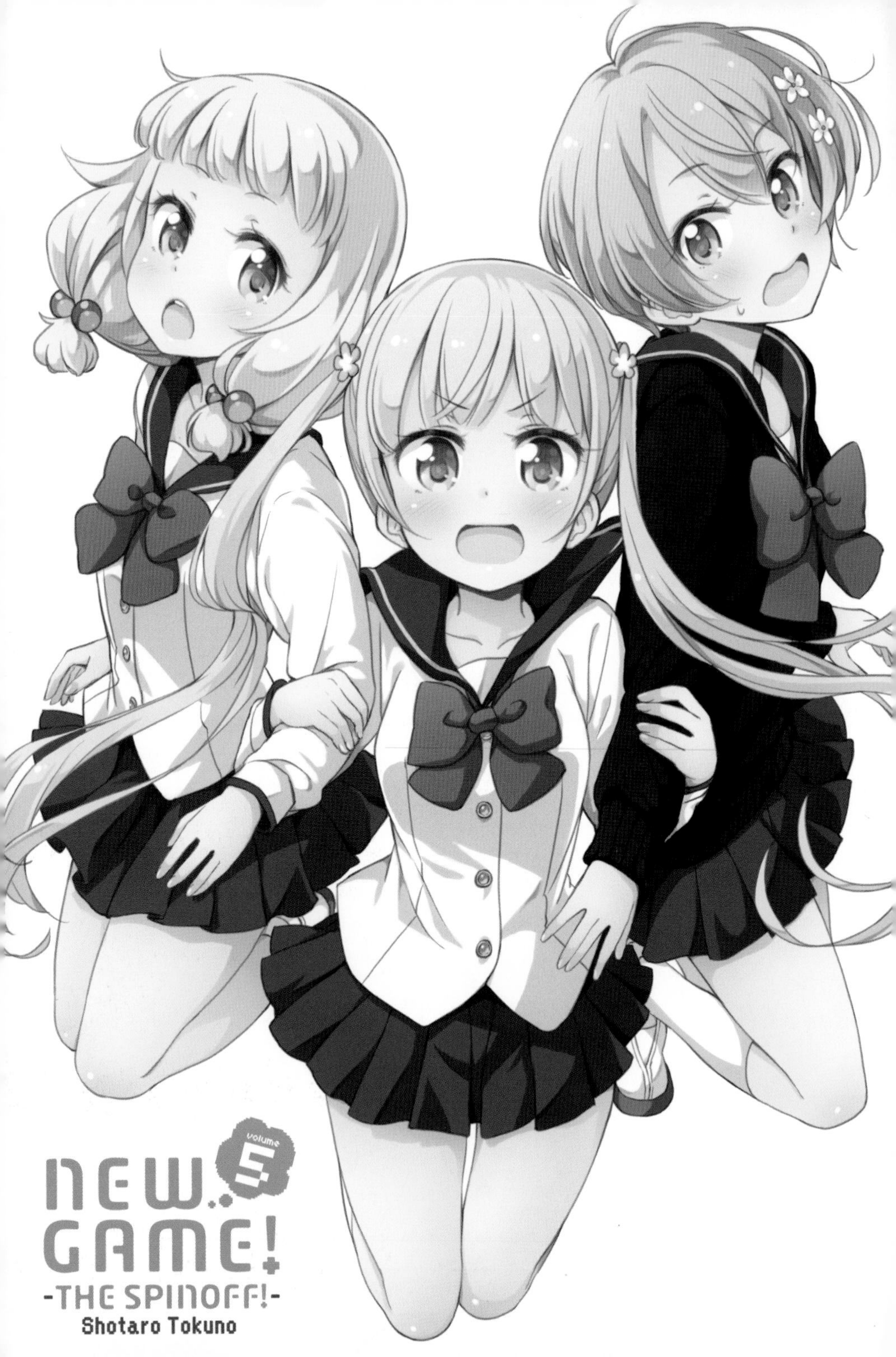
volume 5
NEW GAME!
-THE SPINOFF!-
Shotaro Tokuno

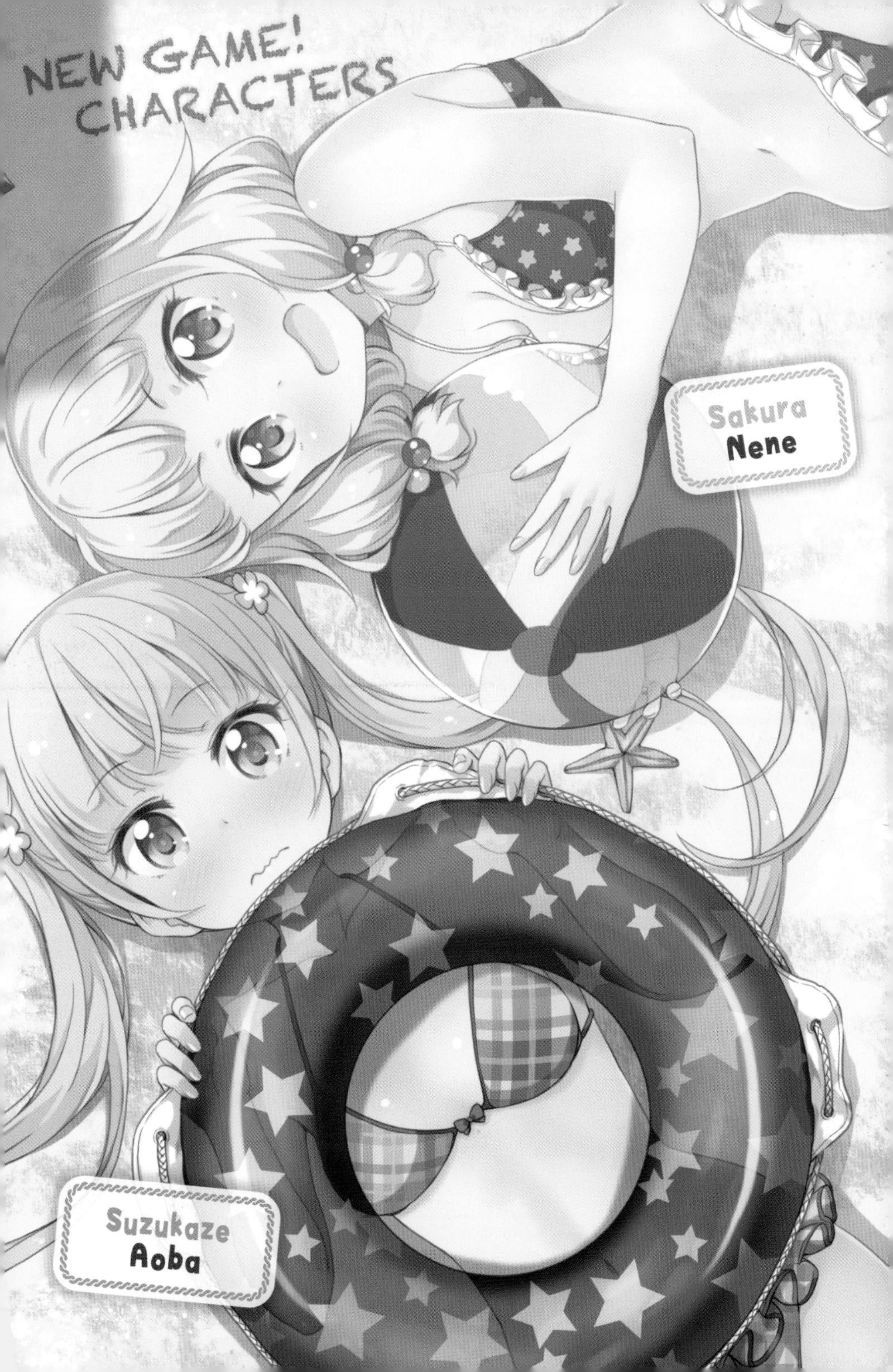
NEW GAME!
CHARACTERS
Sakura
Nene
Suzukaze
Aoba

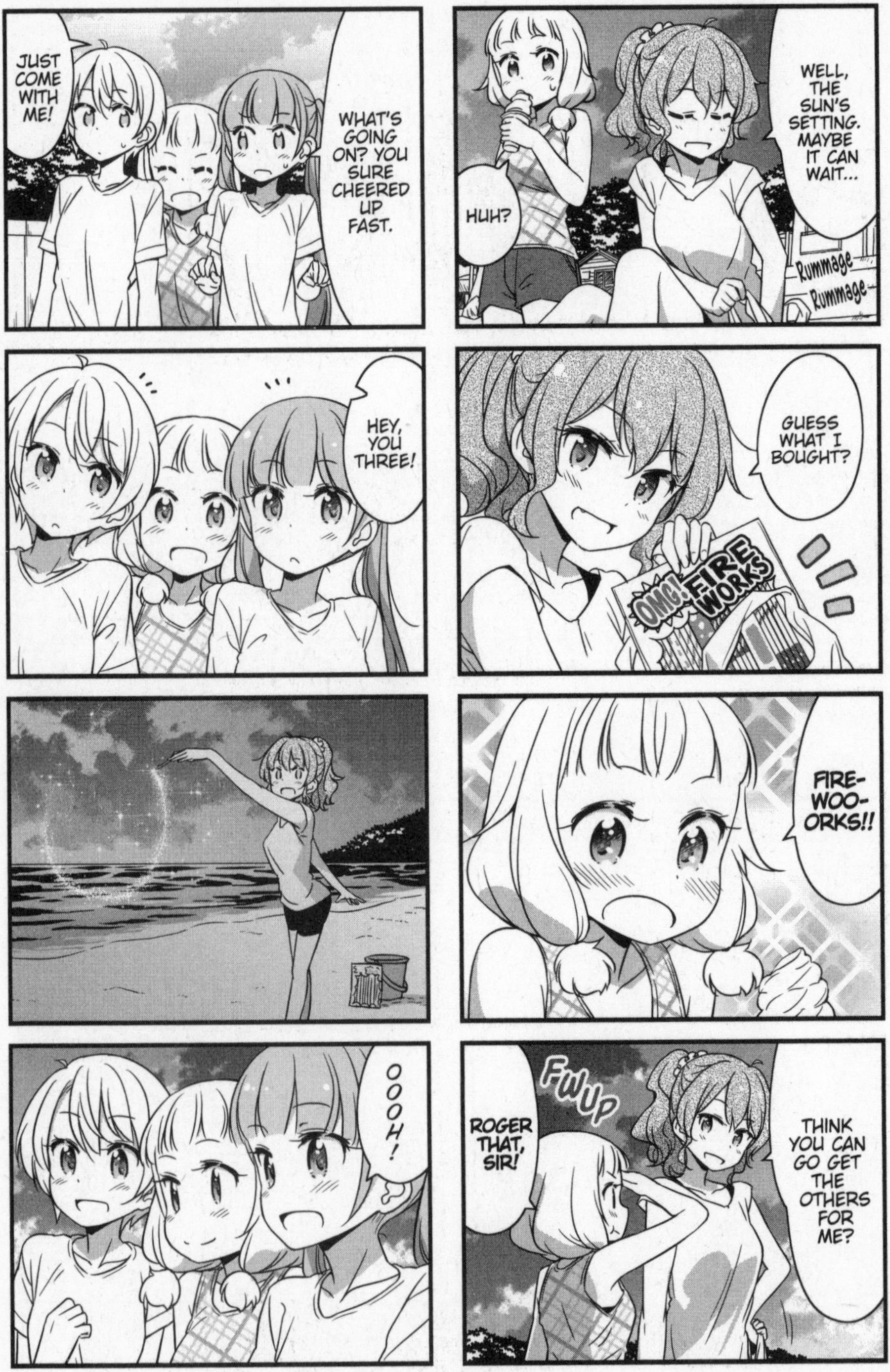
WELL, THE SUN'S SETTING. MAYBE IT CAN WAIT...
HUH?
Rummage
Rummage
GUESS WHAT I BOUGHT?
OMG! FIRE WORKS
FIRE-WOOO-ORKS!!
THINK YOU CAN GO GET THE OTHERS FOR ME?
FWUP
ROGER THAT, SIR!
WHAT'S GOING ON? YOU SURE CHEERED UP FAST.
JUST COME WITH ME!
HEY, YOU THREE!
OOOH!

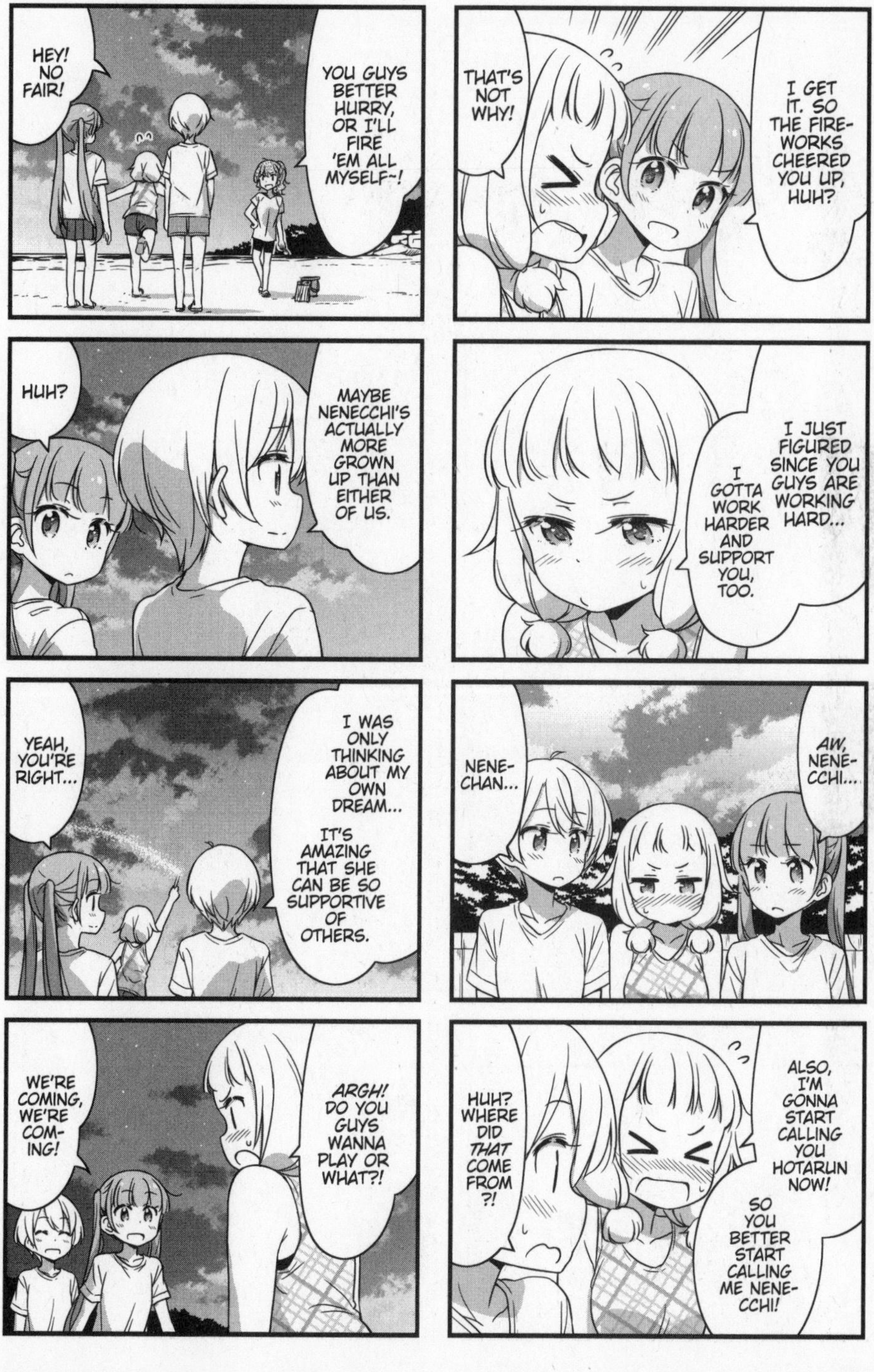
I GET IT. SO THE FIREWORKS CHEERED YOU UP, HUH?
THAT'S NOT WHY!
YOU GUYS BETTER HURRY, OR I'LL FIRE 'EM ALL MYSELF~!
HEY! NO FAIR!
I JUST FIGURED SINCE YOU GUYS ARE WORKING HARD...
I GOTTA WORK HARDER AND SUPPORT YOU, TOO.
MAYBE NENECCHI'S ACTUALLY MORE GROWN UP THAN EITHER OF US.
HUH?
AW, NENECCHI...
NENE-CHAN...
I WAS ONLY THINKING ABOUT MY OWN DREAM...
IT'S AMAZING THAT SHE CAN BE SO SUPPORTIVE OF OTHERS.
YEAH, YOU'RE RIGHT...
ALSO, I'M GONNA START CALLING YOU HOTARUN NOW!
SO YOU BETTER START CALLING ME NENECCHI!
HUH? WHERE DID *THAT* COME FROM?!
ARGH! DO YOU GUYS WANNA PLAY OR WHAT?!
WE'RE COMING, WE'RE COMING!

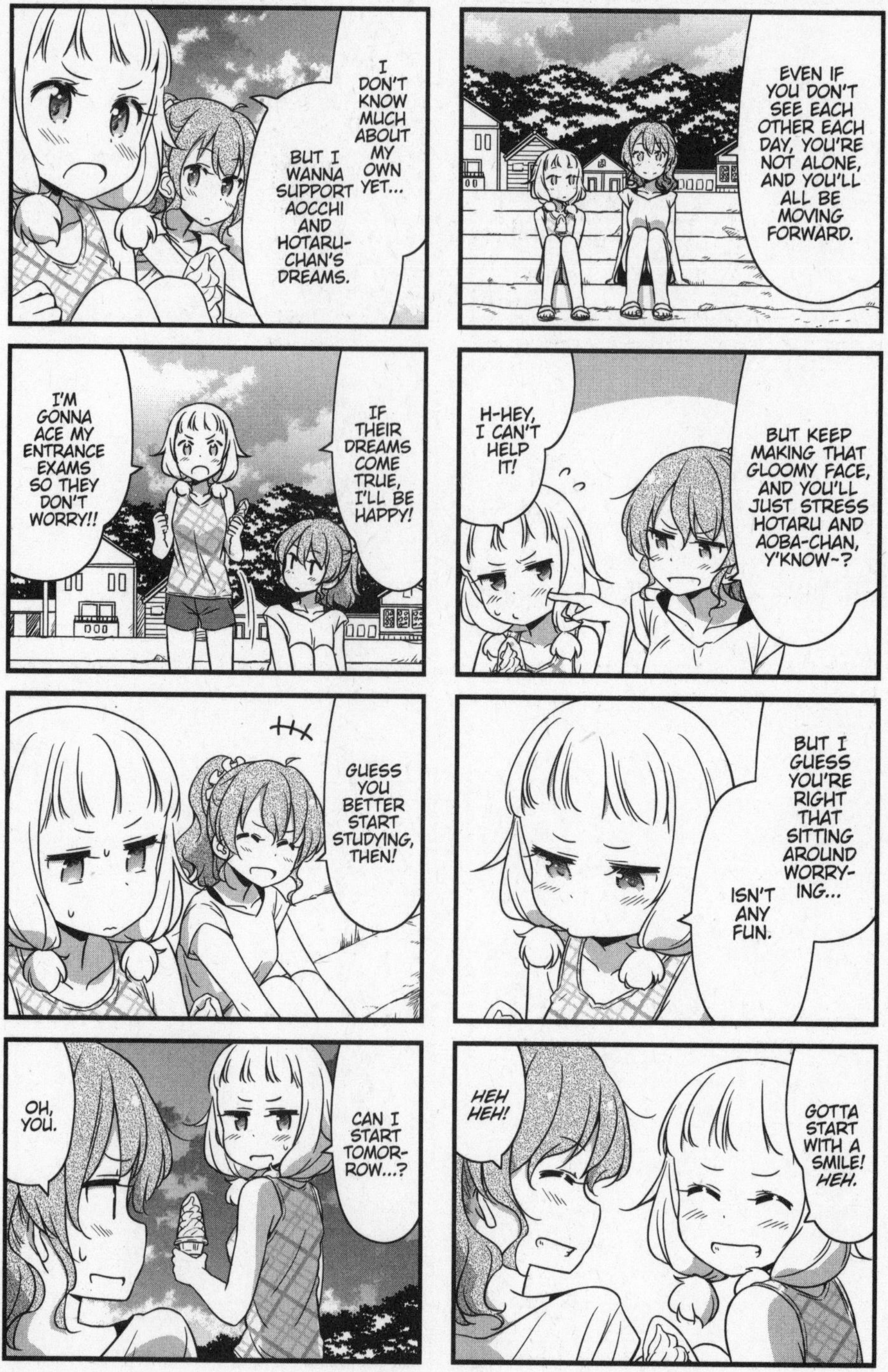
EVEN IF YOU DON'T SEE EACH OTHER EACH DAY, YOU'RE NOT ALONE, AND YOU'LL ALL BE MOVING FORWARD.
I DON'T KNOW MUCH ABOUT MY OWN YET...
BUT I WANNA SUPPORT AOCCHI AND HOTARU-CHAN'S DREAMS.
BUT KEEP MAKING THAT GLOOMY FACE, AND YOU'LL JUST STRESS HOTARU AND AOBA-CHAN, Y'KNOW~?
H-HEY, I CAN'T HELP IT!
IF THEIR DREAMS COME TRUE, I'LL BE HAPPY!
I'M GONNA ACE MY ENTRANCE EXAMS SO THEY DON'T WORRY!!
BUT I GUESS YOU'RE RIGHT THAT SITTING AROUND WORRYING...
ISN'T ANY FUN.
GUESS YOU BETTER START STUDYING, THEN!
GOTTA START WITH A SMILE! HEH.
HEH HEH!
CAN I START TOMORROW...?
OH, YOU.

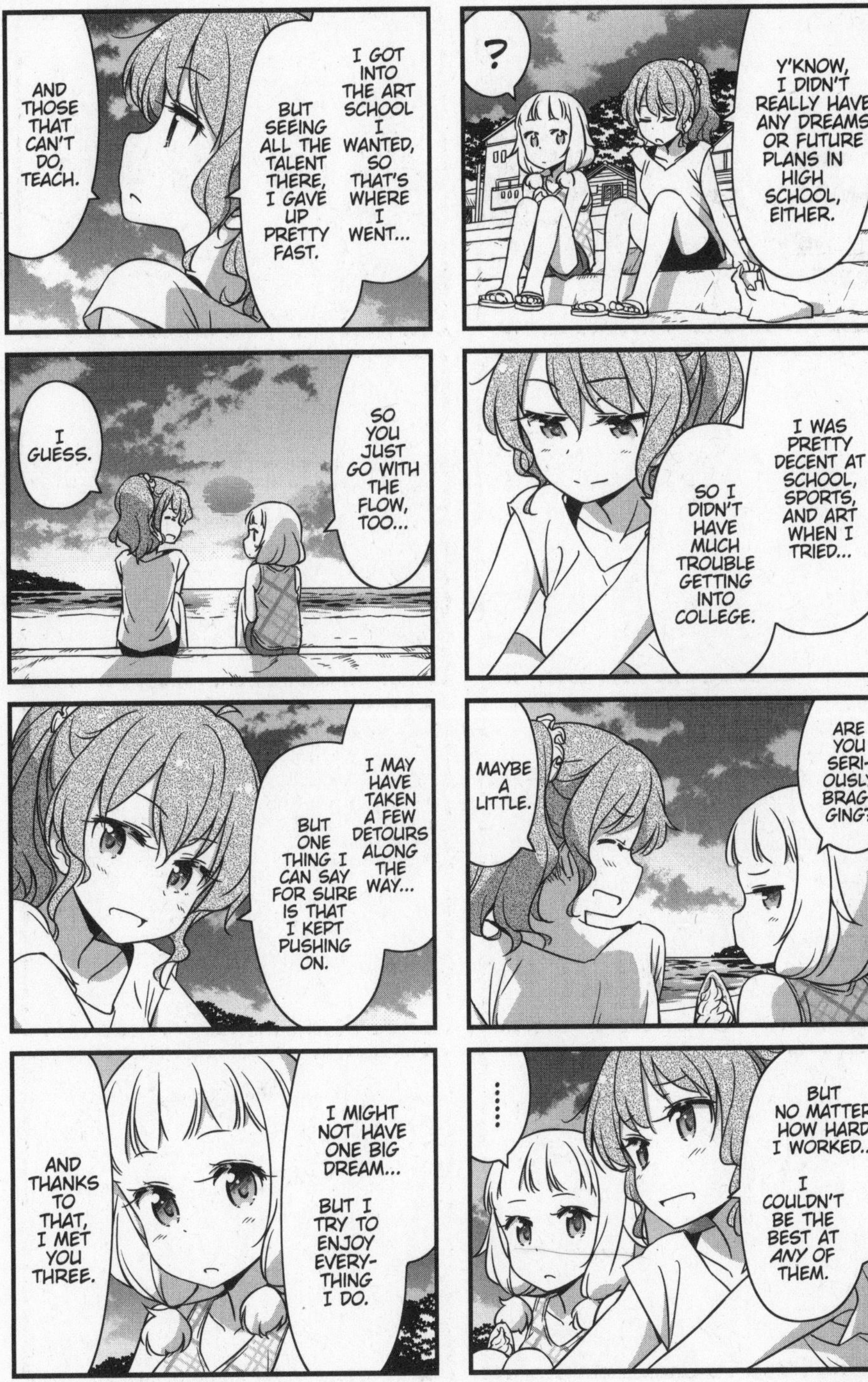
Y'KNOW, I DIDN'T REALLY HAVE ANY DREAMS OR FUTURE PLANS IN HIGH SCHOOL, EITHER.
?
I GOT INTO THE ART SCHOOL I WANTED, SO THAT'S WHERE I WENT...
BUT SEEING ALL THE TALENT THERE, I GAVE UP PRETTY FAST.
AND THOSE THAT CAN'T DO, TEACH.
I WAS PRETTY DECENT AT SCHOOL, SPORTS, AND ART WHEN I TRIED...
SO I DIDN'T HAVE MUCH TROUBLE GETTING INTO COLLEGE.
SO YOU JUST GO WITH THE FLOW, TOO...
I GUESS.
ARE YOU SERI-OUSLY BRAG-GING?
MAYBE A LITTLE.
I MAY HAVE TAKEN A FEW DETOURS ALONG THE WAY...
BUT ONE THING I CAN SAY FOR SURE IS THAT I KEPT PUSHING ON.
BUT NO MATTER HOW HARD I WORKED...
I COULDN'T BE THE BEST AT ANY OF THEM.
......
I MIGHT NOT HAVE ONE BIG DREAM...
BUT I TRY TO ENJOY EVERY-THING I DO.
AND THANKS TO THAT, I MET YOU THREE.

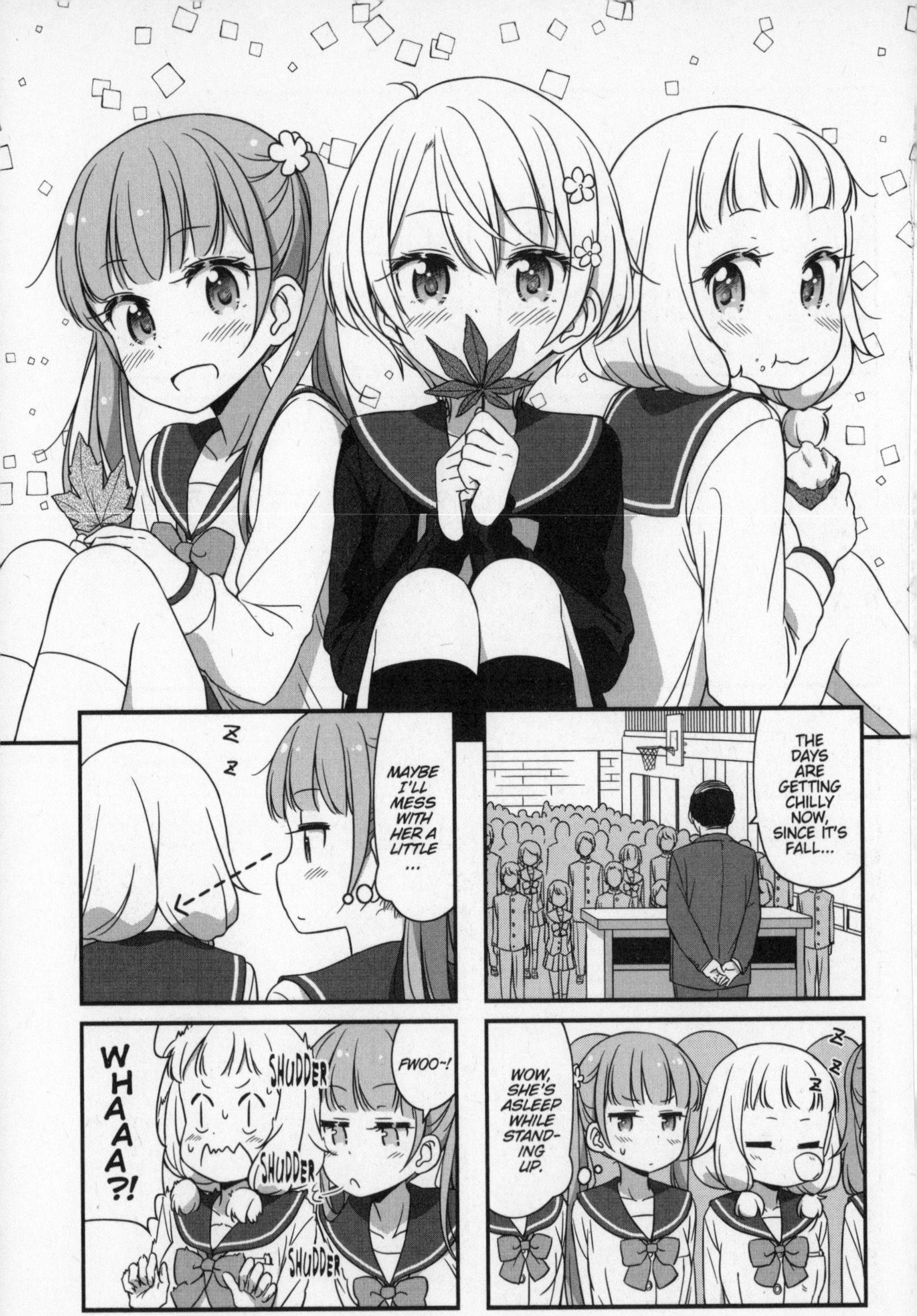
THE DAYS ARE GETTING CHILLY NOW, SINCE IT'S FALL...
Z Z
MAYBE I'LL MESS WITH HER A LITTLE ...
WOW, SHE'S ASLEEP WHILE STANDING UP.
Z Z Z
FWOO~!
SHUDDER
SHUDDER
SHUDDER
WHAAAA?!

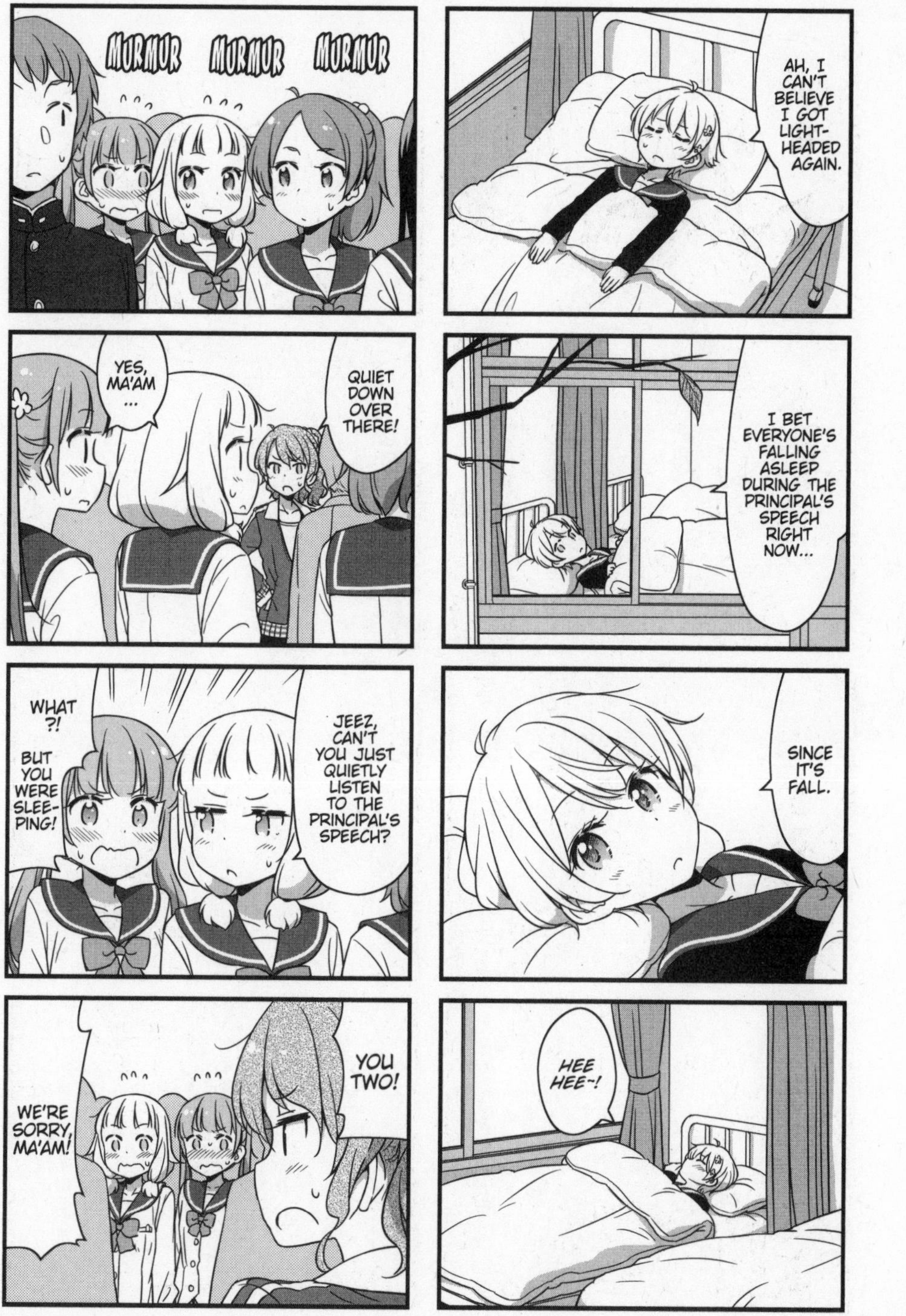
AH, I CAN'T BELIEVE I GOT LIGHT-HEADED AGAIN.
I BET EVERYONE'S FALLING ASLEEP DURING THE PRINCIPAL'S SPEECH RIGHT NOW...
SINCE IT'S FALL.
HEE HEE~!
MURMUR MURMUR MURMUR
QUIET DOWN OVER THERE!
YES, MA'AM...
JEEZ, CAN'T YOU JUST QUIETLY LISTEN TO THE PRINCIPAL'S SPEECH?
WHAT?!
BUT YOU WERE SLEEP-ING!
YOU TWO!
WE'RE SORRY, MA'AM!

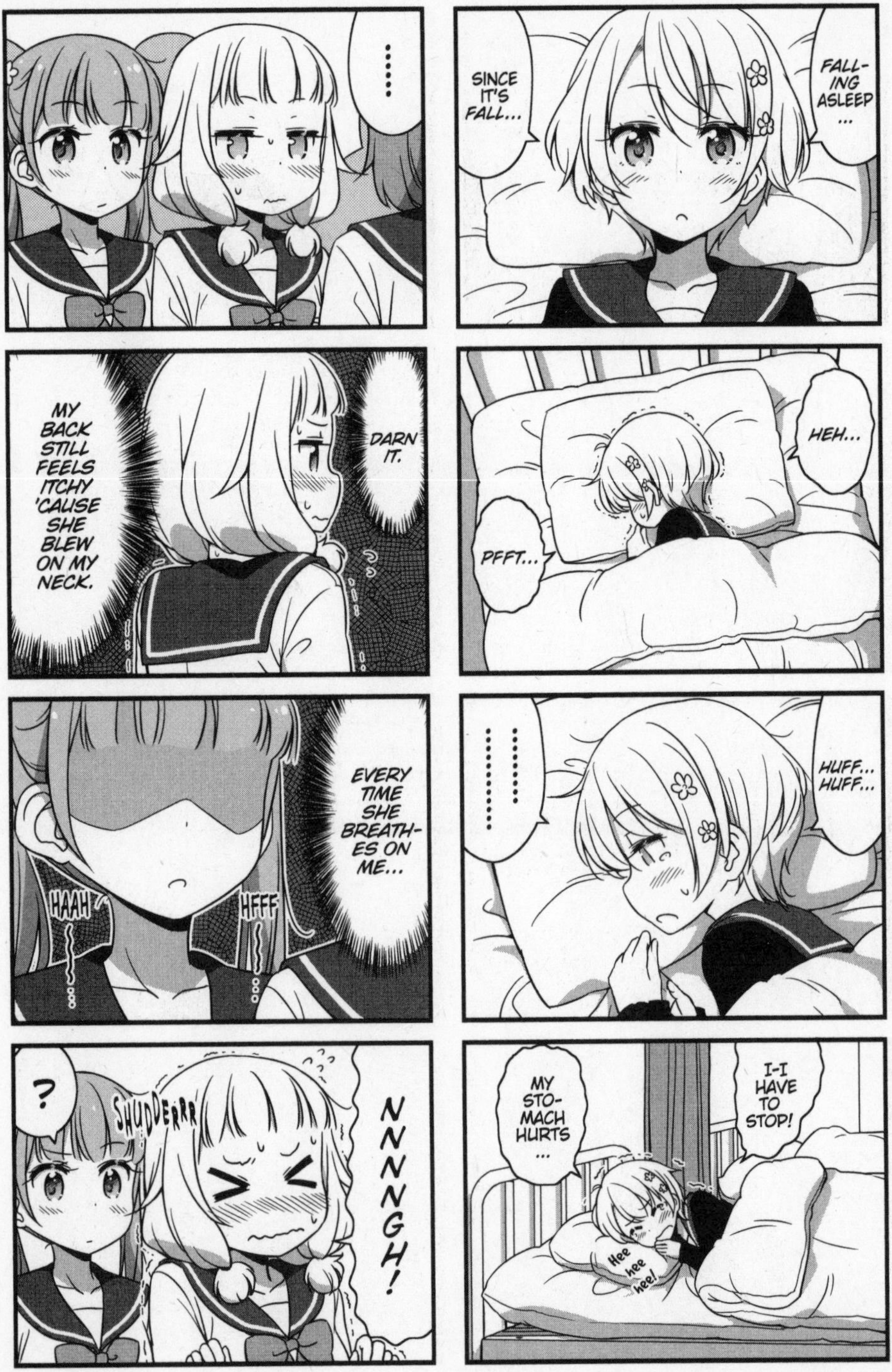
FALL-ING ASLEEP ...
SINCE IT'S FALL...
HEH...
PFFT...
HUFF... HUFF...
......
I-I HAVE TO STOP!
MY STO-MACH HURTS ...
Hee hee hee!
......
DARN IT.
MY BACK STILL FEELS ITCHY 'CAUSE SHE BLEW ON MY NECK.
EVERY TIME SHE BREATH-ES ON ME...
HFFF
HAAH
NNNNGH!
SHUDDERRR
?

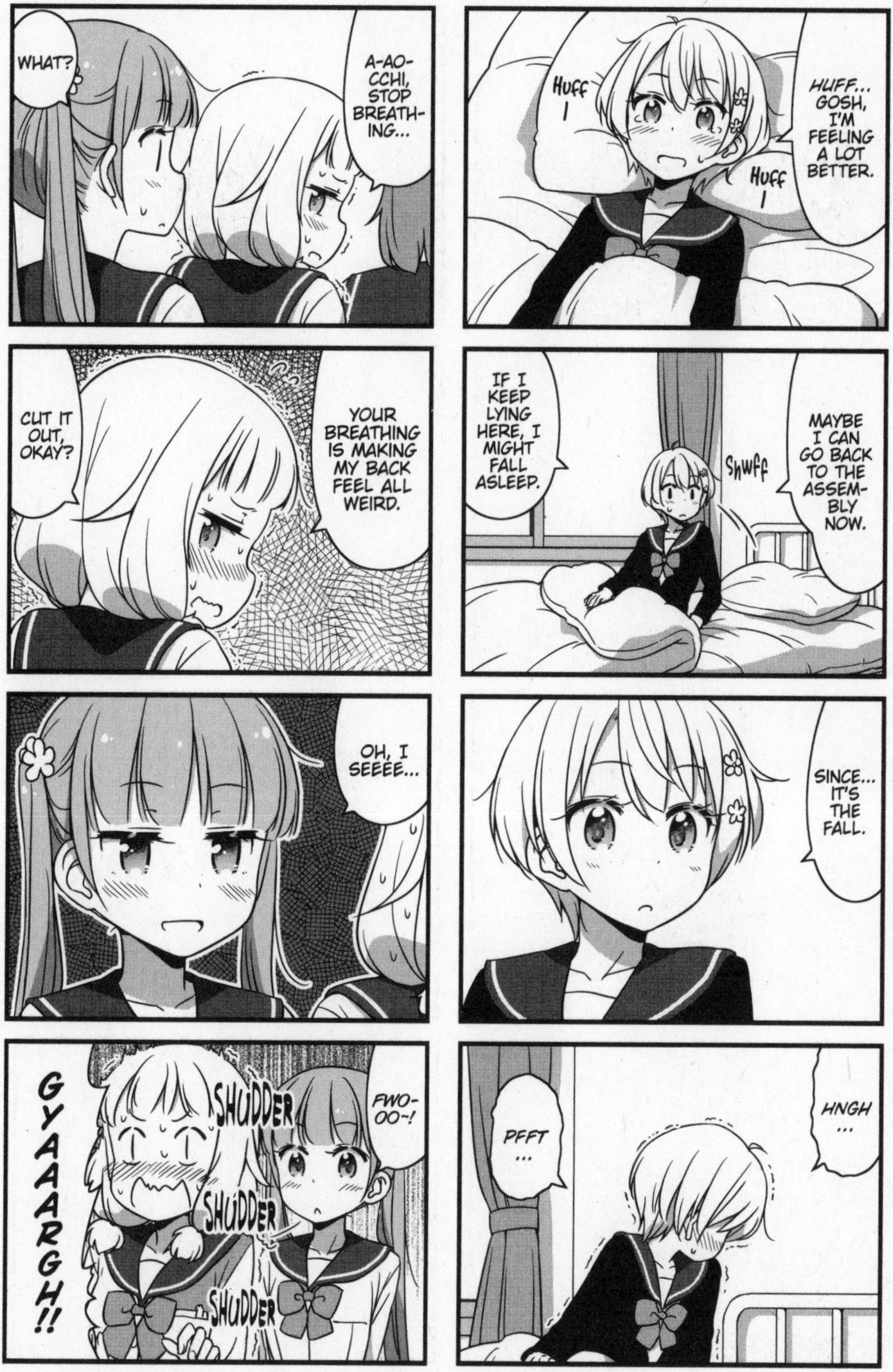
HUFF... GOSH, I'M FEELING A LOT BETTER.
Huff
Huff
MAYBE I CAN GO BACK TO THE ASSEMBLY NOW.
Shwff
IF I KEEP LYING HERE, I MIGHT FALL ASLEEP.
SINCE... IT'S THE FALL.
HNGH...
PFFT...
A-AO-CCHI, STOP BREATHING...
WHAT?
YOUR BREATHING IS MAKING MY BACK FEEL ALL WEIRD.
CUT IT OUT, OKAY?
OH, I SEEEE...
FWOO-OO~!
SHUDDER
SHUDDER
SHUDDER
GYAAARGH!!

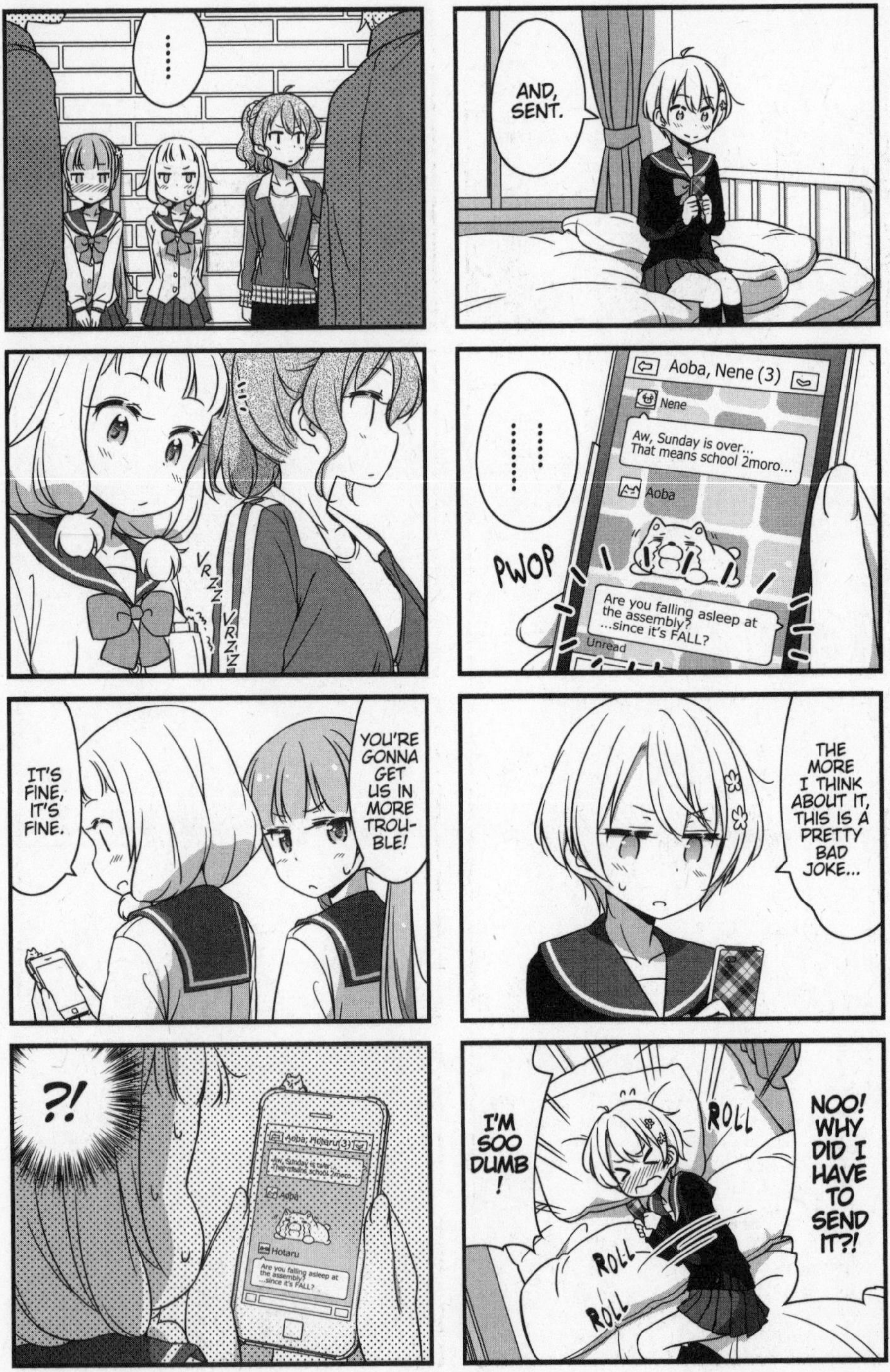
AND, SENT.
……
……!!
Aoba, Nene (3)
Nene
Aw, Sunday is over...
That means school 2moro...
Aoba
PWOP
Are you falling asleep at the assembly?
...since it's FALL?
Unread
VRZZ
VRZZ
THE MORE I THINK ABOUT IT, THIS IS A PRETTY BAD JOKE...
YOU'RE GONNA GET US IN MORE TROUBLE!
IT'S FINE, IT'S FINE.
NOO! WHY DID I HAVE TO SEND IT?!
ROLL
I'M SOO DUMB!
ROLL
ROLL
?!
Aoba, Hotaru (3)
Aoba
Hotaru
Are you falling asleep at the assembly?
...since it's FALL?

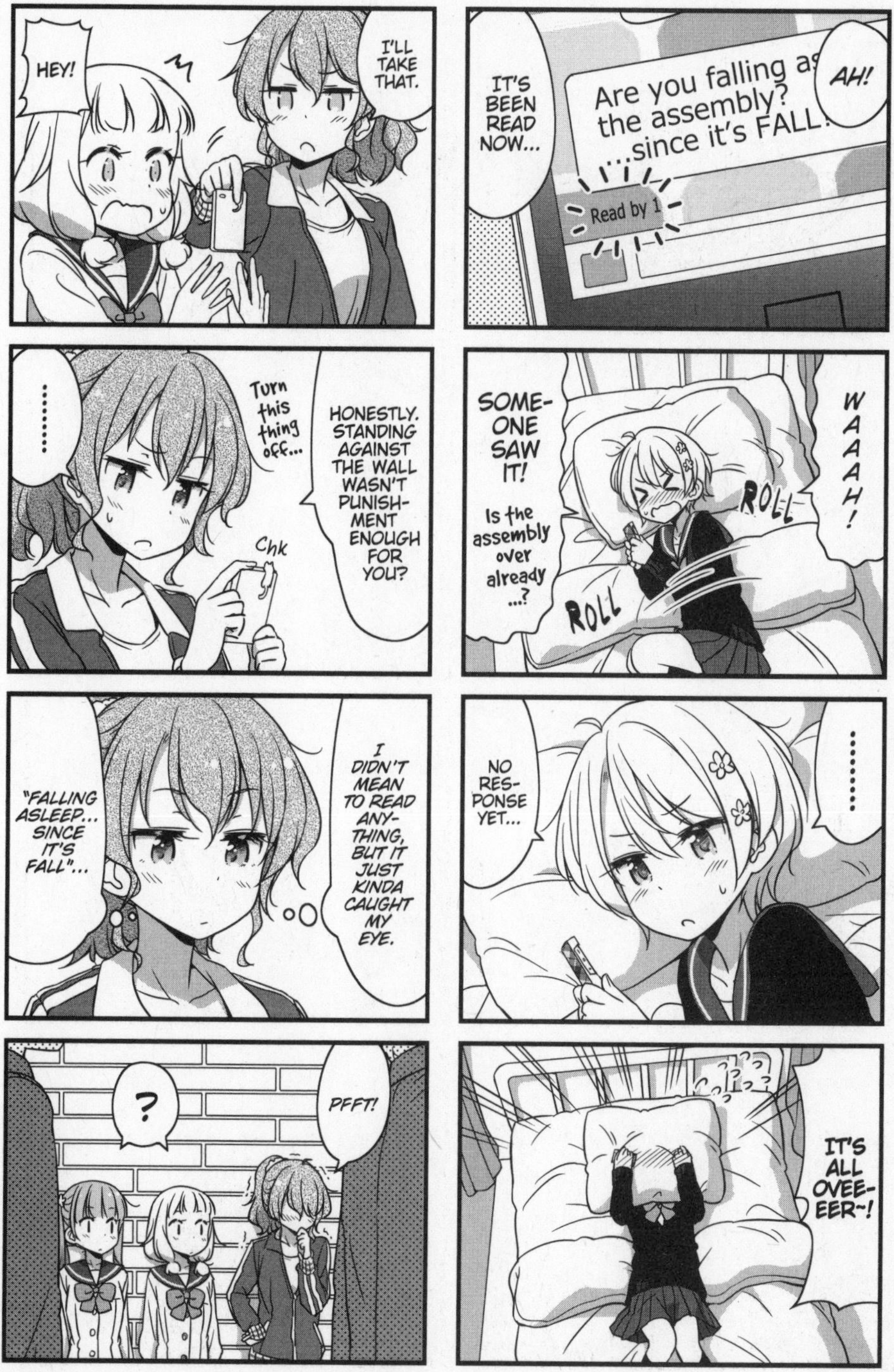
AH!
Are you falling as
the assembly?
...since it's FALL!
Read by 1
IT'S BEEN READ NOW...
I'LL TAKE THAT.
HEY!
WAAAAH!
ROLL
SOME-ONE SAW IT!
Is the assembly over already ...?
ROLL
HONESTLY. STANDING AGAINST THE WALL WASN'T PUNISH-MENT ENOUGH FOR YOU?
Turn this thing off...
Chk
....
....
NO RES-PONSE YET...
I DIDN'T MEAN TO READ ANY-THING, BUT IT JUST KINDA CAUGHT MY EYE.
"FALLING ASLEEP... SINCE IT'S FALL"...
IT'S ALL OVEEE-EER~!
PFFT!
?

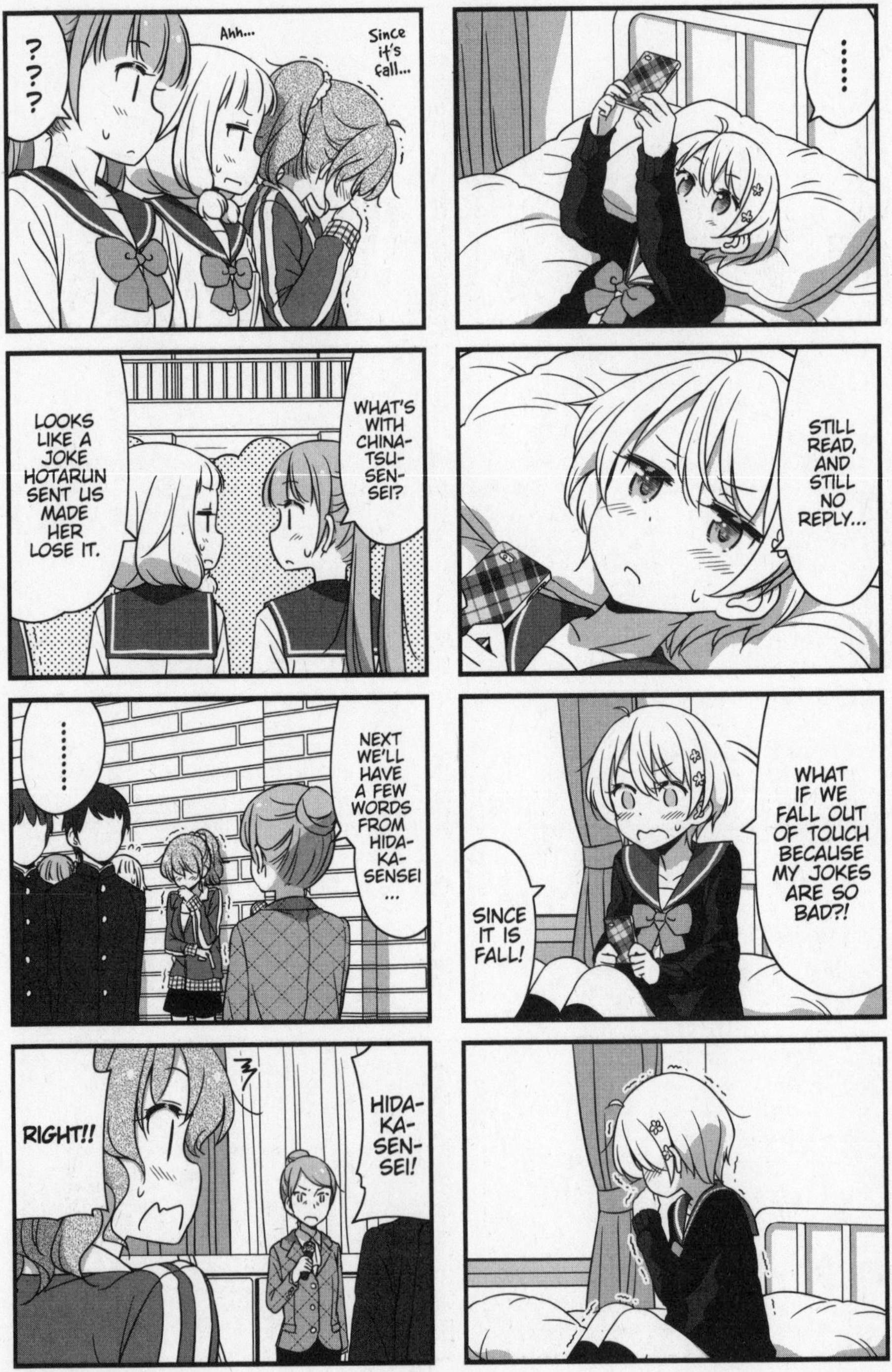

……
STILL READ, AND STILL NO REPLY…
WHAT IF WE FALL OUT OF TOUCH BECAUSE MY JOKES ARE SO BAD?!
SINCE IT IS FALL!
Since it's fall…
Ahh…
?-?-?
WHAT'S WITH CHINATSU-SENSEI?
LOOKS LIKE A JOKE HOTARUN SENT US MADE HER LOSE IT.
NEXT WE'LL HAVE A FEW WORDS FROM HIDAKA-SENSEI …
……
HIDAKA-SENSEI!
RIGHT!!

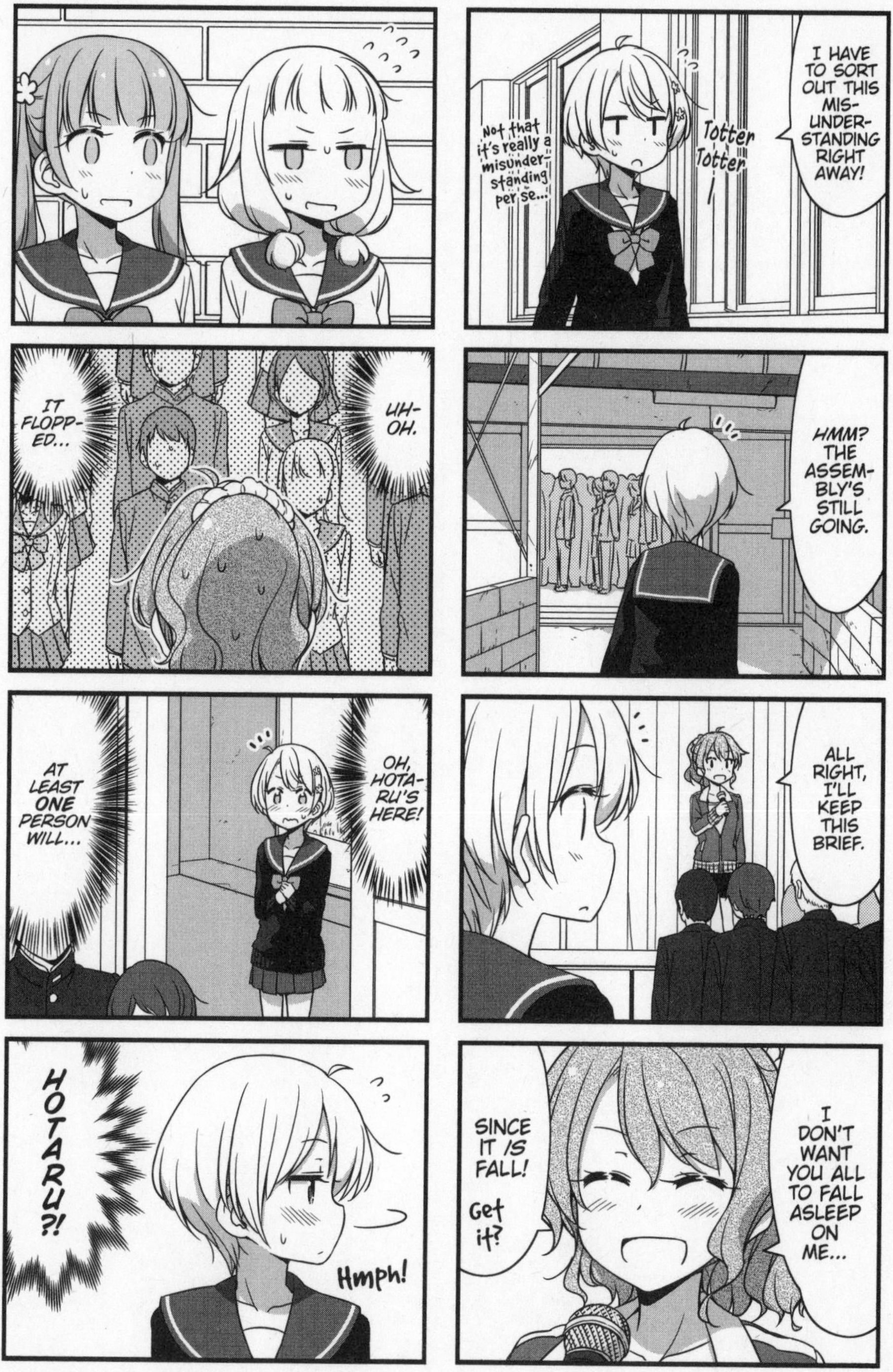
I HAVE TO SORT OUT THIS MISUNDERSTANDING RIGHT AWAY!
Totter Totter
Not that it's really a misunderstanding per se...
HMM? THE ASSEMBLY'S STILL GOING.
ALL RIGHT, I'LL KEEP THIS BRIEF.
I DON'T WANT YOU ALL TO FALL ASLEEP ON ME...
SINCE IT IS FALL!
Get it?
UH-OH.
IT FLOPPED...
OH, HOTARU'S HERE!
AT LEAST ONE PERSON WILL...
HOTARU?!
Hmph!

NEW GAME!

NEW GAME!

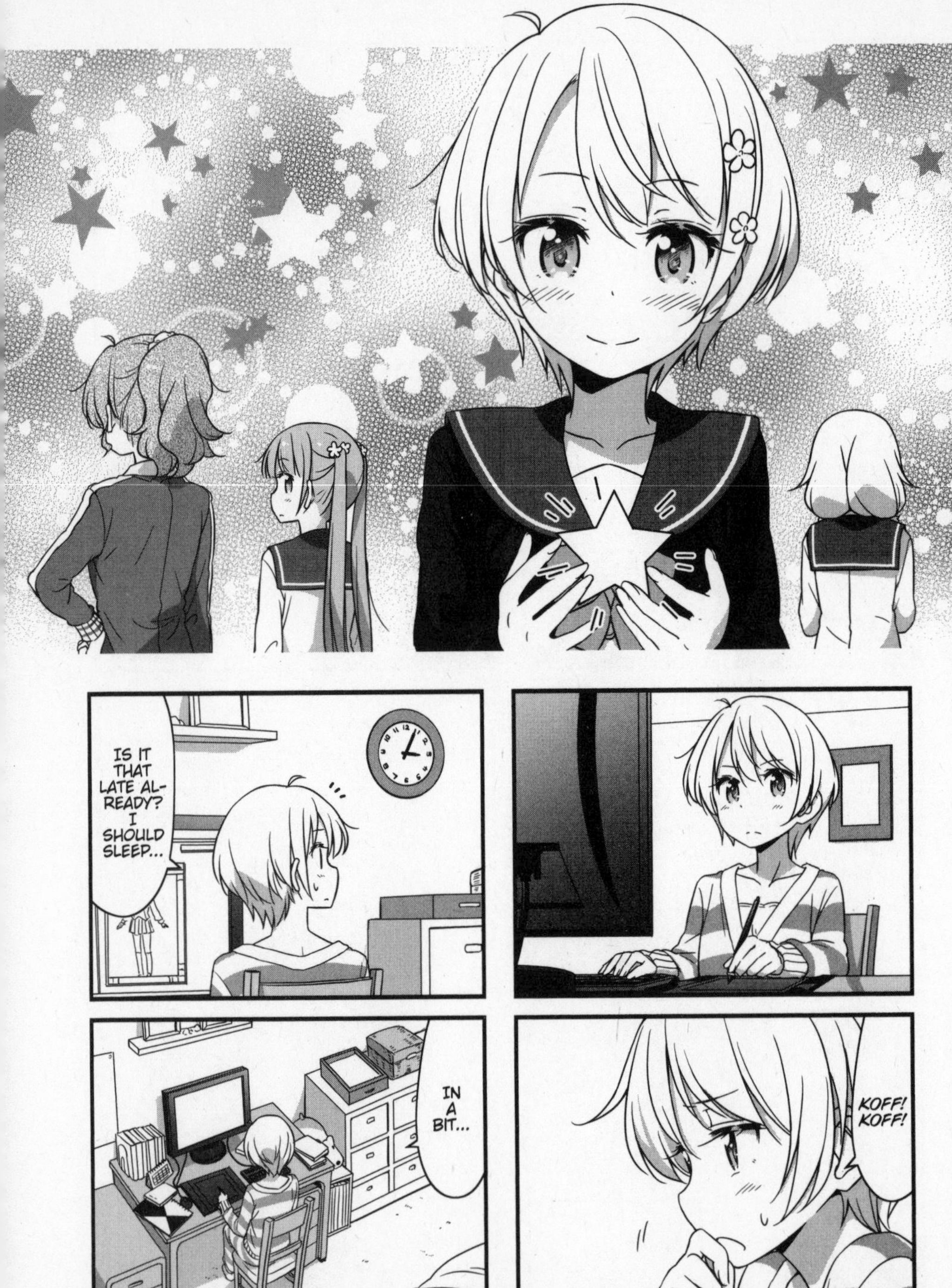
IS IT THAT LATE AL-READY? I SHOULD SLEEP...
KOFF! KOFF!
IN A BIT...

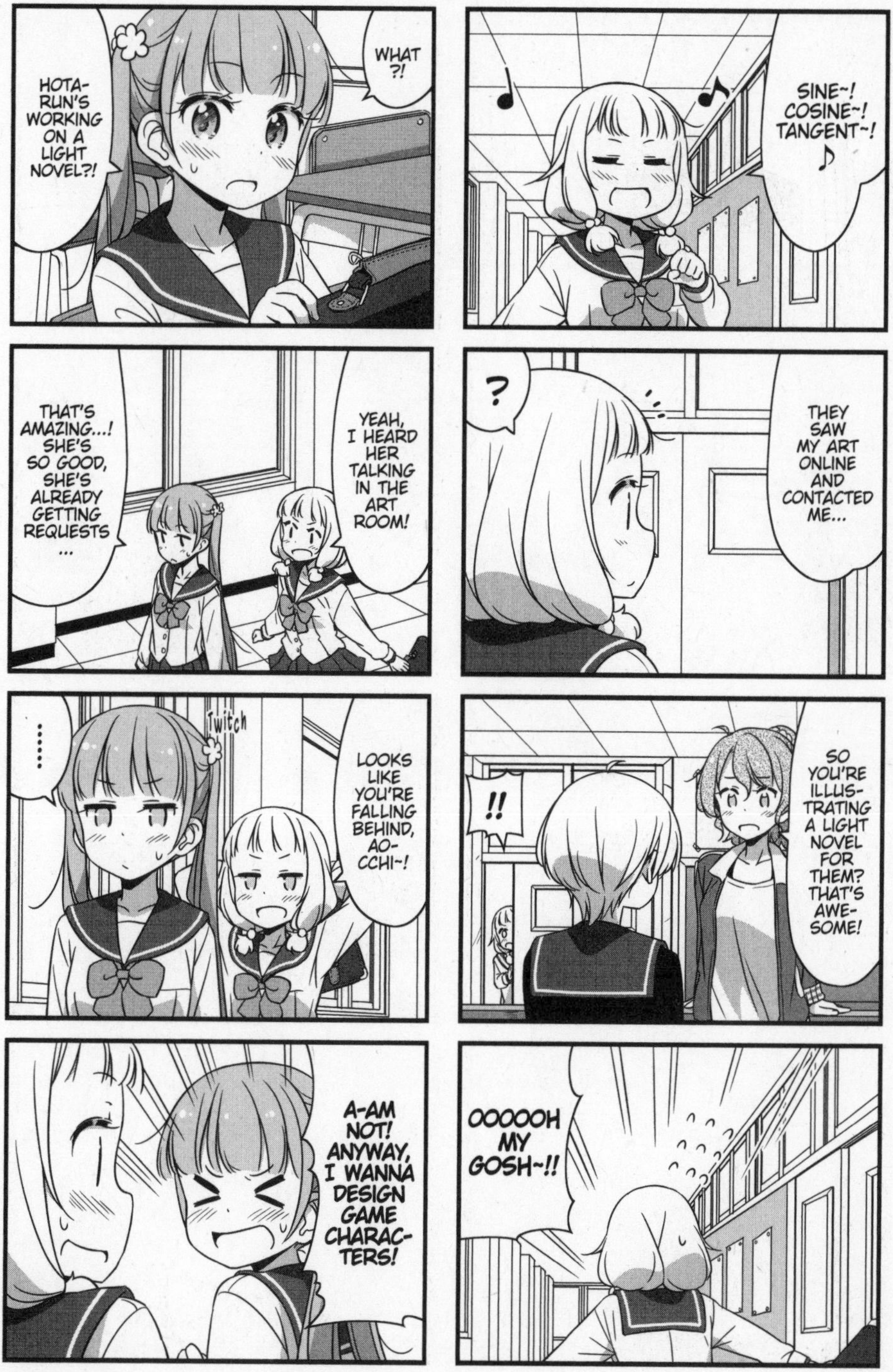
SINE~! COSINE~! TANGENT~! ♪
WHAT ?!
HOTA-RUN'S WORKING ON A LIGHT NOVEL?!
THEY SAW MY ART ONLINE AND CONTACTED ME...
?
YEAH, I HEARD HER TALKING IN THE ART ROOM!
THAT'S AMAZING...! SHE'S SO GOOD, SHE'S ALREADY GETTING REQUESTS ...
SO YOU'RE ILLUS-TRATING A LIGHT NOVEL FOR THEM? THAT'S AWE-SOME!
!!
LOOKS LIKE YOU'RE FALLING BEHIND, AO-CCHI~!
Twitch
......
OOOOOH MY GOSH~!!
A-AM NOT! ANYWAY, I WANNA DESIGN GAME CHARAC-TERS!

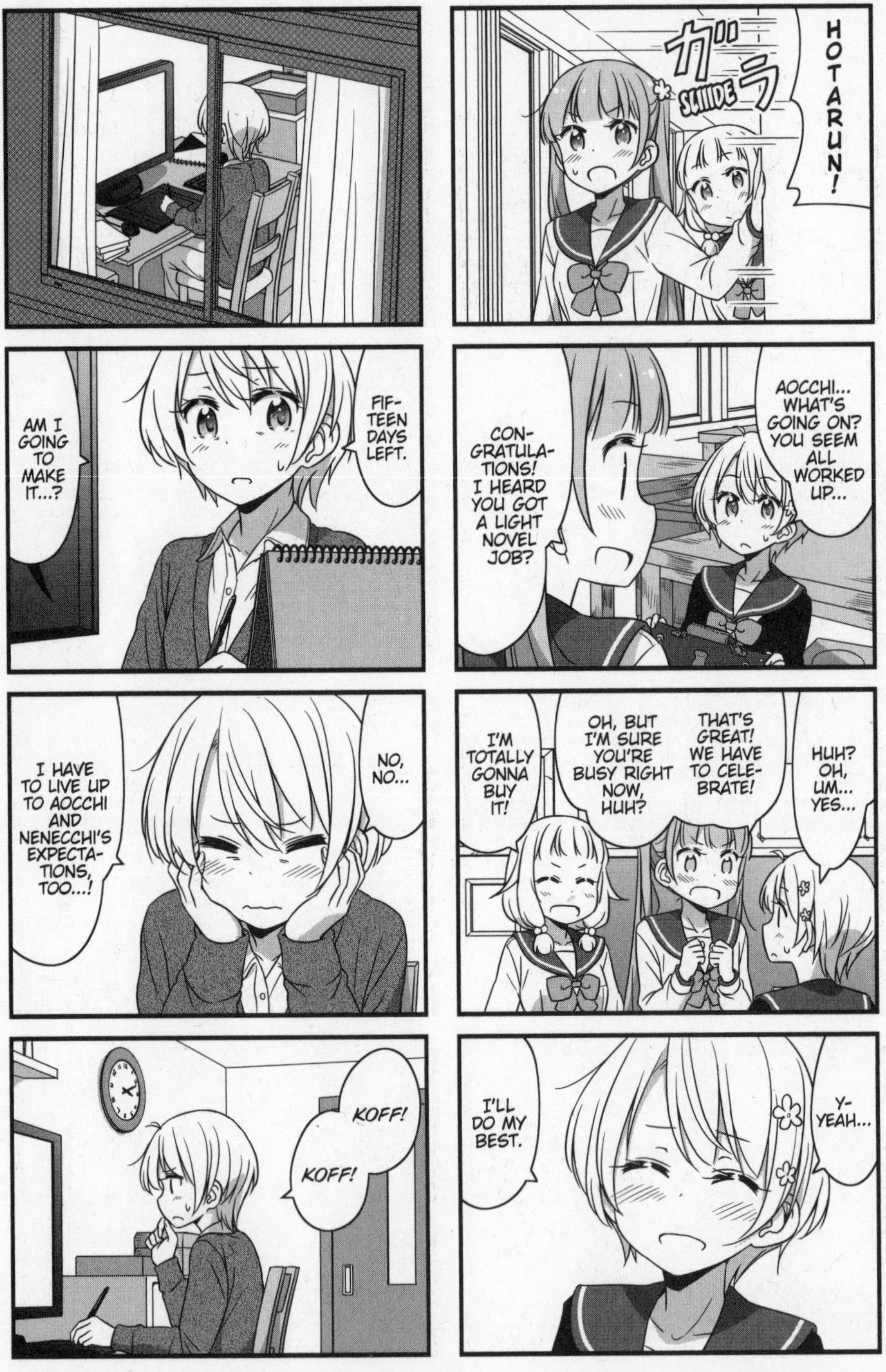
HOTARUN!
ガラ
SLIIIDE
AOCCHI... WHAT'S GOING ON? YOU SEEM ALL WORKED UP...
CONGRATULATIONS! I HEARD YOU GOT A LIGHT NOVEL JOB?
FIFTEEN DAYS LEFT.
AM I GOING TO MAKE IT...?
HUH? OH, UM... YES...
THAT'S GREAT! WE HAVE TO CELEBRATE!
OH, BUT I'M SURE YOU'RE BUSY RIGHT NOW, HUH?
I'M TOTALLY GONNA BUY IT!
NO, NO...
I HAVE TO LIVE UP TO AOCCHI AND NENECCHI'S EXPECTATIONS, TOO...!
Y-YEAH...
I'LL DO MY BEST.
KOFF!
KOFF!

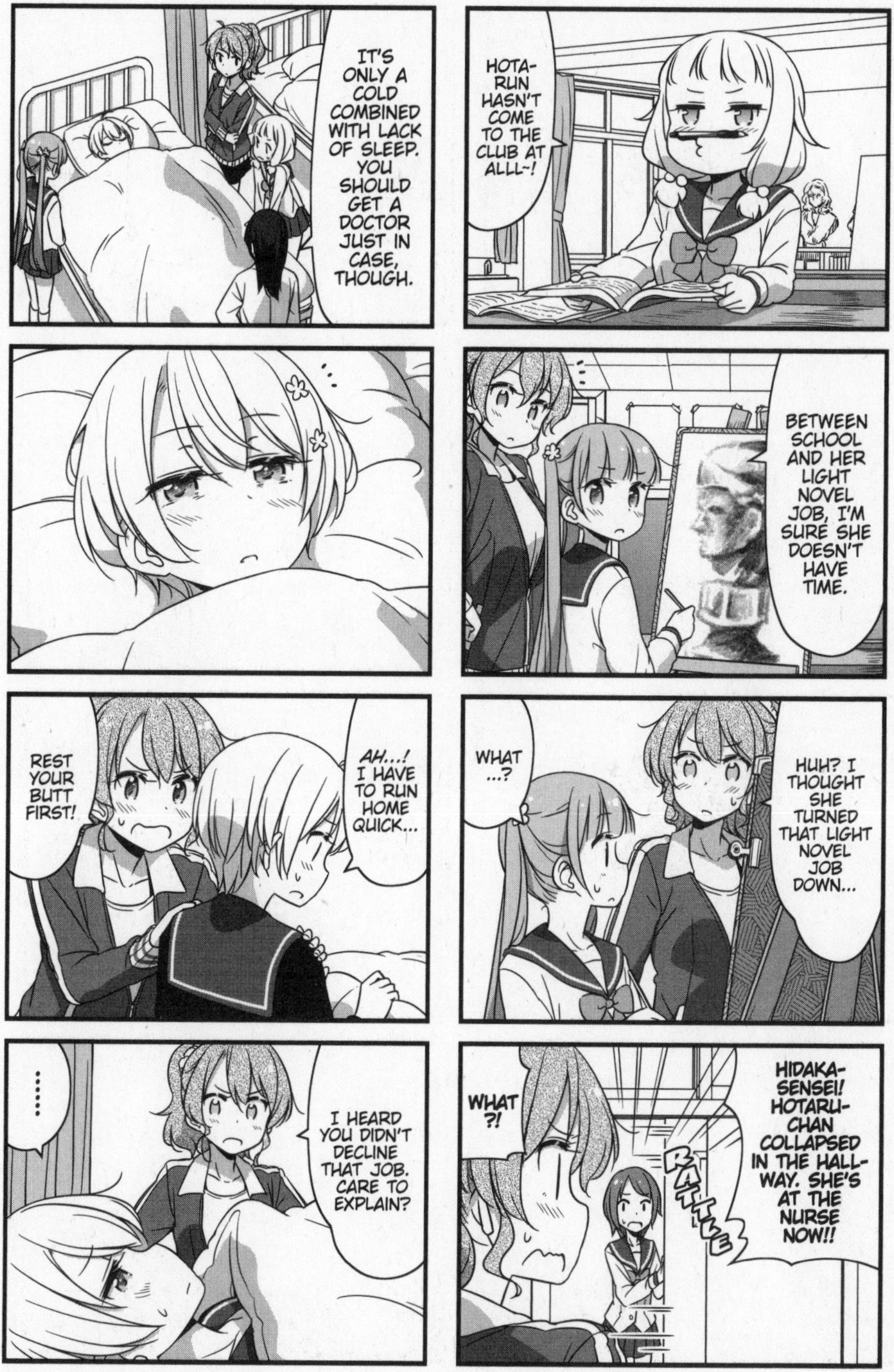
HOTA-RUN HASN'T COME TO THE CLUB AT ALLL~!
BETWEEN SCHOOL AND HER LIGHT NOVEL JOB, I'M SURE SHE DOESN'T HAVE TIME.
HUH? I THOUGHT SHE TURNED THAT LIGHT NOVEL JOB DOWN...
WHAT ...?
HIDAKA-SENSEI! HOTARU-CHAN COLLAPSED IN THE HALLWAY. SHE'S AT THE NURSE NOW!!
RATTLE
WHAT ?!
IT'S ONLY A COLD COMBINED WITH LACK OF SLEEP. YOU SHOULD GET A DOCTOR JUST IN CASE, THOUGH.
AH...! I HAVE TO RUN HOME QUICK...
REST YOUR BUTT FIRST!
I HEARD YOU DIDN'T DECLINE THAT JOB. CARE TO EXPLAIN?
......

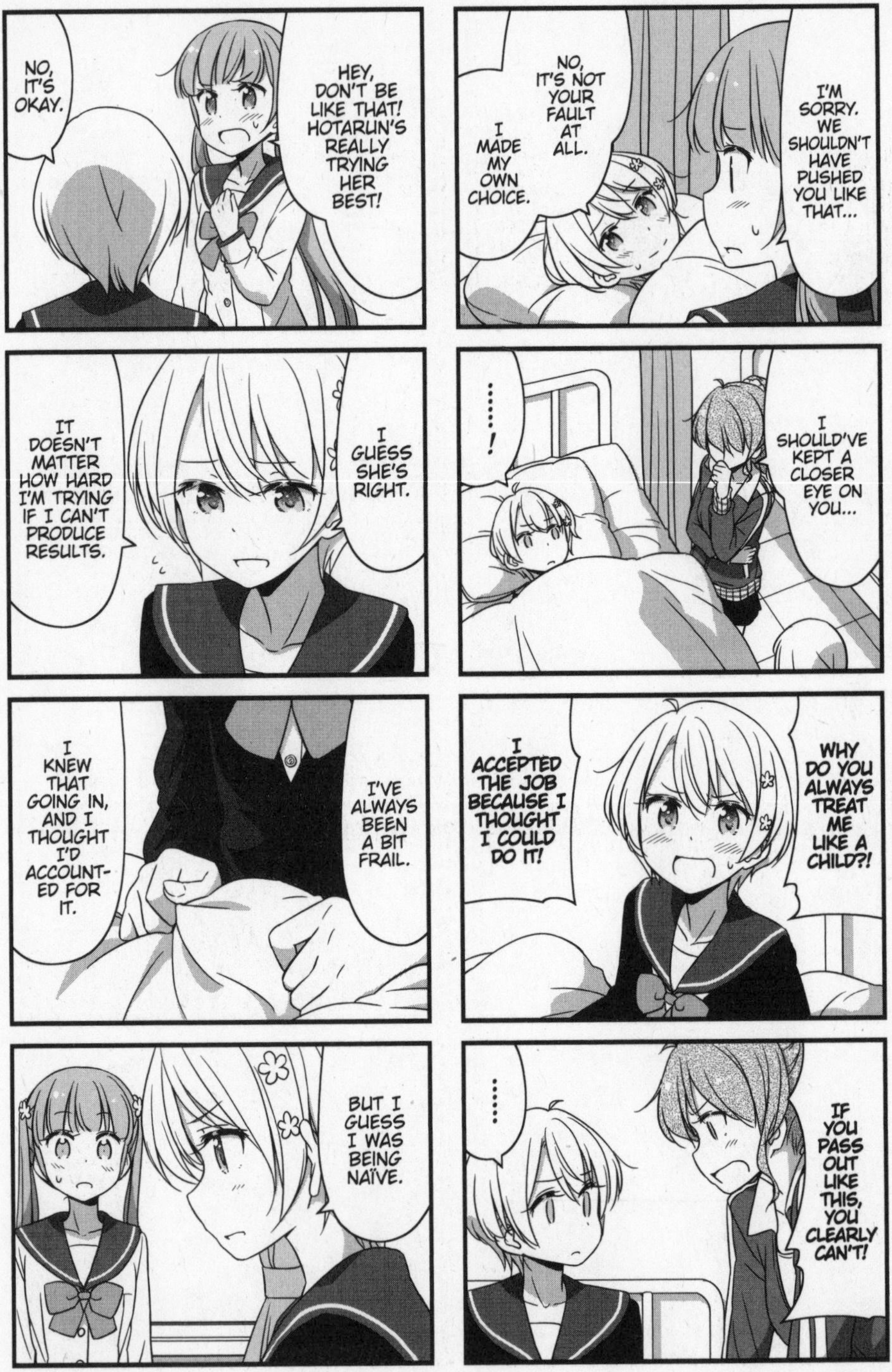
I'M SORRY. WE SHOULDN'T HAVE PUSHED YOU LIKE THAT...
NO, IT'S NOT YOUR FAULT AT ALL.
I MADE MY OWN CHOICE.
I SHOULD'VE KEPT A CLOSER EYE ON YOU...
......!
WHY DO YOU ALWAYS TREAT ME LIKE A CHILD?!
I ACCEPTED THE JOB BECAUSE I THOUGHT I COULD DO IT!
IF YOU PASS OUT LIKE THIS, YOU CLEARLY CAN'T!
......
HEY, DON'T BE LIKE THAT! HOTARUN'S REALLY TRYING HER BEST!
NO, IT'S OKAY.
I GUESS SHE'S RIGHT.
IT DOESN'T MATTER HOW HARD I'M TRYING IF I CAN'T PRODUCE RESULTS.
I'VE ALWAYS BEEN A BIT FRAIL.
I KNEW THAT GOING IN, AND I THOUGHT I'D ACCOUNT-ED FOR IT.
BUT I GUESS I WAS BEING NAÏVE.

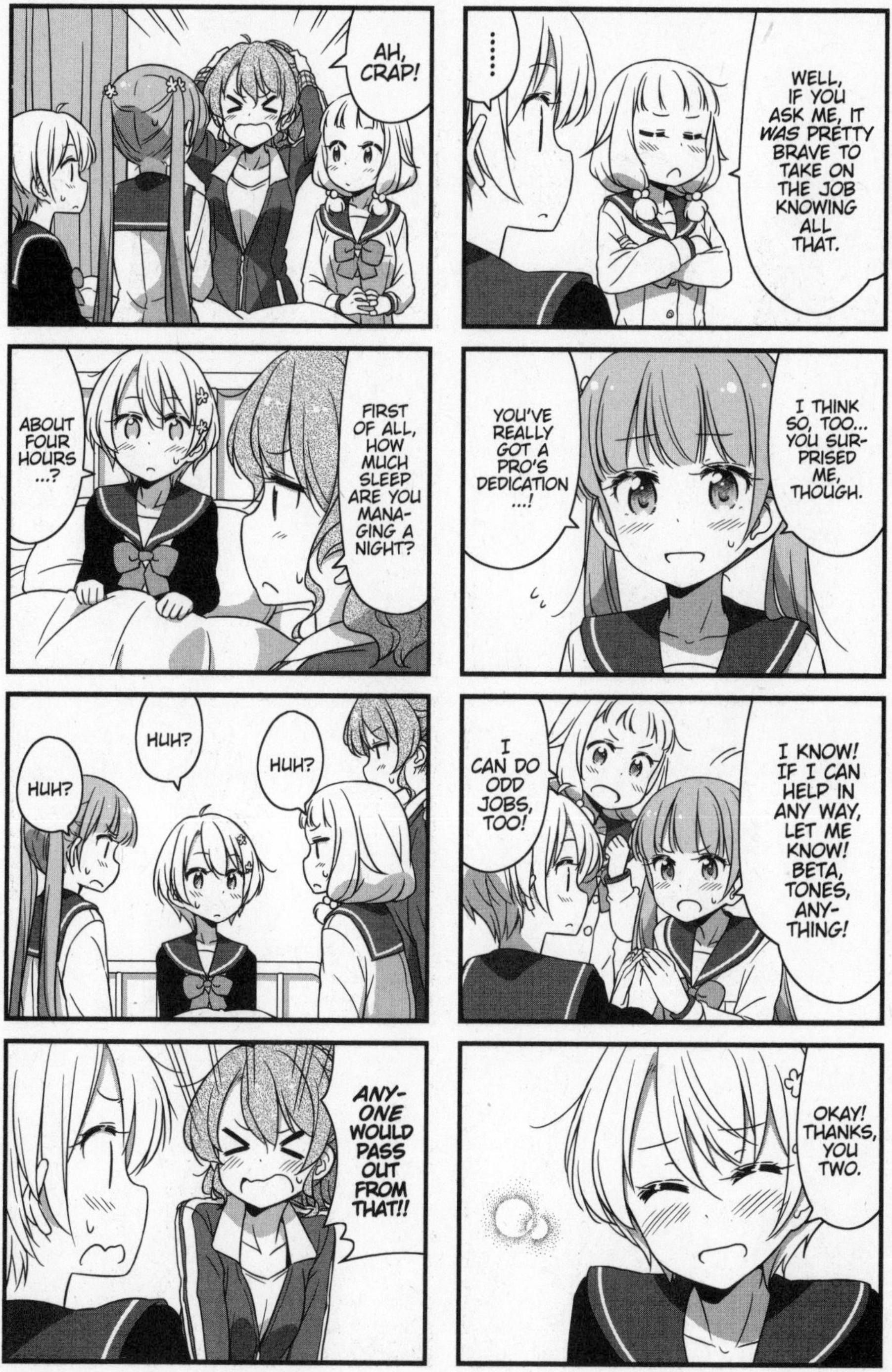
WELL, IF YOU ASK ME, IT WAS PRETTY BRAVE TO TAKE ON THE JOB KNOWING ALL THAT.
……
AH, CRAP!
I THINK SO, TOO... YOU SURPRISED ME, THOUGH.
YOU'VE REALLY GOT A PRO'S DEDICATION ...!
FIRST OF ALL, HOW MUCH SLEEP ARE YOU MANAGING A NIGHT?
ABOUT FOUR HOURS ...?
I KNOW! IF I CAN HELP IN ANY WAY, LET ME KNOW! BETA, TONES, ANYTHING!
I CAN DO ODD JOBS, TOO!
HUH?
HUH?
HUH?
OKAY! THANKS, YOU TWO.
ANYONE WOULD PASS OUT FROM THAT!!

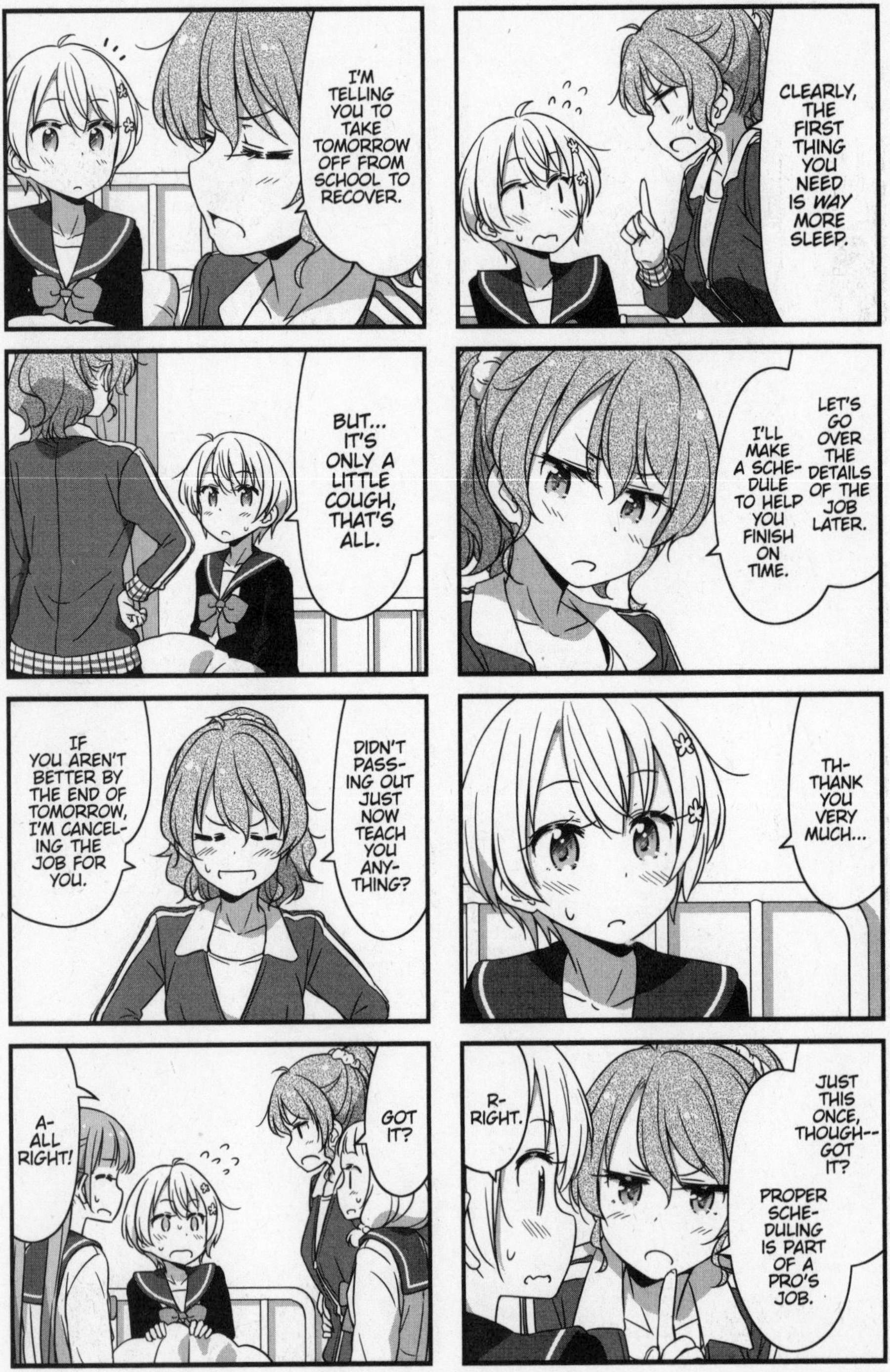
CLEARLY, THE FIRST THING YOU NEED IS WAY MORE SLEEP.
I'M TELLING YOU TO TAKE TOMORROW OFF FROM SCHOOL TO RECOVER.
LET'S GO OVER THE DETAILS OF THE JOB LATER.
I'LL MAKE A SCHEDULE TO HELP YOU FINISH ON TIME.
BUT... IT'S ONLY A LITTLE COUGH, THAT'S ALL.
TH- THANK YOU VERY MUCH...
DIDN'T PASSING OUT JUST NOW TEACH YOU ANYTHING?
IF YOU AREN'T BETTER BY THE END OF TOMORROW, I'M CANCELING THE JOB FOR YOU.
JUST THIS ONCE, THOUGH--GOT IT?
PROPER SCHEDULING IS PART OF A PRO'S JOB.
R- RIGHT.
GOT IT?
A- ALL RIGHT!

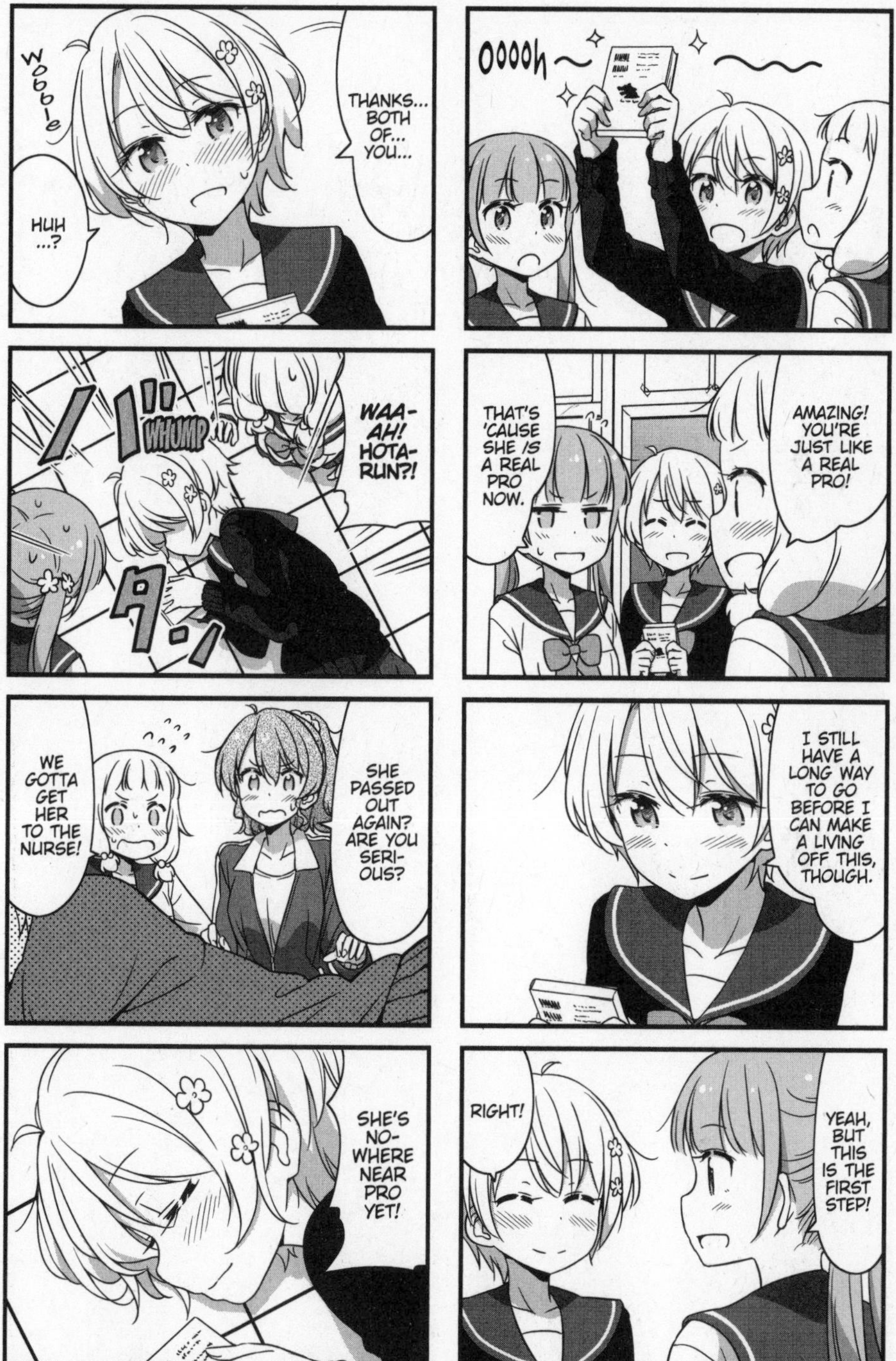
Oooh~ ~~~
AMAZING! YOU'RE JUST LIKE A REAL PRO!
THAT'S 'CAUSE SHE IS A REAL PRO NOW.
I STILL HAVE A LONG WAY TO GO BEFORE I CAN MAKE A LIVING OFF THIS, THOUGH.
YEAH, BUT THIS IS THE FIRST STEP!
RIGHT!
THANKS... BOTH OF... YOU...
Wobble
HUH ...?
WAA-AH! HOTA-RUN?!
WHUMP
SHE PASSED OUT AGAIN? ARE YOU SERI-OUS?
WE GOTTA GET HER TO THE NURSE!
SHE'S NO-WHERE NEAR PRO YET!

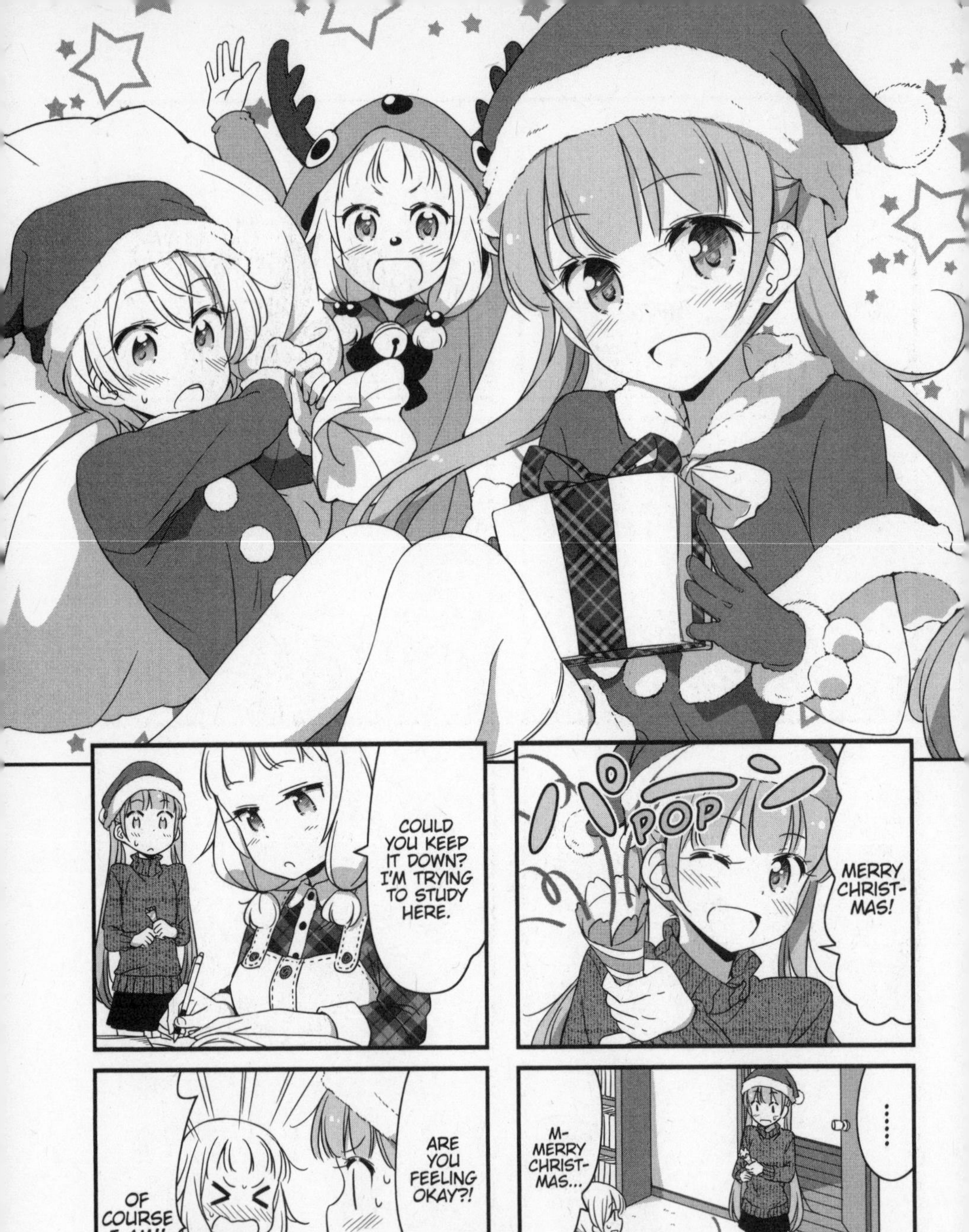
POP
MERRY CHRIST-MAS!
COULD YOU KEEP IT DOWN? I'M TRYING TO STUDY HERE.
......
M-MERRY CHRIST-MAS...
ARE YOU FEELING OKAY?!
OF COURSE I AM!!

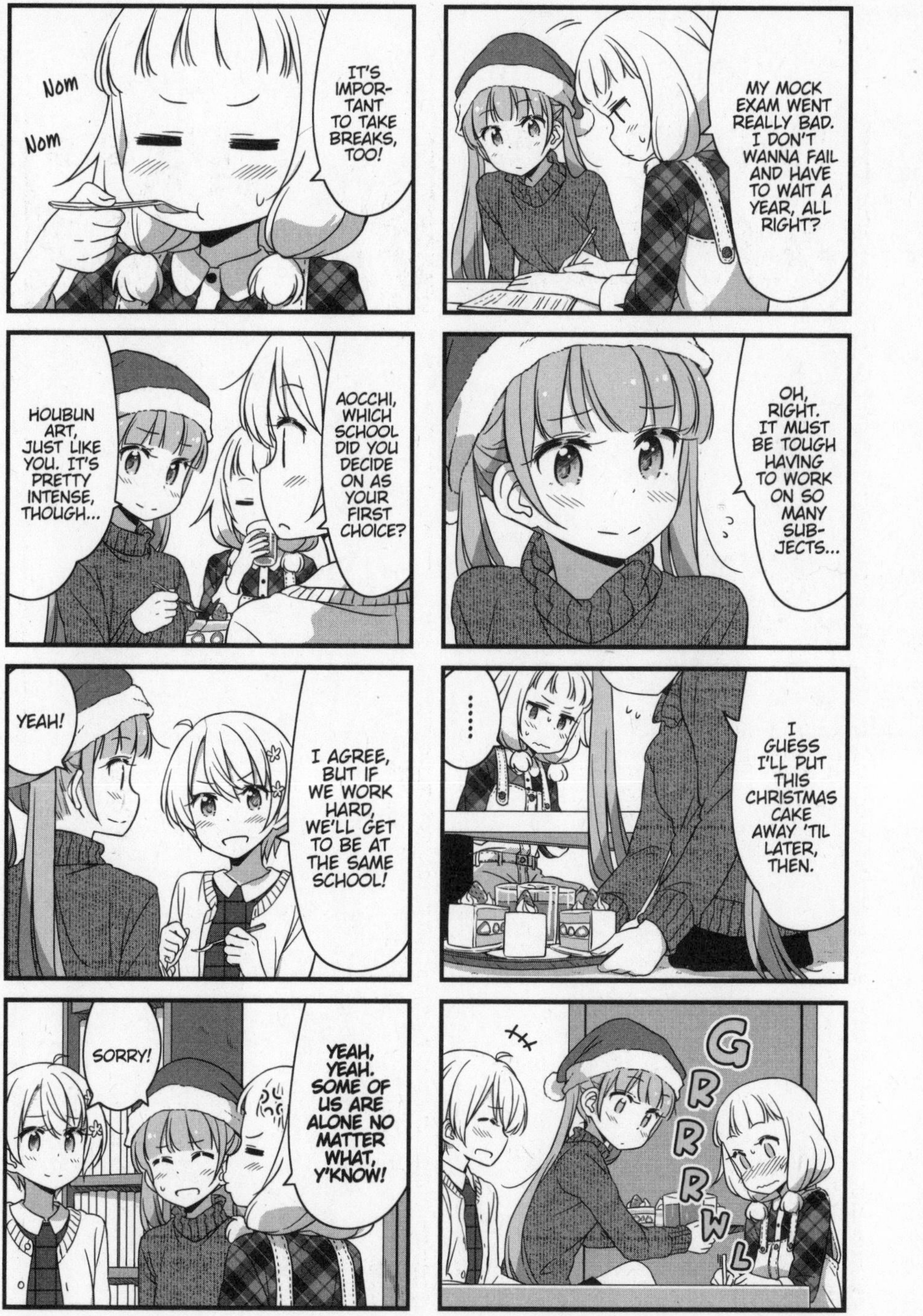
MY MOCK EXAM WENT REALLY BAD. I DON'T WANNA FAIL AND HAVE TO WAIT A YEAR, ALL RIGHT?
OH, RIGHT. IT MUST BE TOUGH HAVING TO WORK ON SO MANY SUBJECTS...
......
I GUESS I'LL PUT THIS CHRISTMAS CAKE AWAY 'TIL LATER, THEN.
GRRRWL
IT'S IMPORTANT TO TAKE BREAKS, TOO!
Nom
Nom
AOCCHI, WHICH SCHOOL DID YOU DECIDE ON AS YOUR FIRST CHOICE?
HOUBUN ART, JUST LIKE YOU. IT'S PRETTY INTENSE, THOUGH...
I AGREE, BUT IF WE WORK HARD, WE'LL GET TO BE AT THE SAME SCHOOL!
YEAH!
YEAH, YEAH. SOME OF US ARE ALONE NO MATTER WHAT, Y'KNOW!
SORRY!

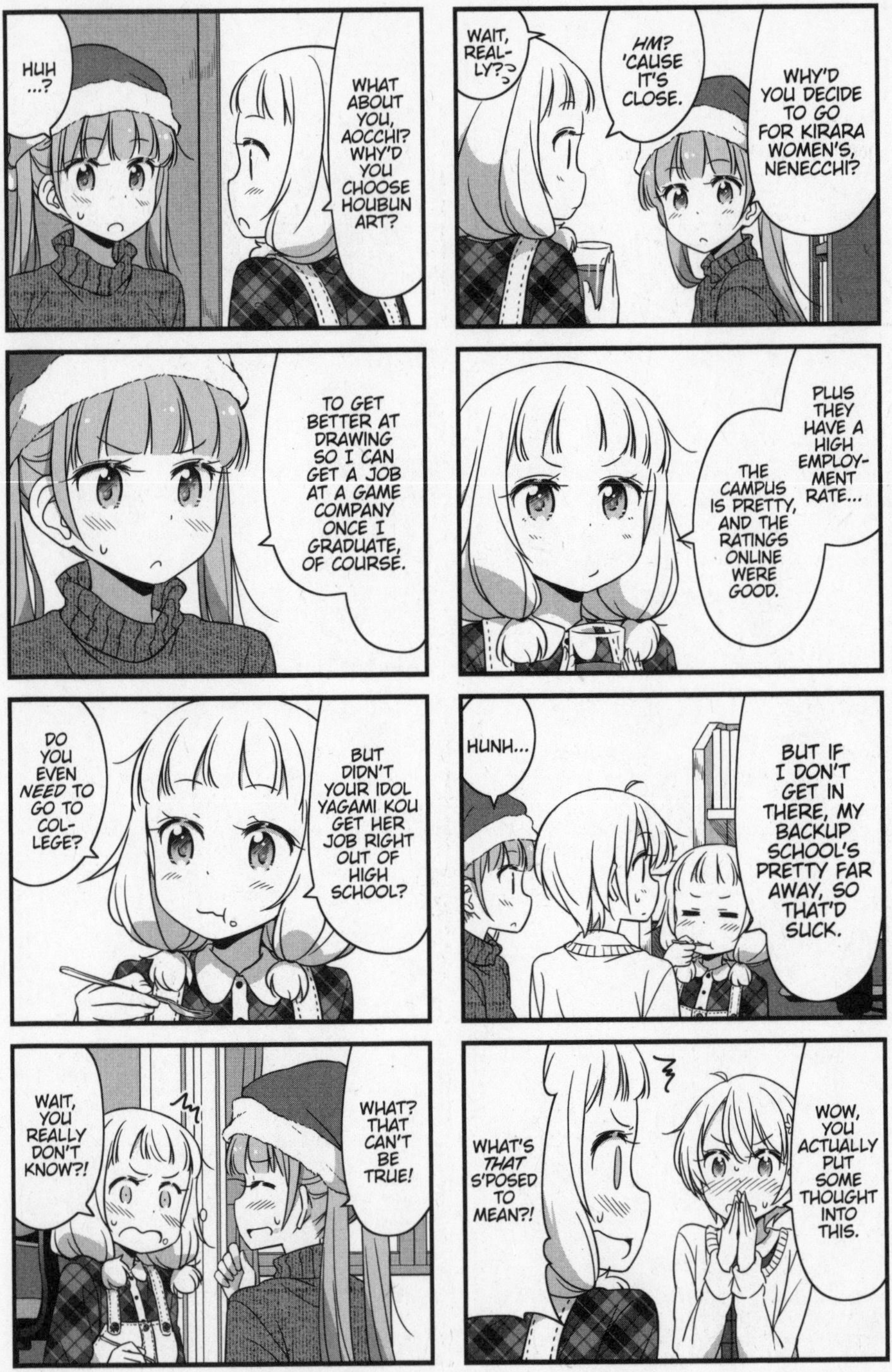
WHY'D YOU DECIDE TO GO FOR KIRARA WOMEN'S, NENECCHI?
HM? 'CAUSE IT'S CLOSE.
WAIT, REALLY?
WHAT ABOUT YOU, AOCCHI? WHY'D YOU CHOOSE HOUBUN ART?
HUH ...?
PLUS THEY HAVE A HIGH EMPLOYMENT RATE...
THE CAMPUS IS PRETTY, AND THE RATINGS ONLINE WERE GOOD.
TO GET BETTER AT DRAWING SO I CAN GET A JOB AT A GAME COMPANY ONCE I GRADUATE, OF COURSE.
BUT IF I DON'T GET IN THERE, MY BACKUP SCHOOL'S PRETTY FAR AWAY, SO THAT'D SUCK.
HUNH...
BUT DIDN'T YOUR IDOL YAGAMI KOU GET HER JOB RIGHT OUT OF HIGH SCHOOL?
DO YOU EVEN *NEED* TO GO TO COLLEGE?
WOW, YOU ACTUALLY PUT SOME THOUGHT INTO THIS.
WHAT'S *THAT* S'POSED TO MEAN?!
WHAT? THAT CAN'T BE TRUE!
WAIT, YOU REALLY DON'T KNOW?!

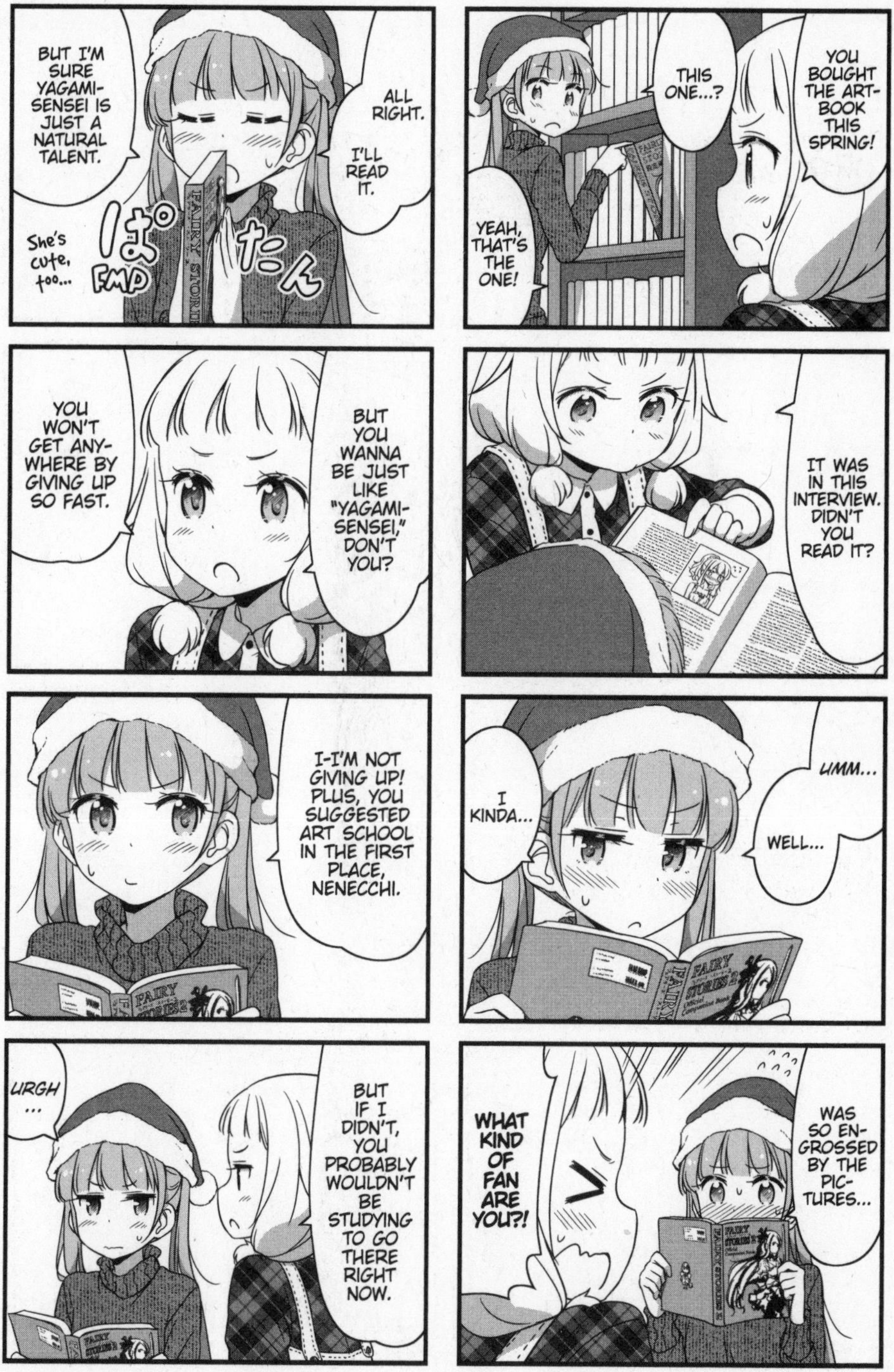
YOU BOUGHT THE ART-BOOK THIS SPRING!
THIS ONE...?
YEAH, THAT'S THE ONE!
ALL RIGHT.
I'LL READ IT.
BUT I'M SURE YAGAMI-SENSEI IS JUST A NATURAL TALENT.
ぱたん
FMP
She's cute, too...
IT WAS IN THIS INTERVIEW. DIDN'T YOU READ IT?
BUT YOU WANNA BE JUST LIKE "YAGAMI-SENSEI," DON'T YOU?
YOU WON'T GET ANYWHERE BY GIVING UP SO FAST.
UMM...
WELL...
I KINDA...
I-I'M NOT GIVING UP! PLUS, YOU SUGGESTED ART SCHOOL IN THE FIRST PLACE, NENECCHI.
WAS SO ENGROSSED BY THE PICTURES...
WHAT KIND OF FAN ARE YOU?!
BUT IF I DIDN'T, YOU PROBABLY WOULDN'T BE STUDYING TO GO THERE RIGHT NOW.
URGH...

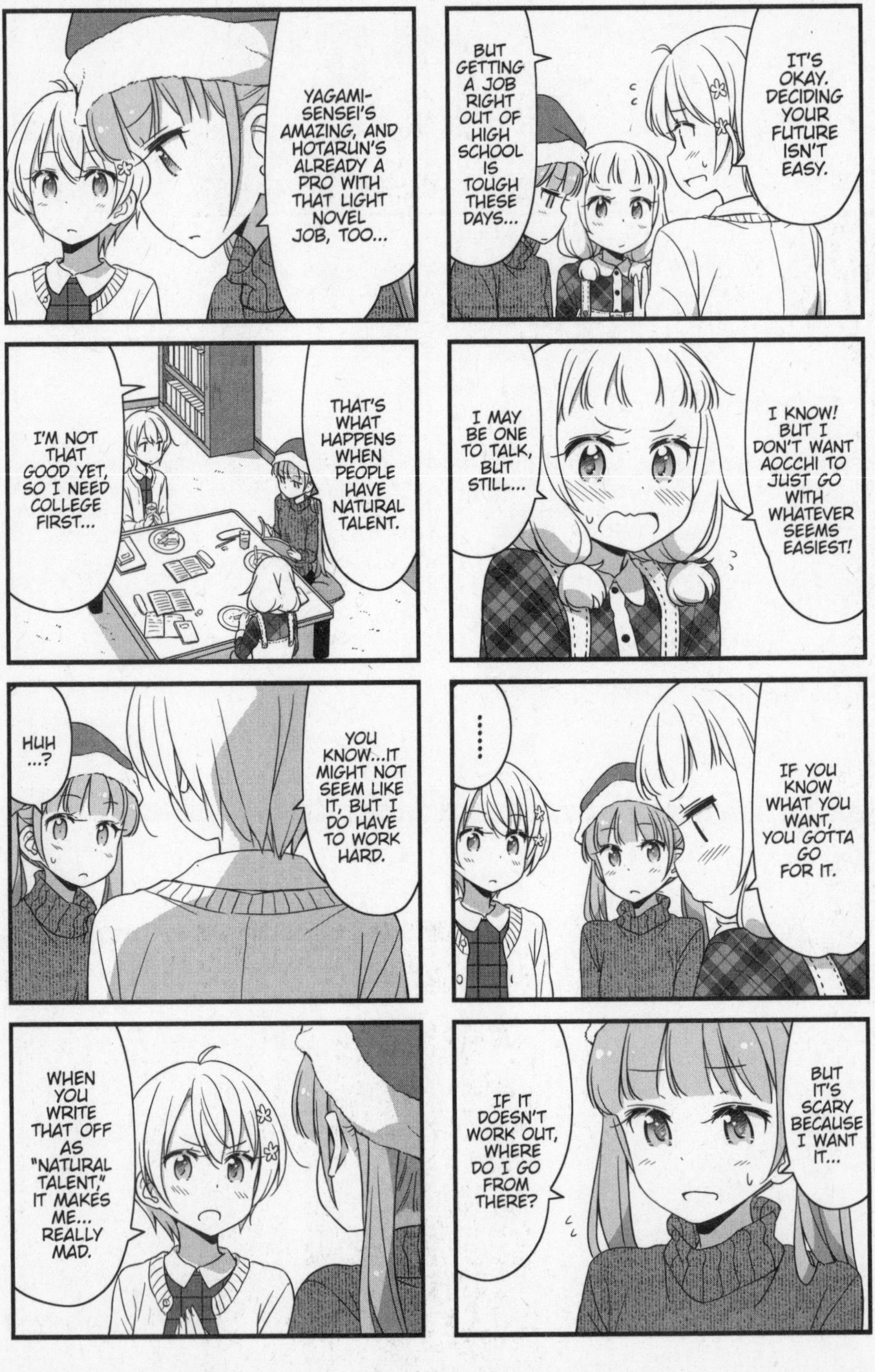
IT'S OKAY. DECIDING YOUR FUTURE ISN'T EASY.
BUT GETTING A JOB RIGHT OUT OF HIGH SCHOOL IS TOUGH THESE DAYS...
YAGAMI-SENSEI'S AMAZING, AND HOTARUN'S ALREADY A PRO WITH THAT LIGHT NOVEL JOB, TOO...
I KNOW! BUT I DON'T WANT AOCCHI TO JUST GO WITH WHATEVER SEEMS EASIEST!
I MAY BE ONE TO TALK, BUT STILL...
THAT'S WHAT HAPPENS WHEN PEOPLE HAVE NATURAL TALENT.
I'M NOT THAT GOOD YET, SO I NEED COLLEGE FIRST...
IF YOU KNOW WHAT YOU WANT, YOU GOTTA GO FOR IT.
......
YOU KNOW...IT MIGHT NOT SEEM LIKE IT, BUT I DO HAVE TO WORK HARD.
HUH ...?
BUT IT'S SCARY BECAUSE I WANT IT...
IF IT DOESN'T WORK OUT, WHERE DO I GO FROM THERE?
WHEN YOU WRITE THAT OFF AS "NATURAL TALENT," IT MAKES ME... REALLY MAD.

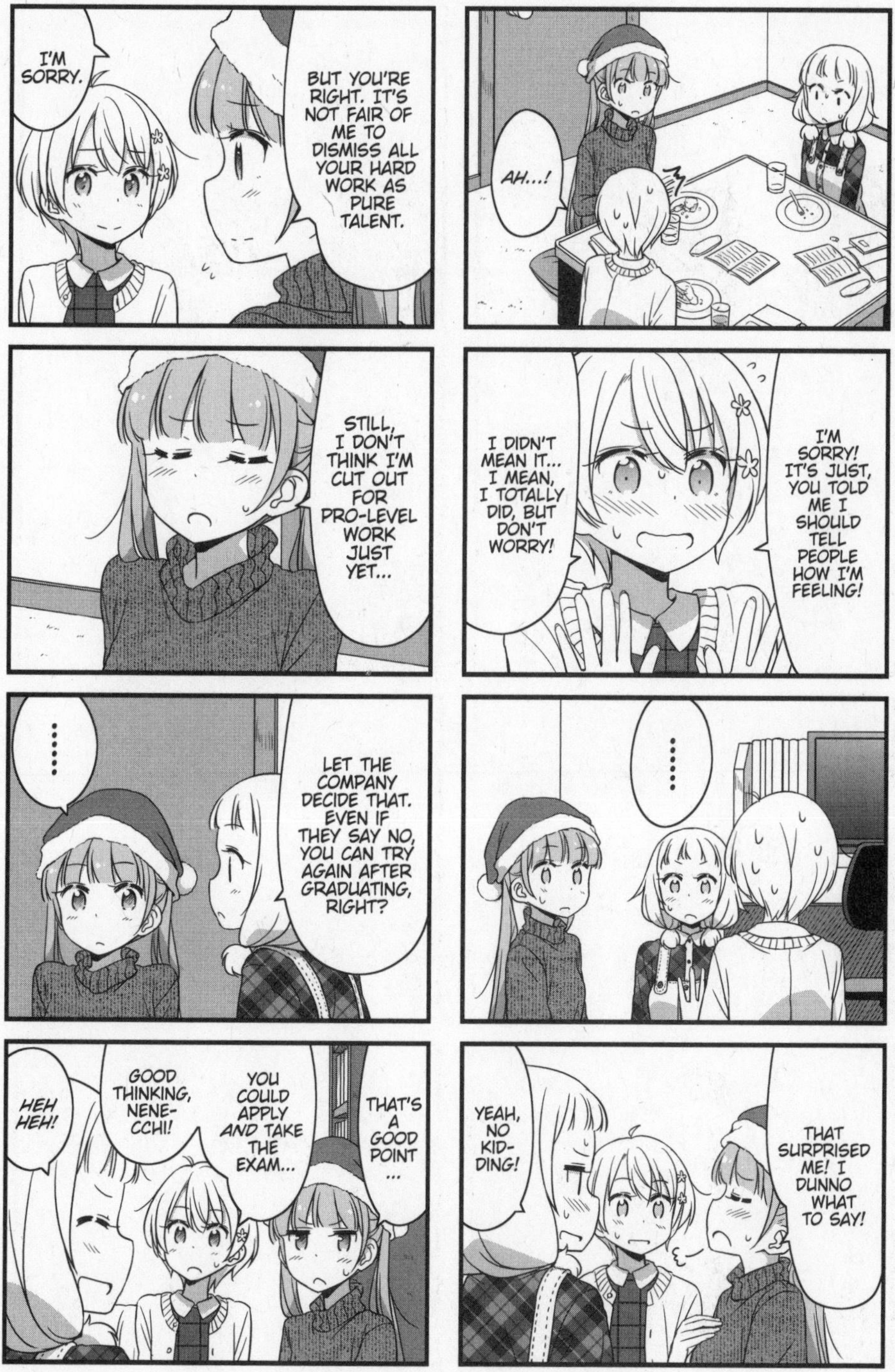
AH...!
BUT YOU'RE RIGHT. IT'S NOT FAIR OF ME TO DISMISS ALL YOUR HARD WORK AS PURE TALENT.
I'M SORRY.
I'M SORRY! IT'S JUST, YOU TOLD ME I SHOULD TELL PEOPLE HOW I'M FEELING!
I DIDN'T MEAN IT... I MEAN, I TOTALLY DID, BUT DON'T WORRY!
STILL, I DON'T THINK I'M CUT OUT FOR PRO-LEVEL WORK JUST YET...
......
LET THE COMPANY DECIDE THAT. EVEN IF THEY SAY NO, YOU CAN TRY AGAIN AFTER GRADUATING, RIGHT?
......
THAT SURPRISED ME! I DUNNO WHAT TO SAY!
YEAH, NO KID-DING!
THAT'S A GOOD POINT ...
YOU COULD APPLY AND TAKE THE EXAM...
GOOD THINKING, NENE-CCHI!
HEH HEH!

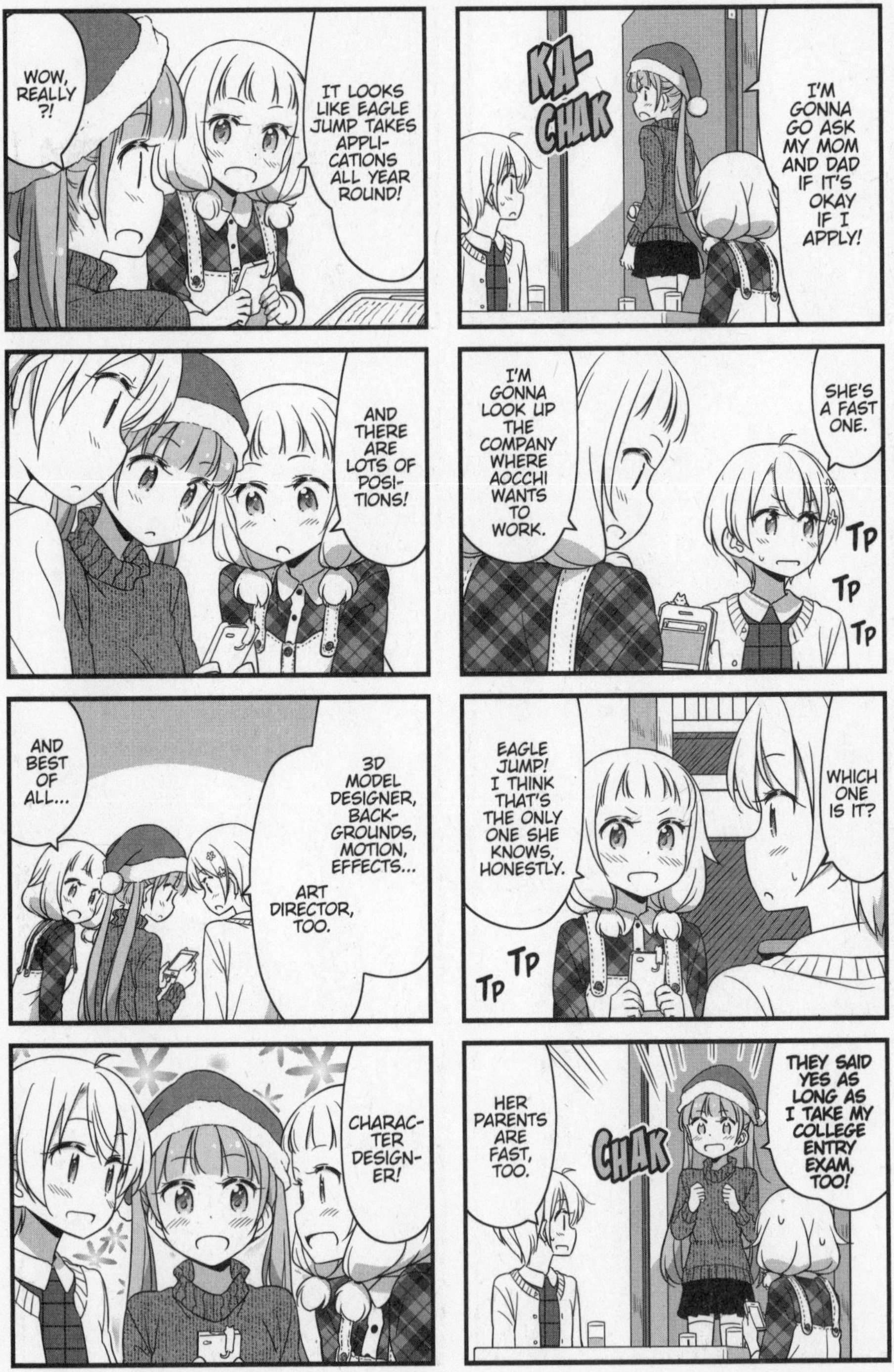

I'M GONNA GO ASK MY MOM AND DAD IF IT'S OKAY IF I APPLY!
KA-CHAK
SHE'S A FAST ONE.
I'M GONNA LOOK UP THE COMPANY WHERE AOCCHI WANTS TO WORK.
Tp Tp Tp
WHICH ONE IS IT?
EAGLE JUMP! I THINK THAT'S THE ONLY ONE SHE KNOWS, HONESTLY.
Tp Tp
THEY SAID YES AS LONG AS I TAKE MY COLLEGE ENTRY EXAM, TOO!
CHAK
HER PARENTS ARE FAST, TOO.
IT LOOKS LIKE EAGLE JUMP TAKES APPLI-CATIONS ALL YEAR ROUND!
WOW, REALLY ?!
AND THERE ARE LOTS OF POSI-TIONS!
3D MODEL DESIGNER, BACK-GROUNDS, MOTION, EFFECTS...
ART DIRECTOR, TOO.
AND BEST OF ALL...
CHARAC-TER DESIGN-ER!

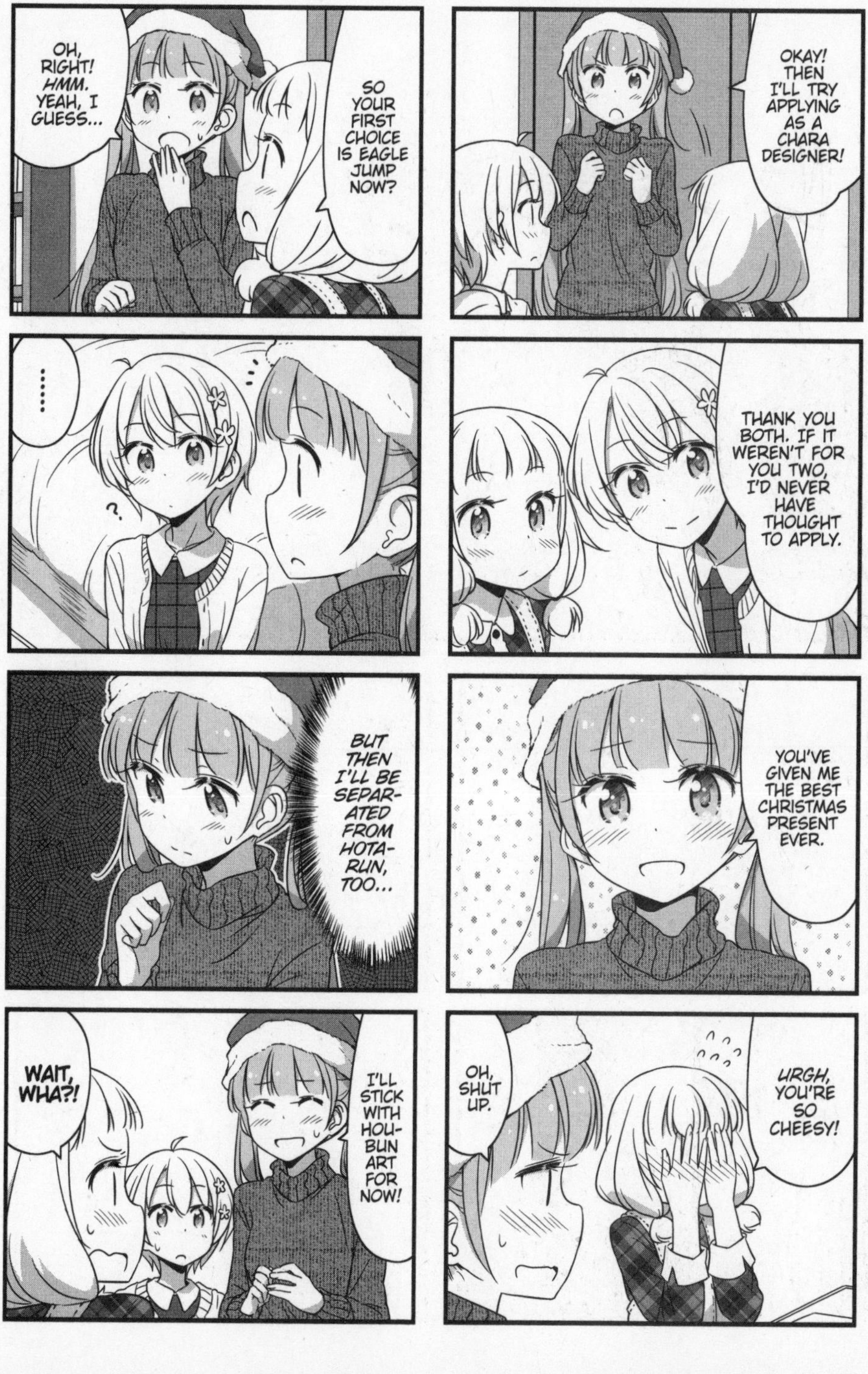
OKAY! THEN I'LL TRY APPLYING AS A CHARA DESIGNER!
SO YOUR FIRST CHOICE IS EAGLE JUMP NOW?
OH, RIGHT! *HMM.* YEAH, I GUESS...
THANK YOU BOTH. IF IT WEREN'T FOR YOU TWO, I'D NEVER HAVE THOUGHT TO APPLY.
......
YOU'VE GIVEN ME THE BEST CHRISTMAS PRESENT EVER.
BUT THEN I'LL BE SEPARATED FROM HOTARUN, TOO...
URGH, YOU'RE SO CHEESY!
OH, SHUT UP.
I'LL STICK WITH HOUBUN ART FOR NOW!
WAIT, WHA?!

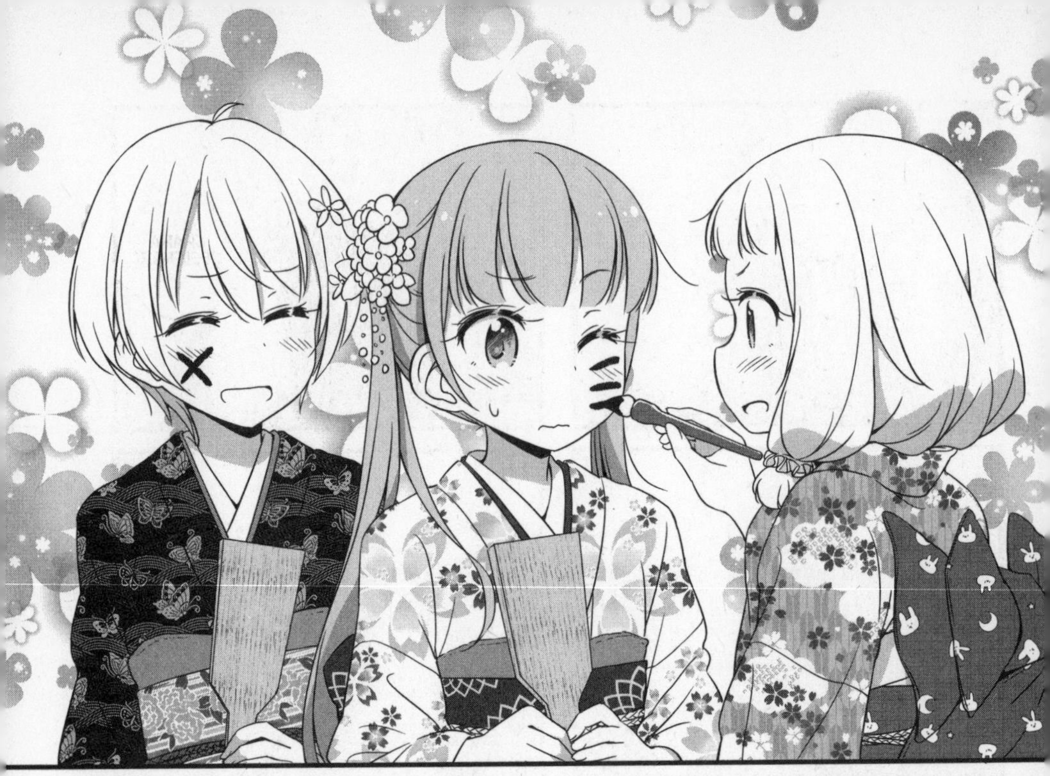

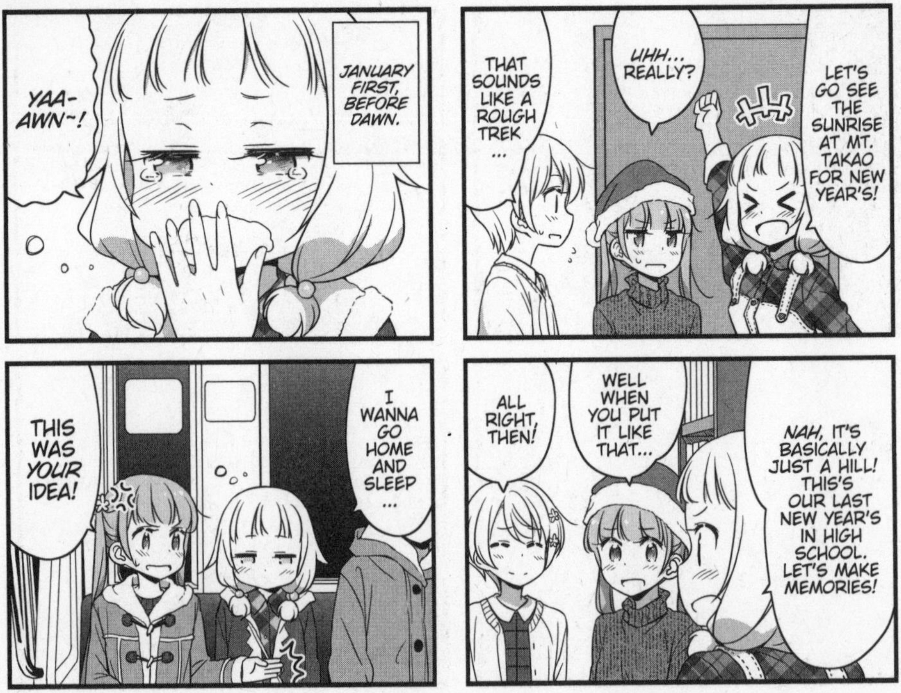
LET'S GO SEE THE SUNRISE AT MT. TAKAO FOR NEW YEAR'S!
UHH... REALLY?
THAT SOUNDS LIKE A ROUGH TREK...
NAH, IT'S BASICALLY JUST A HILL! THIS'S OUR LAST NEW YEAR'S IN HIGH SCHOOL. LET'S MAKE MEMORIES!
WELL WHEN YOU PUT IT LIKE THAT...
ALL RIGHT, THEN!
JANUARY FIRST, BEFORE DAWN.
YAA-AWN~!
I WANNA GO HOME AND SLEEP...
THIS WAS YOUR IDEA!

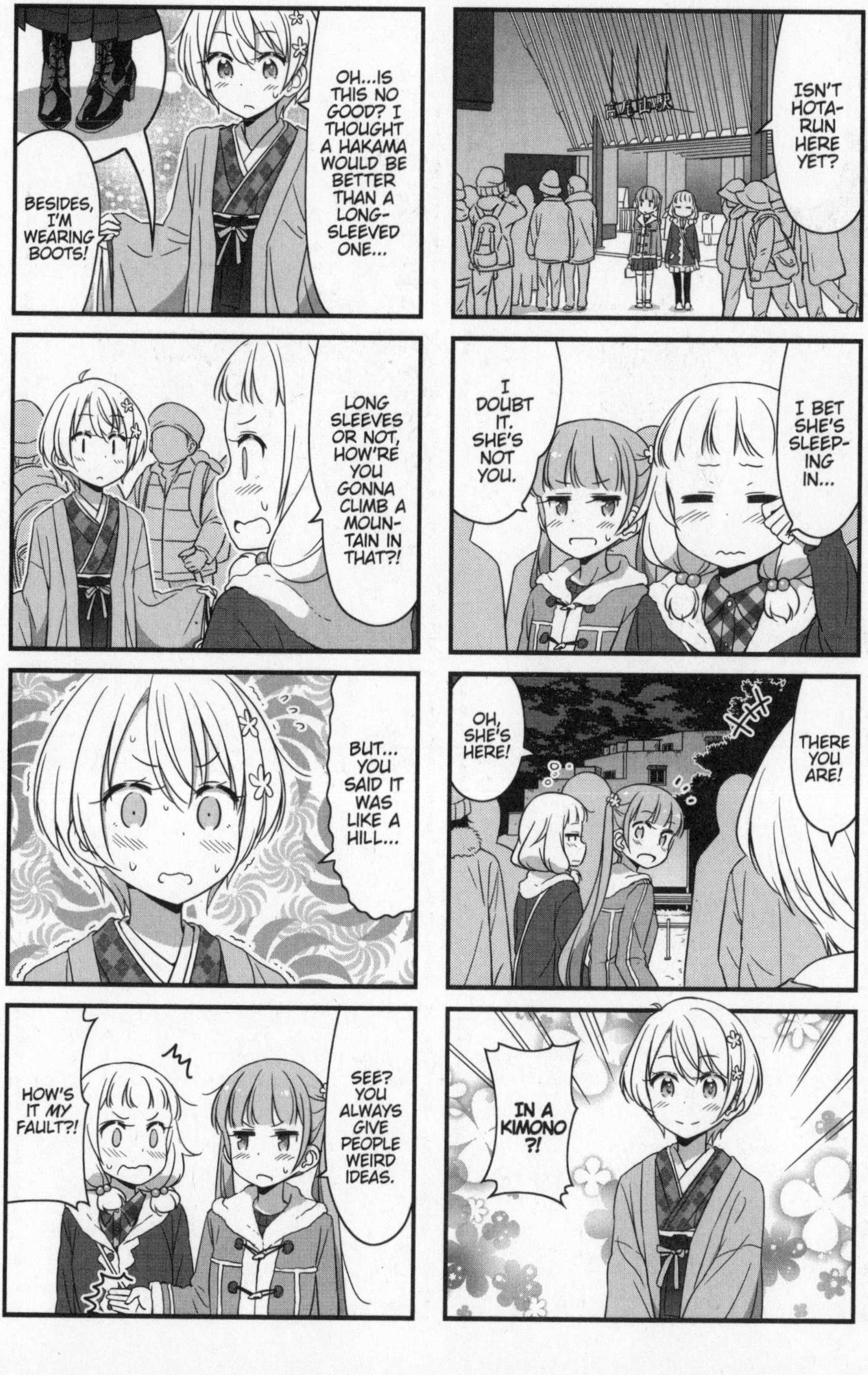
ISN'T HOTARUN HERE YET?
I BET SHE'S SLEEPING IN...
I DOUBT IT. SHE'S NOT YOU.
THERE YOU ARE!
OH, SHE'S HERE!
IN A KIMONO?!
OH...IS THIS NO GOOD? I THOUGHT A HAKAMA WOULD BE BETTER THAN A LONG-SLEEVED ONE...
BESIDES, I'M WEARING BOOTS!
LONG SLEEVES OR NOT, HOW'RE YOU GONNA CLIMB A MOUNTAIN IN THAT?!
BUT... YOU SAID IT WAS LIKE A HILL...
SEE? YOU ALWAYS GIVE PEOPLE WEIRD IDEAS.
HOW'S IT MY FAULT?!

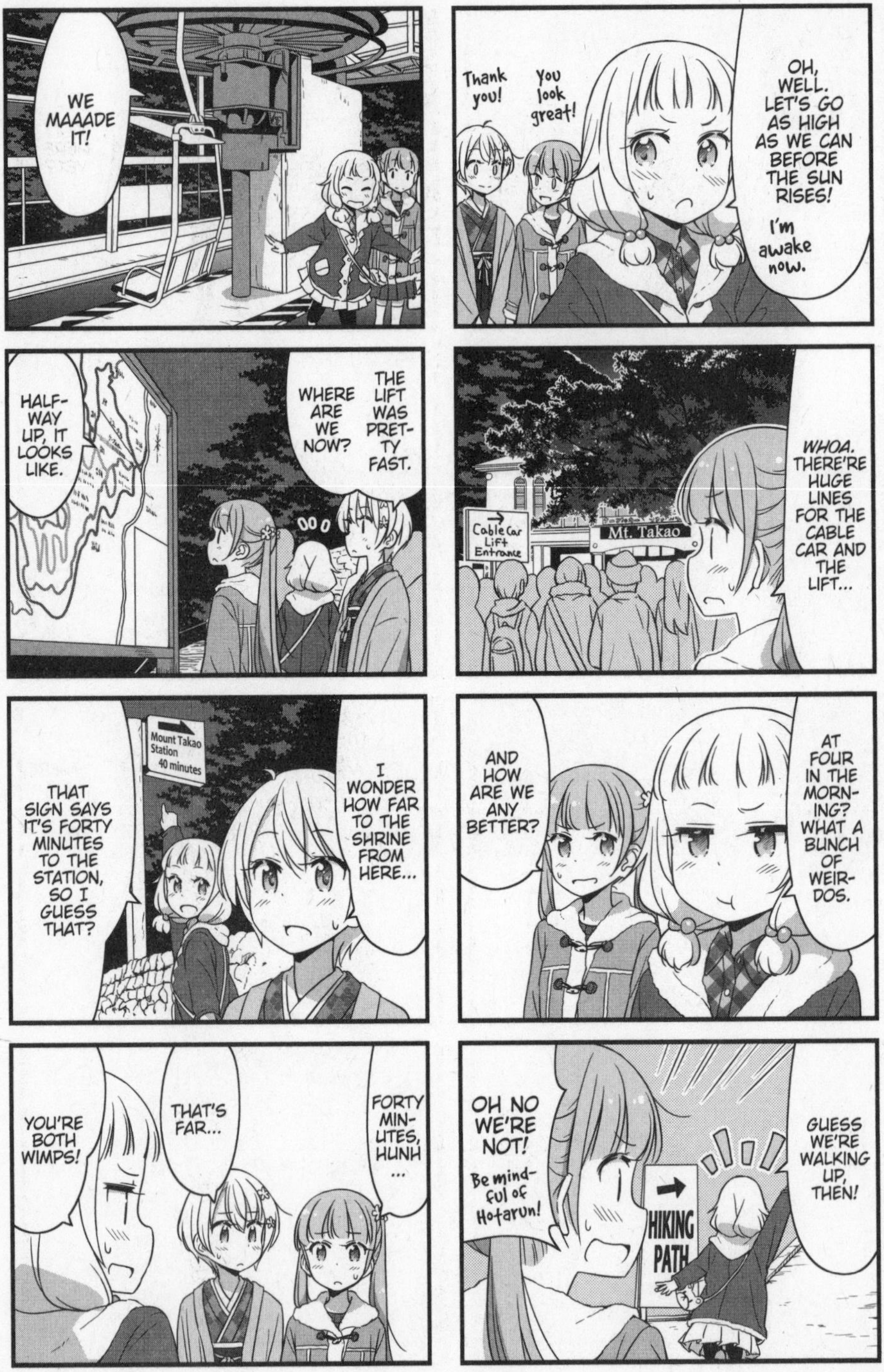
OH, WELL. LET'S GO AS HIGH AS WE CAN BEFORE THE SUN RISES!
I'm awake now.
You look great!
Thank you!
WE MAAADE IT!
WHOA. THERE'RE HUGE LINES FOR THE CABLE CAR AND THE LIFT...
Mt. Takao
Cable Car Lift Entrance
THE LIFT WAS PRETTY FAST.
WHERE ARE WE NOW?
HALF-WAY UP, IT LOOKS LIKE.
AT FOUR IN THE MORNING? WHAT A BUNCH OF WEIRDOS.
AND HOW ARE WE ANY BETTER?
I WONDER HOW FAR TO THE SHRINE FROM HERE...
Mount Takao Station 40 minutes
THAT SIGN SAYS IT'S FORTY MINUTES TO THE STATION, SO I GUESS THAT?
GUESS WE'RE WALKING UP, THEN!
HIKING PATH
OH NO WE'RE NOT!
Be mindful of Hotarun!
FORTY MINUTES, HUNH...
THAT'S FAR...
YOU'RE BOTH WIMPS!

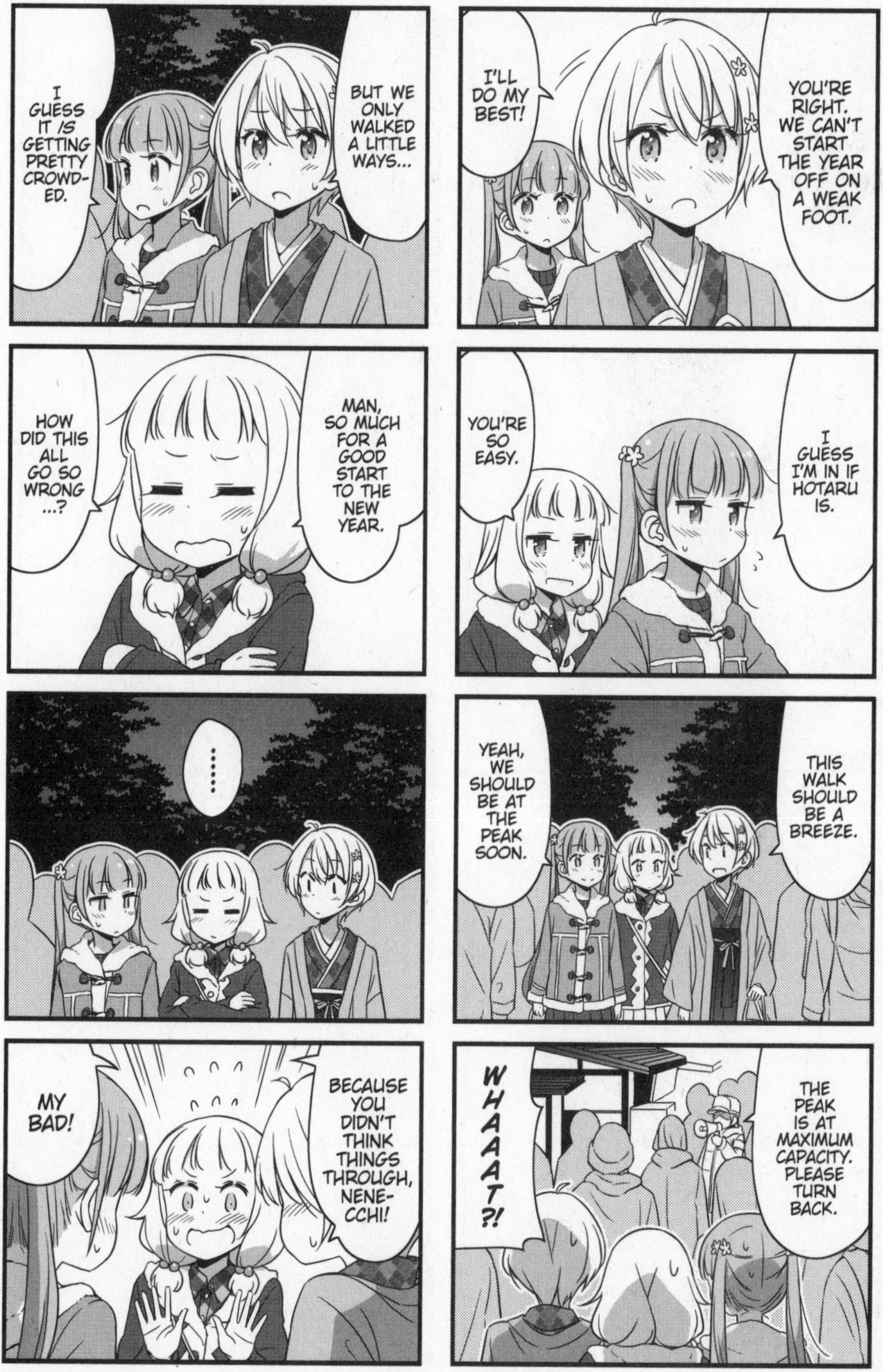
YOU'RE RIGHT. WE CAN'T START THE YEAR OFF ON A WEAK FOOT.
I'LL DO MY BEST!
BUT WE ONLY WALKED A LITTLE WAYS...
I GUESS IT IS GETTING PRETTY CROWD-ED.
I GUESS I'M IN IF HOTARU IS.
YOU'RE SO EASY.
MAN, SO MUCH FOR A GOOD START TO THE NEW YEAR.
HOW DID THIS ALL GO SO WRONG ...?
THIS WALK SHOULD BE A BREEZE.
YEAH, WE SHOULD BE AT THE PEAK SOON.
......
THE PEAK IS AT MAXIMUM CAPACITY. PLEASE TURN BACK.
WHAAAAT?!
BECAUSE YOU DIDN'T THINK THINGS THROUGH, NENE-CCHI!
MY BAD!

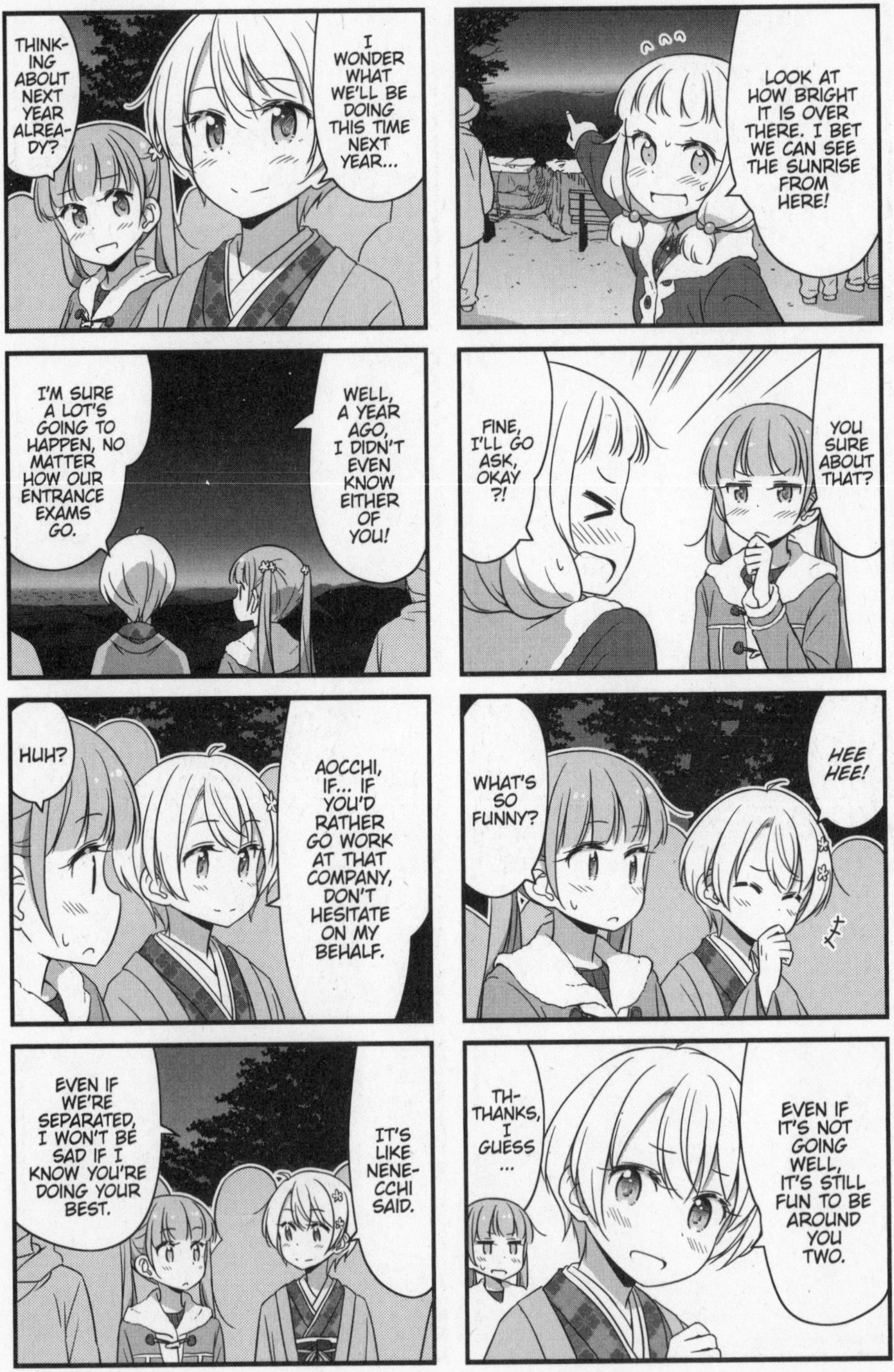

LOOK AT HOW BRIGHT IT IS OVER THERE. I BET WE CAN SEE THE SUNRISE FROM HERE!
YOU SURE ABOUT THAT?
FINE, I'LL GO ASK, OKAY?!
HEE HEE!
WHAT'S SO FUNNY?
EVEN IF IT'S NOT GOING WELL, IT'S STILL FUN TO BE AROUND YOU TWO.
TH-THANKS, I GUESS...
I WONDER WHAT WE'LL BE DOING THIS TIME NEXT YEAR...
THINKING ABOUT NEXT YEAR ALREADY?
WELL, A YEAR AGO, I DIDN'T EVEN KNOW EITHER OF YOU!
I'M SURE A LOT'S GOING TO HAPPEN, NO MATTER HOW OUR ENTRANCE EXAMS GO.
AOCCHI, IF... IF YOU'D RATHER GO WORK AT THAT COMPANY, DON'T HESITATE ON MY BEHALF.
HUH?
IT'S LIKE NENECCHI SAID.
EVEN IF WE'RE SEPARATED, I WON'T BE SAD IF I KNOW YOU'RE DOING YOUR BEST.

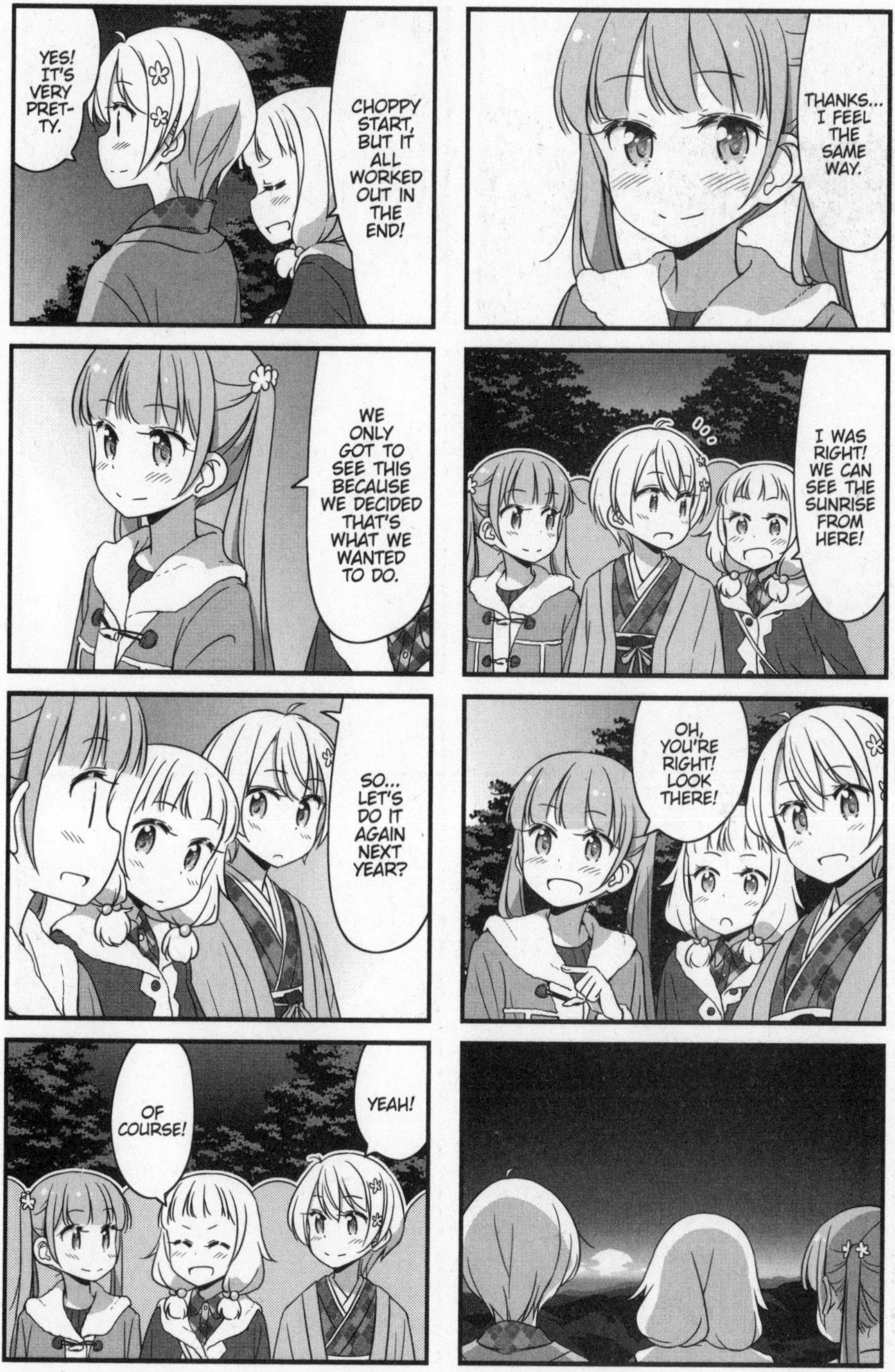
THANKS... I FEEL THE SAME WAY.
CHOPPY START, BUT IT ALL WORKED OUT IN THE END!
YES! IT'S VERY PRET-TY.
I WAS RIGHT! WE CAN SEE THE SUNRISE FROM HERE!
WE ONLY GOT TO SEE THIS BECAUSE WE DECIDED THAT'S WHAT WE WANTED TO DO.
OH, YOU'RE RIGHT! LOOK THERE!
SO... LET'S DO IT AGAIN NEXT YEAR?
YEAH!
OF COURSE!

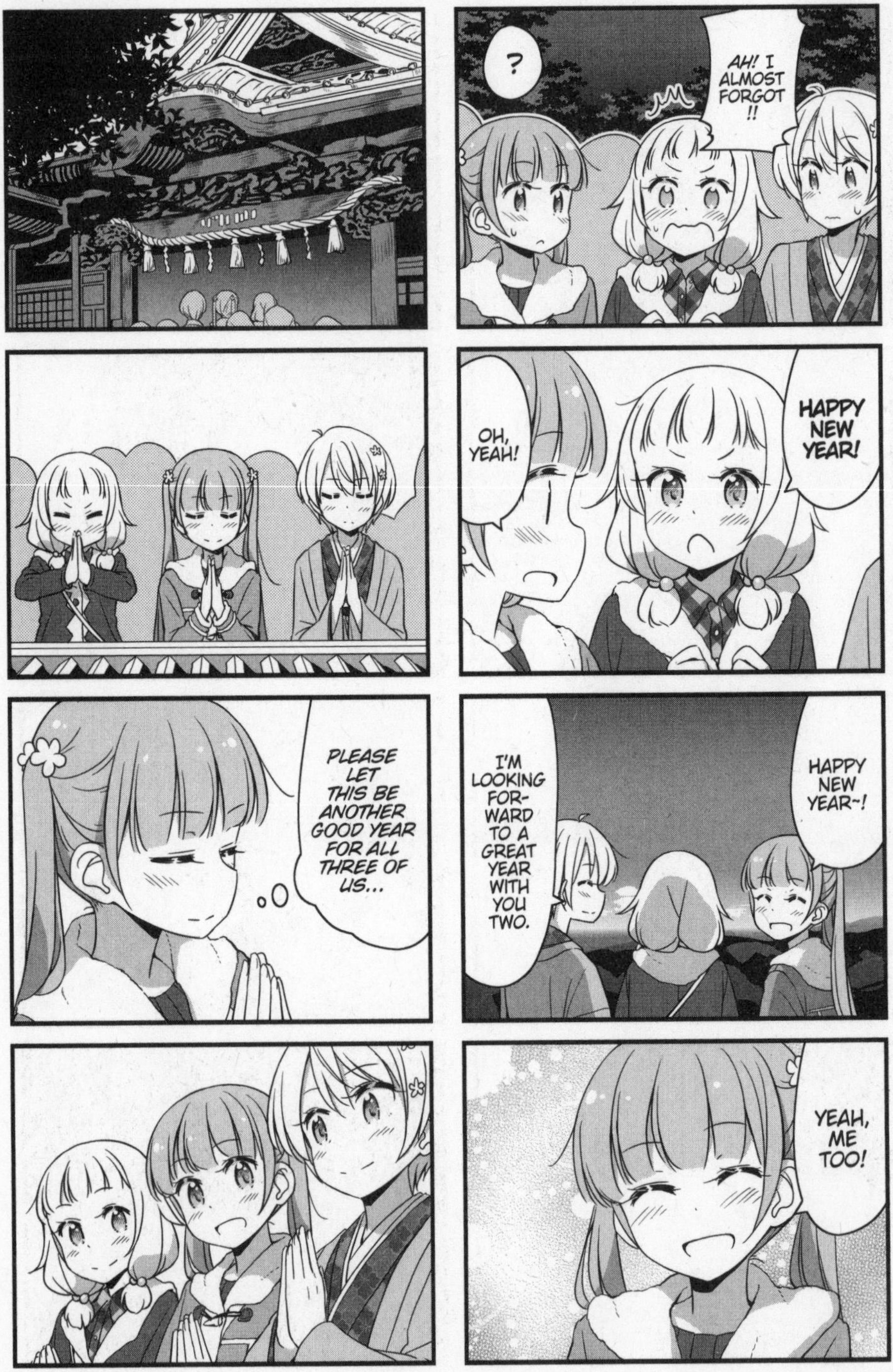
AH! I ALMOST FORGOT !!
?
HAPPY NEW YEAR!
OH, YEAH!
HAPPY NEW YEAR~!
I'M LOOKING FOR-WARD TO A GREAT YEAR WITH YOU TWO.
PLEASE LET THIS BE ANOTHER GOOD YEAR FOR ALL THREE OF US...
YEAH, ME TOO!

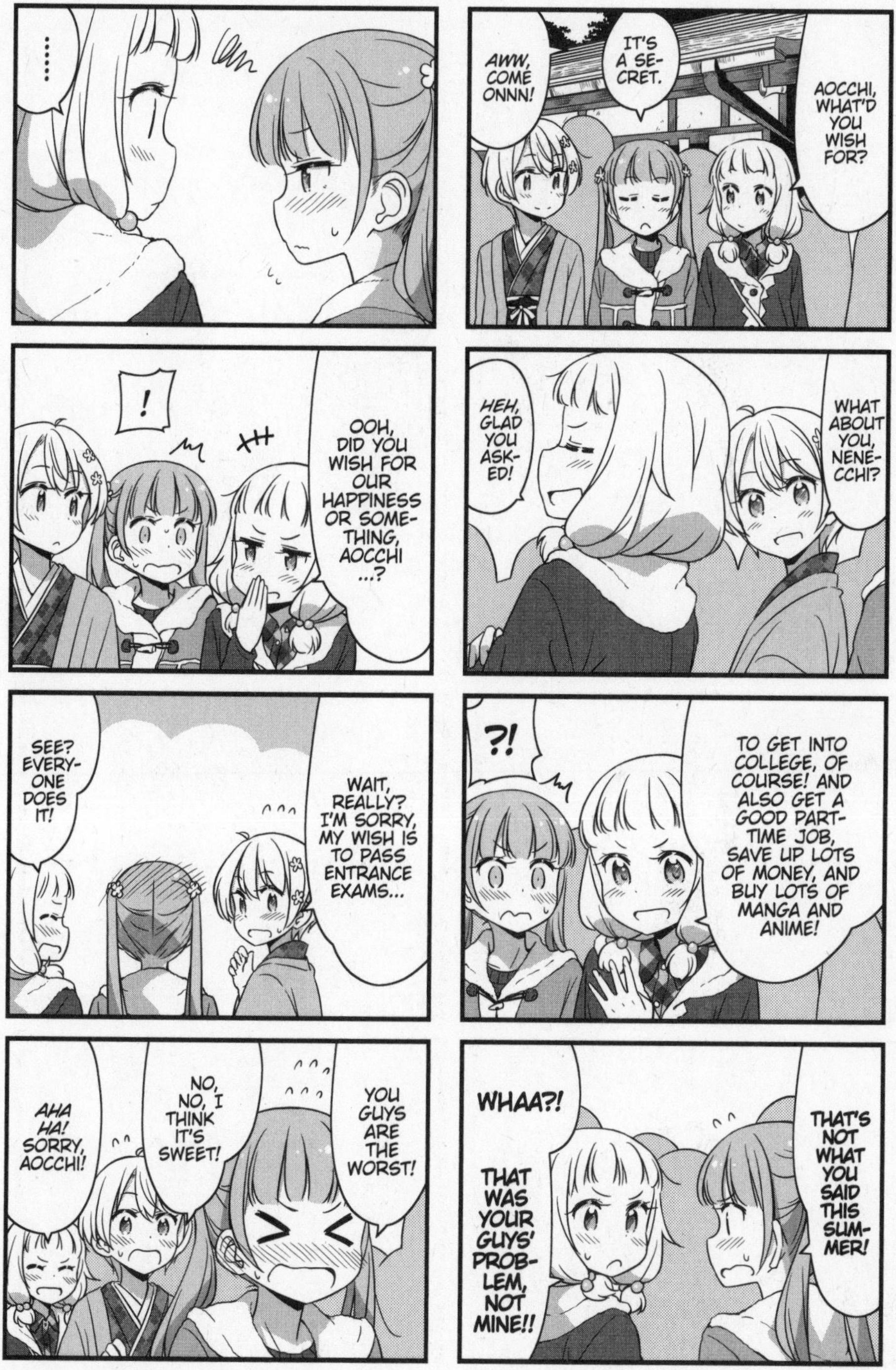
AOCCHI, WHAT'D YOU WISH FOR?
IT'S A SE-CRET.
AWW, COME ONNN!
......
WHAT ABOUT YOU, NENE-CCHI?
HEH, GLAD YOU ASK-ED!
OOH, DID YOU WISH FOR OUR HAPPINESS OR SOME-THING, AOCCHI ...?
!
TO GET INTO COLLEGE, OF COURSE! AND ALSO GET A GOOD PART-TIME JOB, SAVE UP LOTS OF MONEY, AND BUY LOTS OF MANGA AND ANIME!
?!
WAIT, REALLY? I'M SORRY, MY WISH IS TO PASS ENTRANCE EXAMS...
SEE? EVERY-ONE DOES IT!
THAT'S NOT WHAT YOU SAID THIS SUM-MER!
WHAA?!
THAT WAS YOUR GUYS' PROB-LEM, NOT MINE!!
YOU GUYS ARE THE WORST!
NO, NO, I THINK IT'S SWEET!
AHA HA! SORRY, AOCCHI!

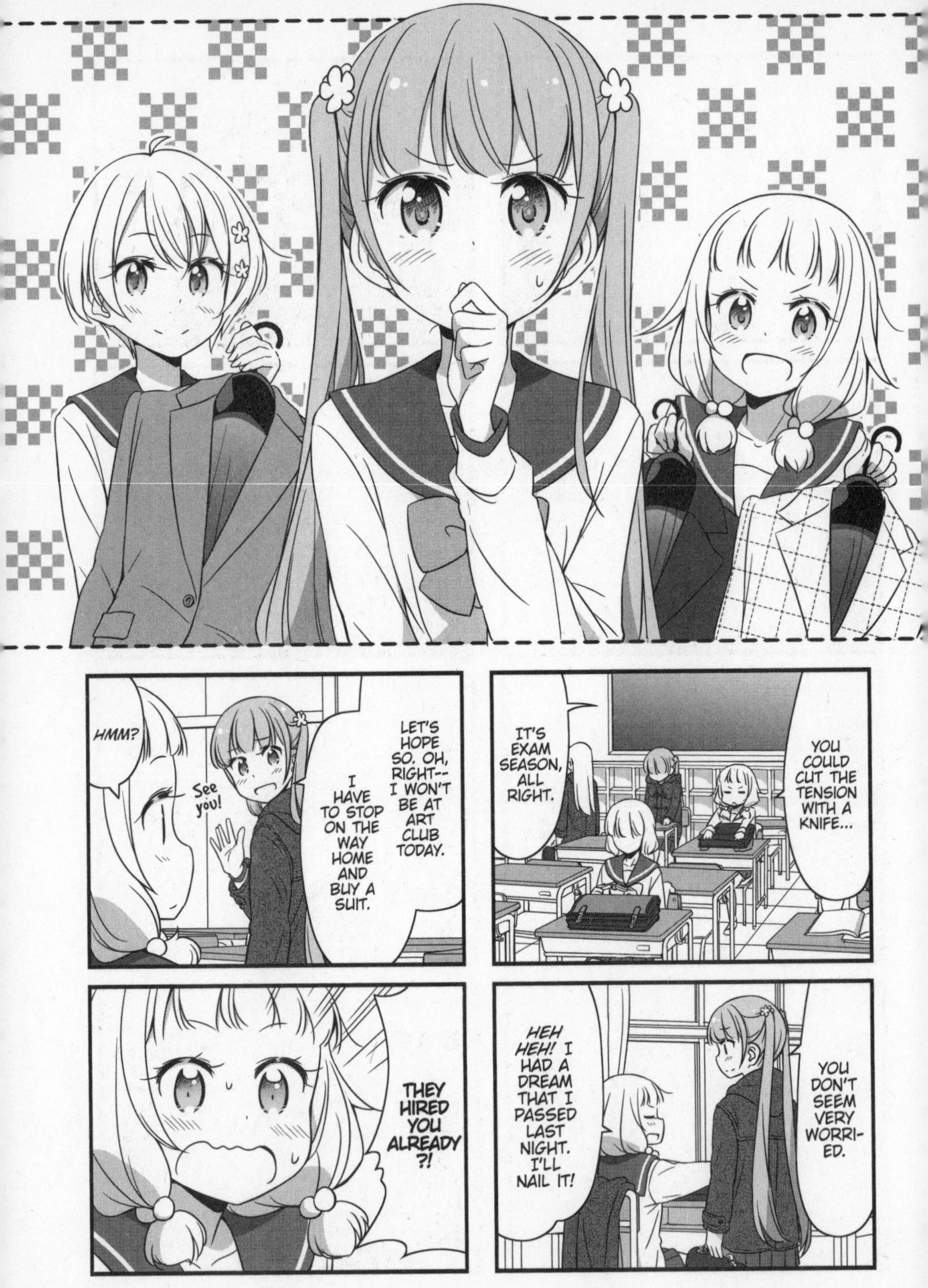
YOU COULD CUT THE TENSION WITH A KNIFE...
IT'S EXAM SEASON, ALL RIGHT.
YOU DON'T SEEM VERY WORRI-ED.
HEH HEH! I HAD A DREAM THAT I PASSED LAST NIGHT. I'LL NAIL IT!
LET'S HOPE SO. OH, RIGHT-- I WON'T BE AT ART CLUB TODAY.
I HAVE TO STOP ON THE WAY HOME AND BUY A SUIT.
See you!
HMM?
THEY HIRED YOU ALREADY?!

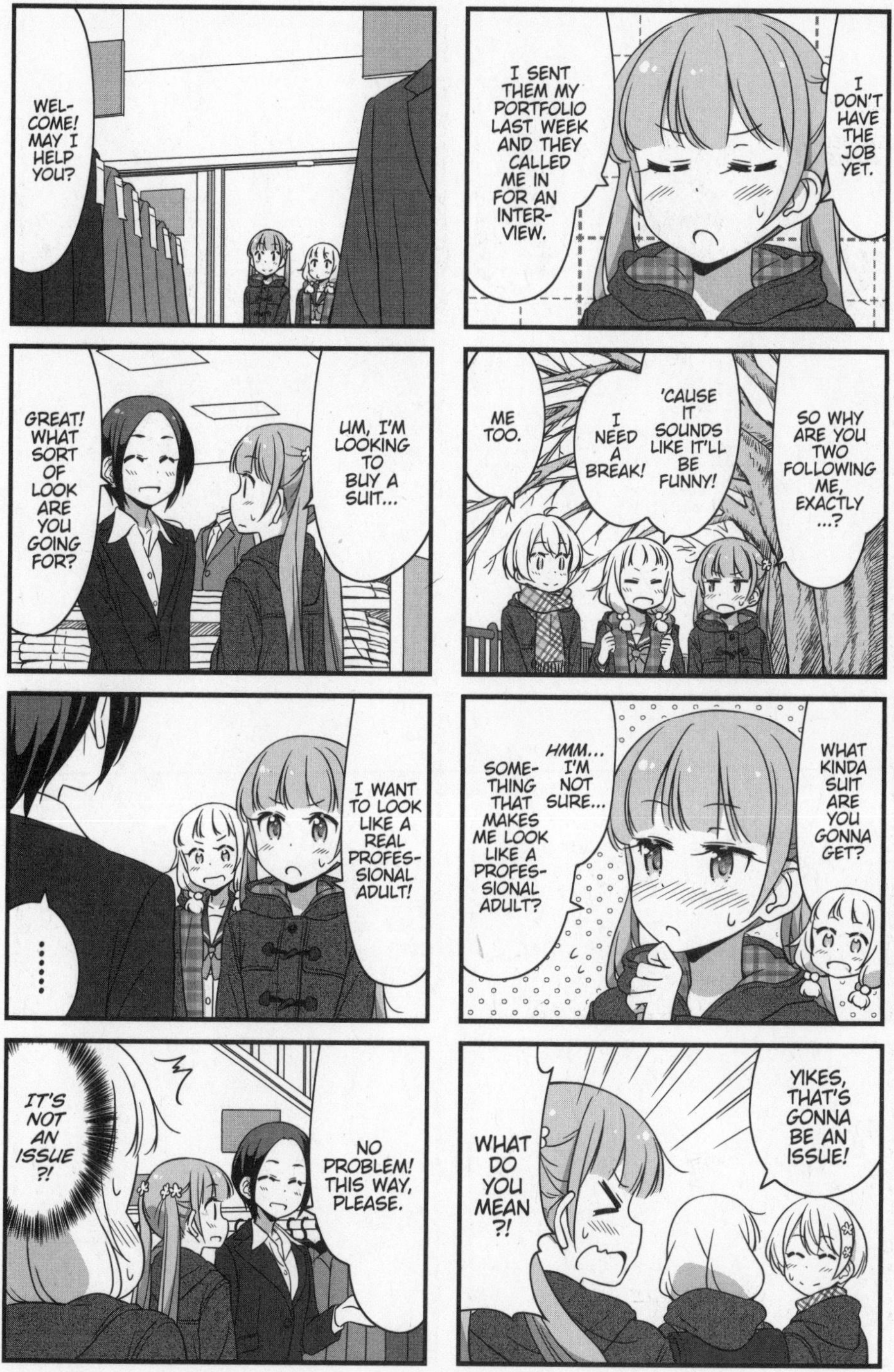
I DON'T HAVE THE JOB YET.
I SENT THEM MY PORTFOLIO LAST WEEK AND THEY CALLED ME IN FOR AN INTERVIEW.
SO WHY ARE YOU TWO FOLLOWING ME, EXACTLY ...?
'CAUSE IT SOUNDS LIKE IT'LL BE FUNNY!
I NEED A BREAK!
ME TOO.
WHAT KINDA SUIT ARE YOU GONNA GET?
HMM... I'M NOT SURE...
SOMETHING THAT MAKES ME LOOK LIKE A PROFESSIONAL ADULT?
YIKES, THAT'S GONNA BE AN ISSUE!
WHAT DO YOU MEAN?!
WELCOME! MAY I HELP YOU?
UM, I'M LOOKING TO BUY A SUIT...
GREAT! WHAT SORT OF LOOK ARE YOU GOING FOR?
I WANT TO LOOK LIKE A REAL PROFESSIONAL ADULT!
......
NO PROBLEM! THIS WAY, PLEASE.
IT'S NOT AN ISSUE?!

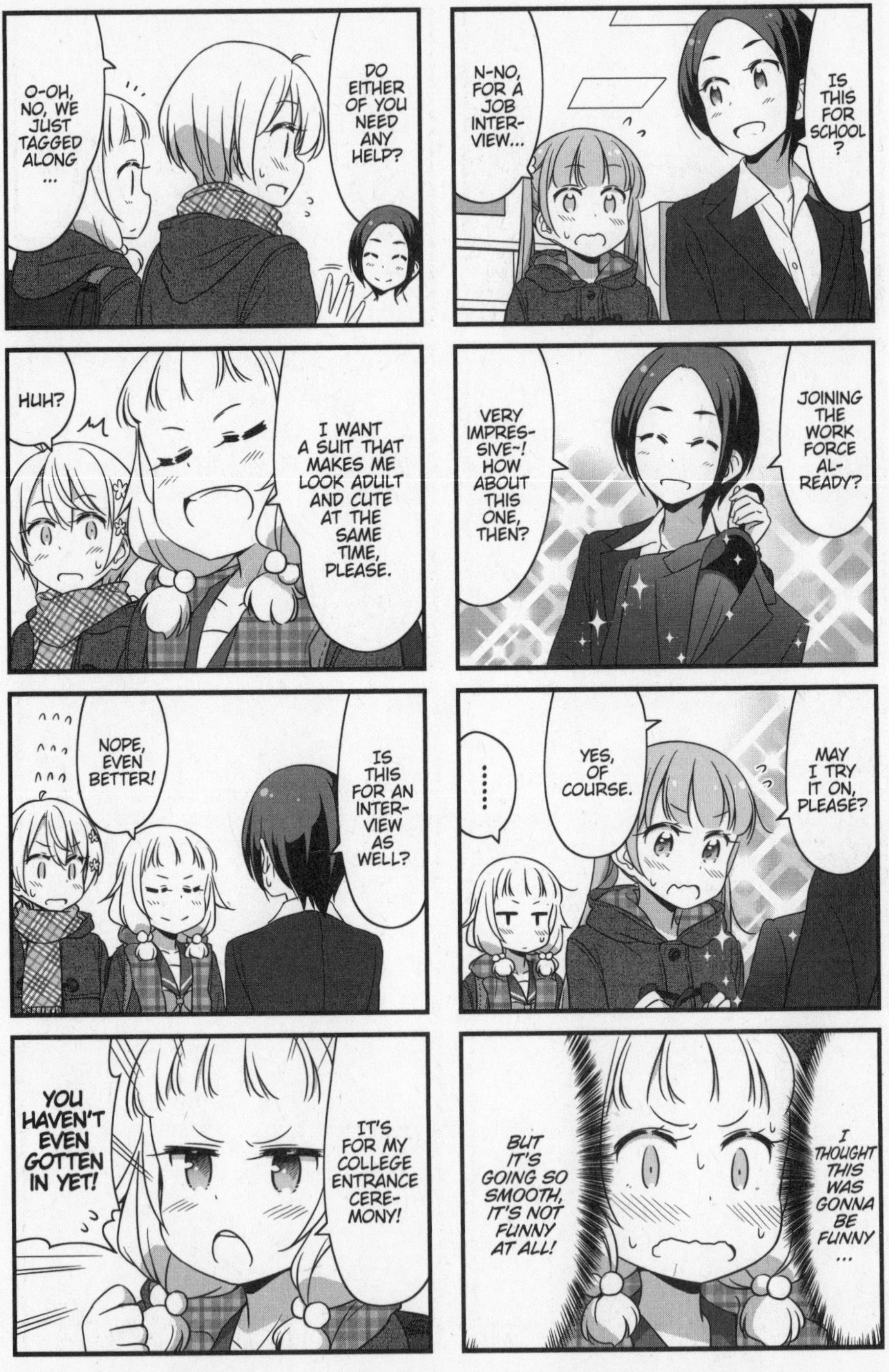
IS THIS FOR SCHOOL?
N-NO, FOR A JOB INTERVIEW...
JOINING THE WORK FORCE AL-READY?
VERY IMPRES-SIVE~! HOW ABOUT THIS ONE, THEN?
MAY I TRY IT ON, PLEASE?
YES, OF COURSE.
......
I THOUGHT THIS WAS GONNA BE FUNNY...
BUT IT'S GOING SO SMOOTH, IT'S NOT FUNNY AT ALL!
DO EITHER OF YOU NEED ANY HELP?
O-OH, NO, WE JUST TAGGED ALONG...
I WANT A SUIT THAT MAKES ME LOOK ADULT AND CUTE AT THE SAME TIME, PLEASE.
HUH?
IS THIS FOR AN INTERVIEW AS WELL?
NOPE, EVEN BETTER!
IT'S FOR MY COLLEGE ENTRANCE CERE-MONY!
YOU HAVEN'T EVEN GOTTEN IN YET!

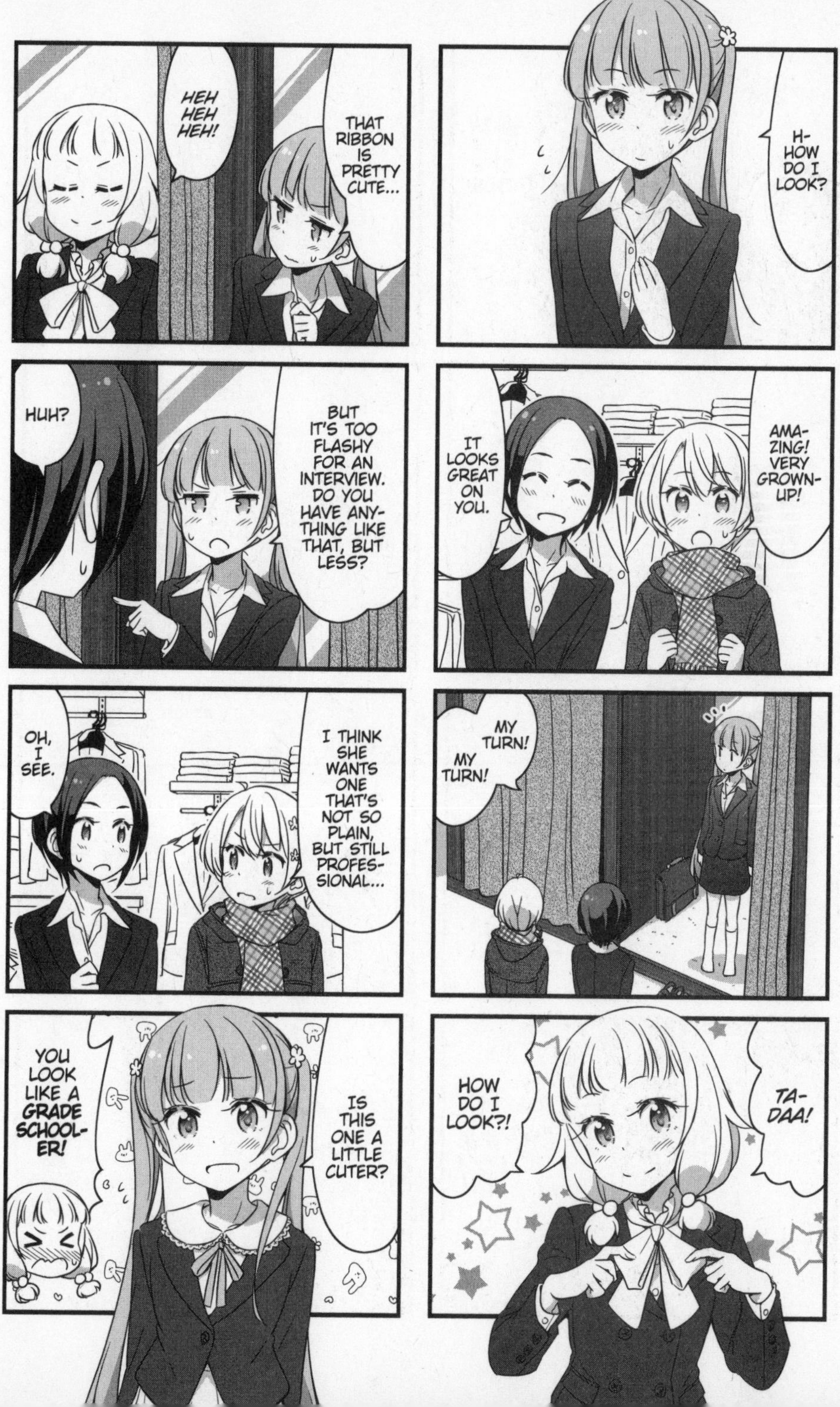

H-HOW DO I LOOK?
THAT RIBBON IS PRETTY CUTE...
HEH HEH HEH!
AMA-ZING! VERY GROWN-UP!
IT LOOKS GREAT ON YOU.
BUT IT'S TOO FLASHY FOR AN INTERVIEW. DO YOU HAVE ANY-THING LIKE THAT, BUT LESS?
HUH?
MY TURN!
MY TURN!
I THINK SHE WANTS ONE THAT'S NOT SO PLAIN, BUT STILL PROFES-SIONAL...
OH, I SEE.
TA-DAA!
HOW DO I LOOK?!
IS THIS ONE A LITTLE CUTER?
YOU LOOK LIKE A GRADE SCHOOL-ER!

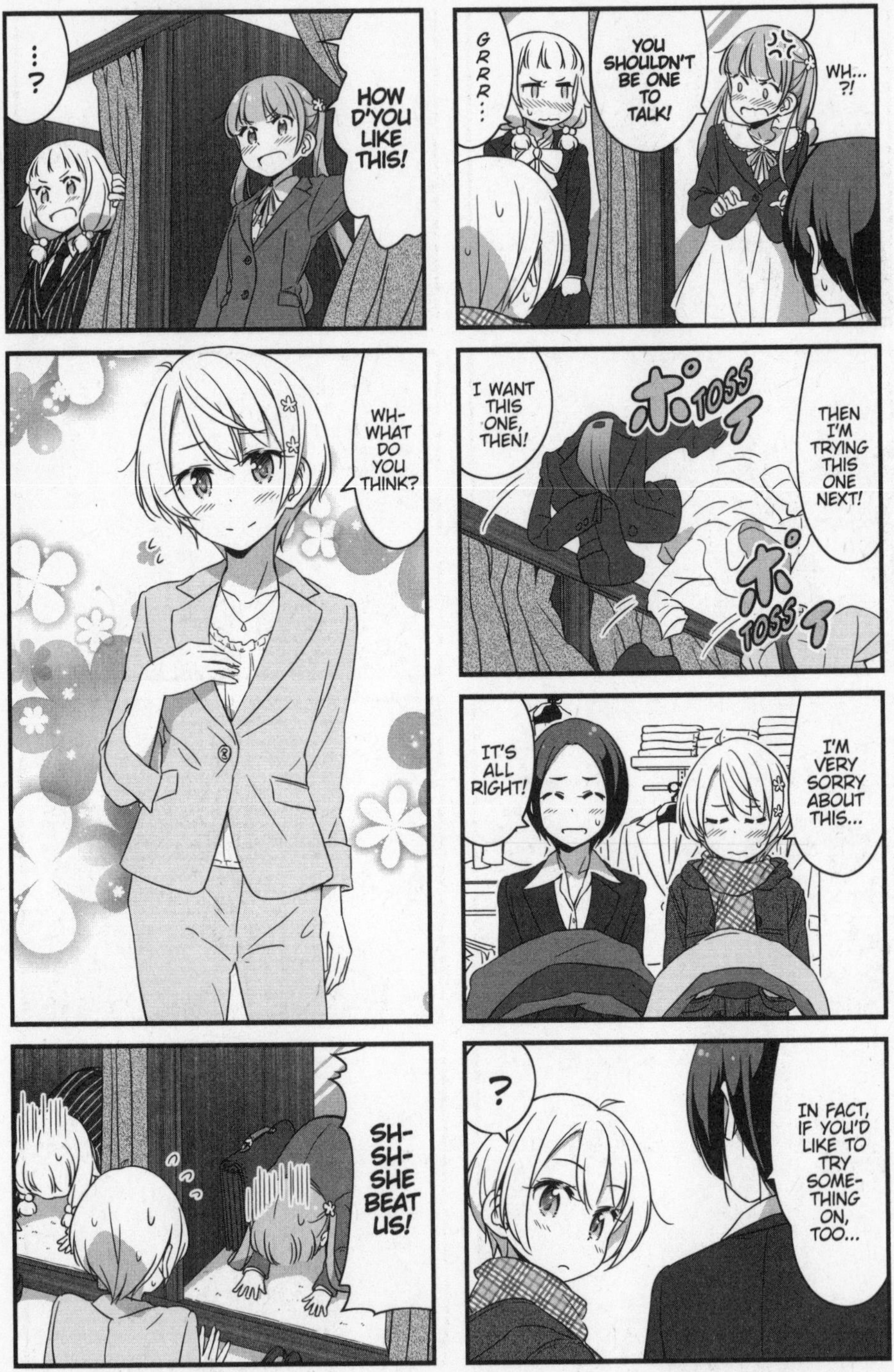
WH... ?!
YOU SHOULDN'T BE ONE TO TALK!
GRRR...
THEN I'M TRYING THIS ONE NEXT!
TOSS
TOSS
I WANT THIS ONE, THEN!
I'M VERY SORRY ABOUT THIS...
IT'S ALL RIGHT!
IN FACT, IF YOU'D LIKE TO TRY SOME-THING ON, TOO...
?
HOW D'YOU LIKE THIS!
...?
WH-WHAT DO YOU THINK?
SH-SH-SHE BEAT US!

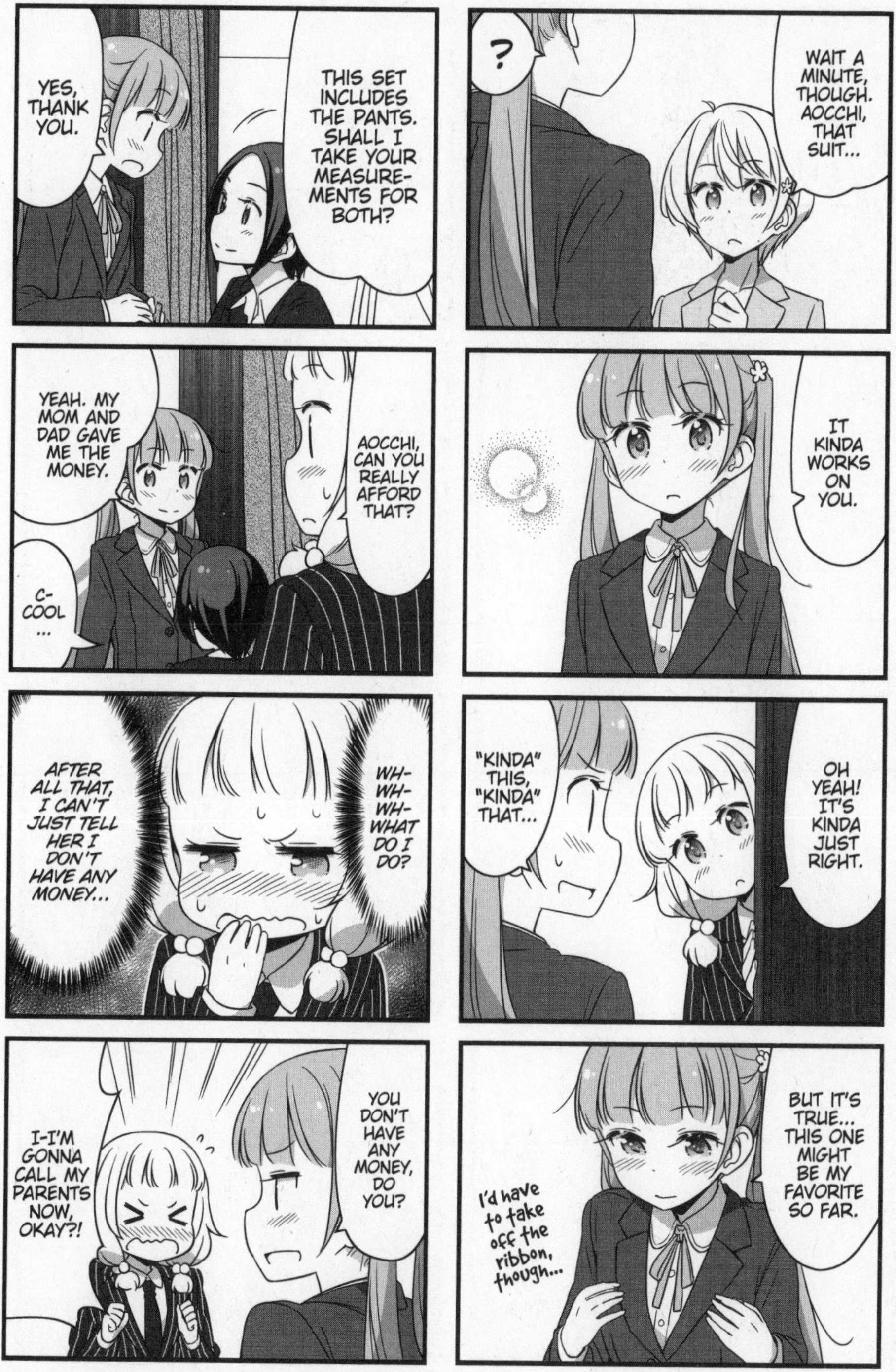
WAIT A MINUTE, THOUGH. AOCCHI, THAT SUIT...
?
THIS SET INCLUDES THE PANTS. SHALL I TAKE YOUR MEASUREMENTS FOR BOTH?
YES, THANK YOU.
IT KINDA WORKS ON YOU.
AOCCHI, CAN YOU REALLY AFFORD THAT?
YEAH. MY MOM AND DAD GAVE ME THE MONEY.
C-COOL...
OH YEAH! IT'S KINDA JUST RIGHT.
"KINDA" THIS, "KINDA" THAT...
WH-WH-WH-WHAT DO I DO?
AFTER ALL THAT, I CAN'T JUST TELL HER I DON'T HAVE ANY MONEY...
BUT IT'S TRUE... THIS ONE MIGHT BE MY FAVORITE SO FAR.
I'd have to take off the ribbon, though...
YOU DON'T HAVE ANY MONEY, DO YOU?
I-I'M GONNA CALL MY PARENTS NOW, OKAY?!

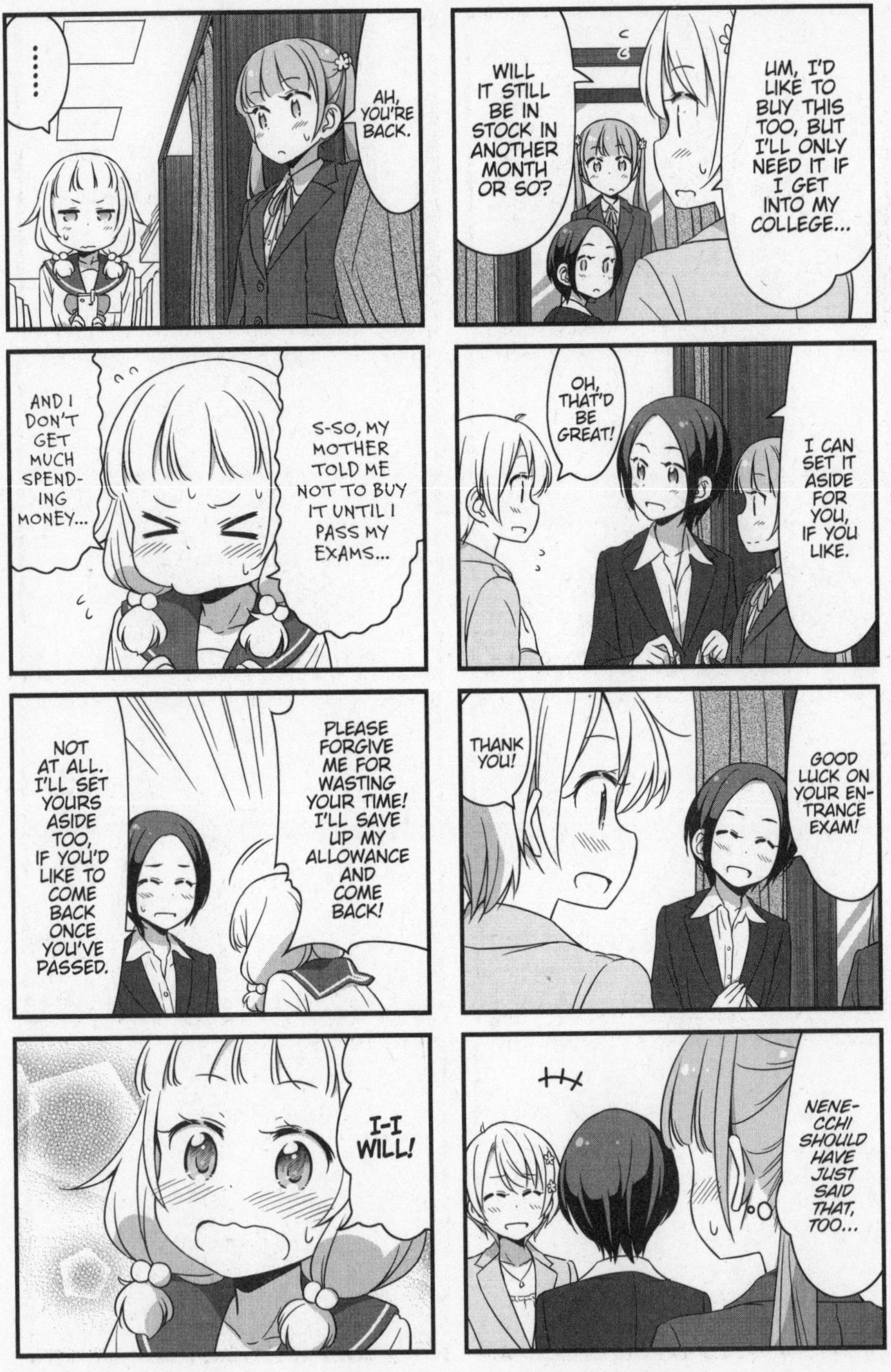
UM, I'D LIKE TO BUY THIS TOO, BUT I'LL ONLY NEED IT IF I GET INTO MY COLLEGE...
WILL IT STILL BE IN STOCK IN ANOTHER MONTH OR SO?
AH, YOU'RE BACK.
......
I CAN SET IT ASIDE FOR YOU, IF YOU LIKE.
OH, THAT'D BE GREAT!
S-SO, MY MOTHER TOLD ME NOT TO BUY IT UNTIL I PASS MY EXAMS...
AND I DON'T GET MUCH SPEND-ING MONEY...
GOOD LUCK ON YOUR EN-TRANCE EXAM!
THANK YOU!
PLEASE FORGIVE ME FOR WASTING YOUR TIME! I'LL SAVE UP MY ALLOWANCE AND COME BACK!
NOT AT ALL. I'LL SET YOURS ASIDE TOO, IF YOU'D LIKE TO COME BACK ONCE YOU'VE PASSED.
NENE-CCHI SHOULD HAVE JUST SAID THAT, TOO...
I-I WILL!

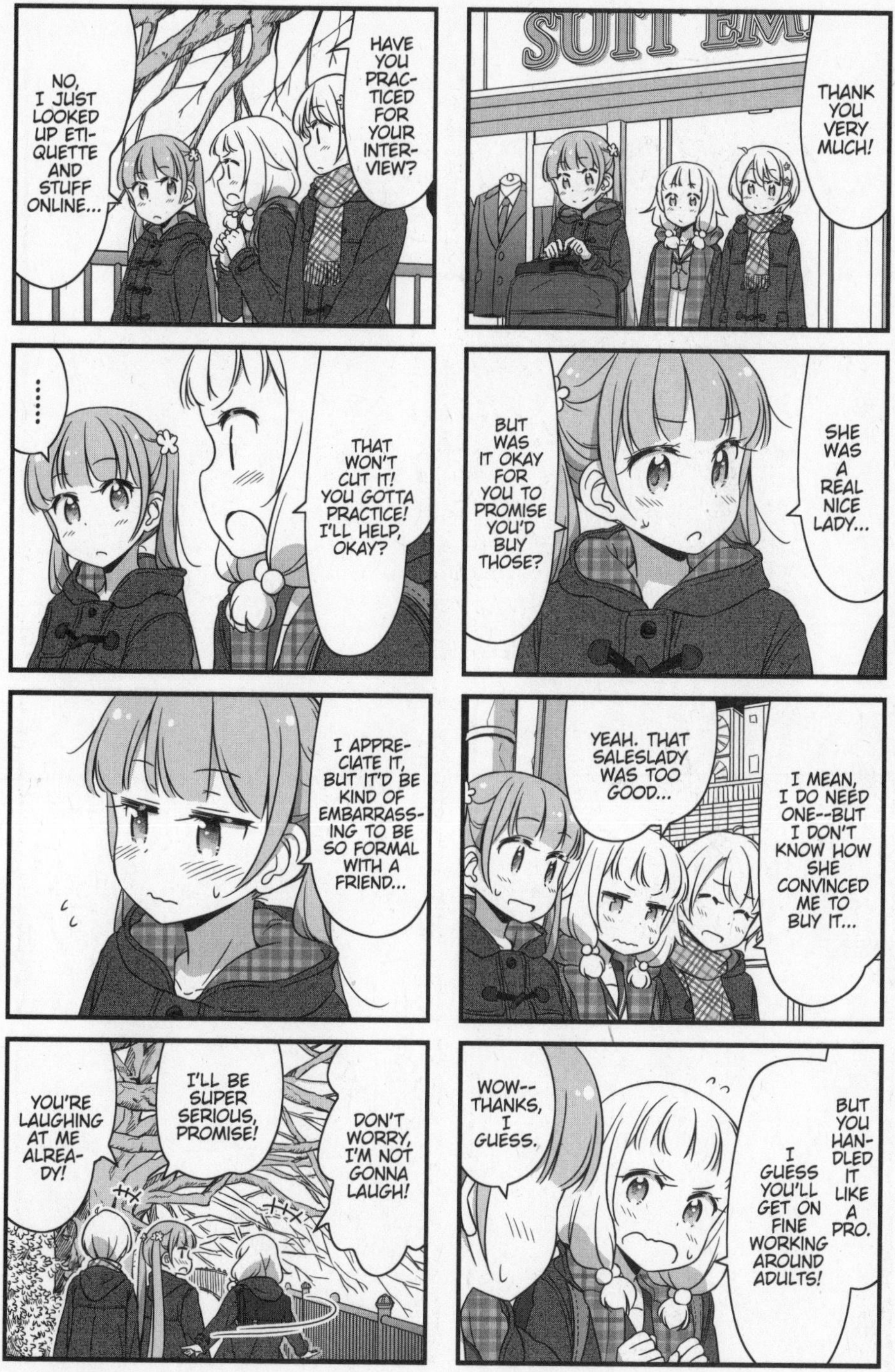
THANK YOU VERY MUCH!
SHE WAS A REAL NICE LADY...
BUT WAS IT OKAY FOR YOU TO PROMISE YOU'D BUY THOSE?
I MEAN, I DO NEED ONE--BUT I DON'T KNOW HOW SHE CONVINCED ME TO BUY IT...
YEAH. THAT SALESLADY WAS TOO GOOD...
BUT YOU HANDLED IT LIKE A PRO.
I GUESS YOU'LL GET ON FINE WORKING AROUND ADULTS!
WOW--THANKS, I GUESS.
HAVE YOU PRACTICED FOR YOUR INTERVIEW?
NO, I JUST LOOKED UP ETIQUETTE AND STUFF ONLINE...
THAT WON'T CUT IT! YOU GOTTA PRACTICE! I'LL HELP, OKAY?
......
I APPRECIATE IT, BUT IT'D BE KIND OF EMBARRASSING TO BE SO FORMAL WITH A FRIEND...
DON'T WORRY, I'M NOT GONNA LAUGH!
I'LL BE SUPER SERIOUS, PROMISE!
YOU'RE LAUGHING AT ME ALREADY!

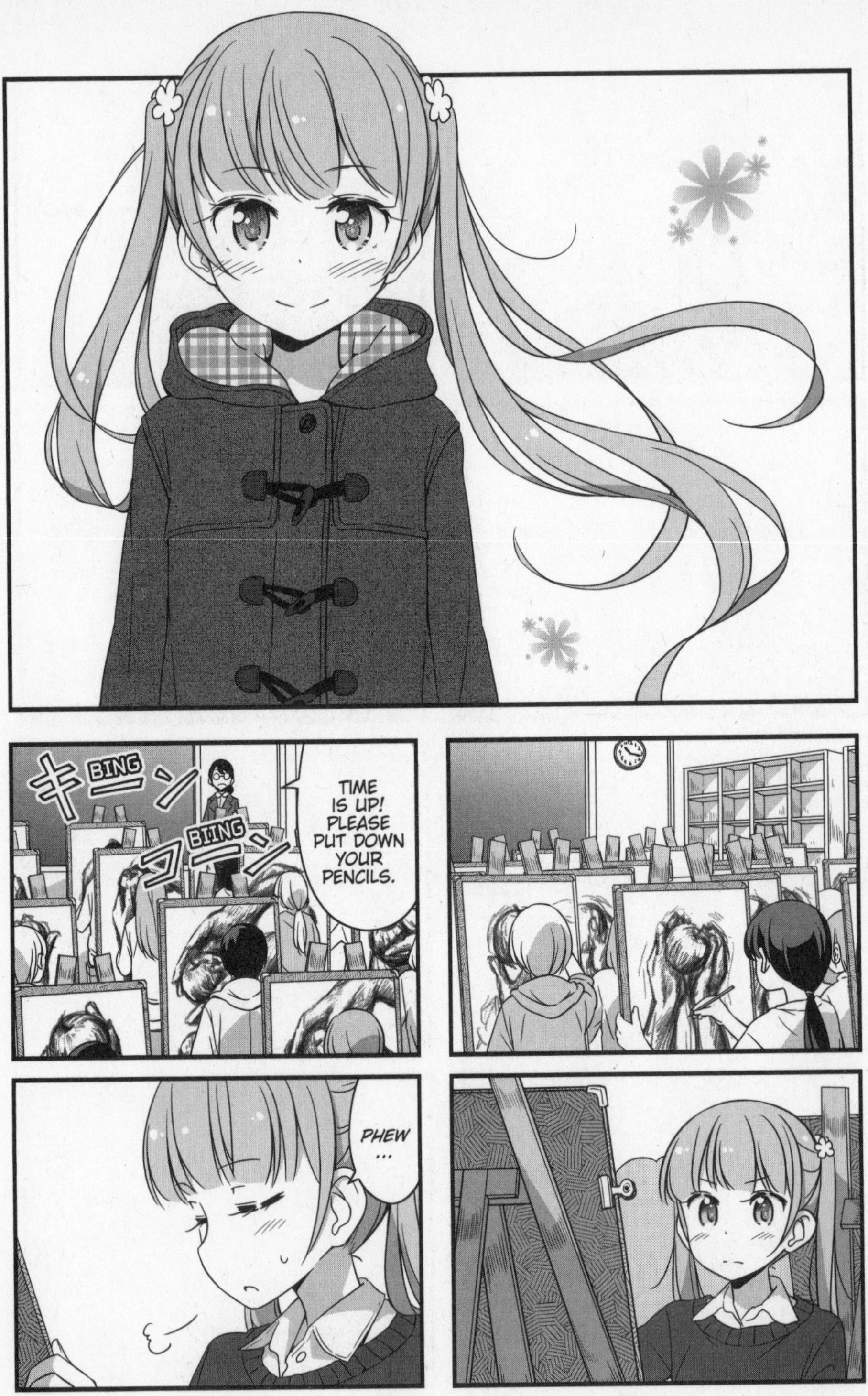
BING
BIING
TIME IS UP! PLEASE PUT DOWN YOUR PENCILS.
PHEW ...

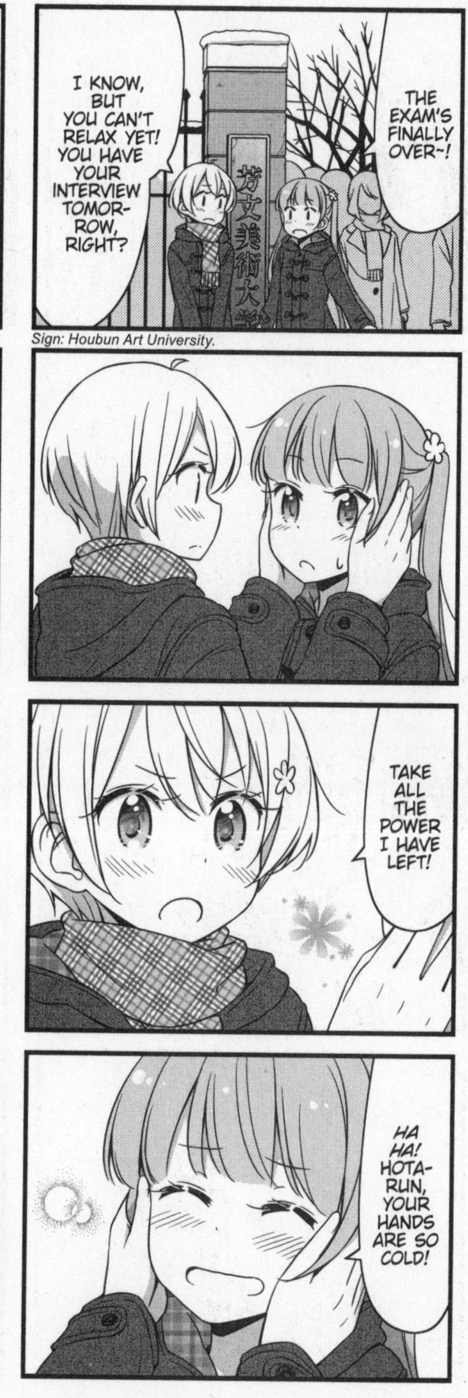
THE EXAM'S FINALLY OVER~!
I KNOW, BUT YOU CAN'T RELAX YET! YOU HAVE YOUR INTERVIEW TOMOR-ROW, RIGHT?
TAKE ALL THE POWER I HAVE LEFT!
HA HA! HOTA-RUN, YOUR HANDS ARE SO COLD!
Sign: Houbun Art University.

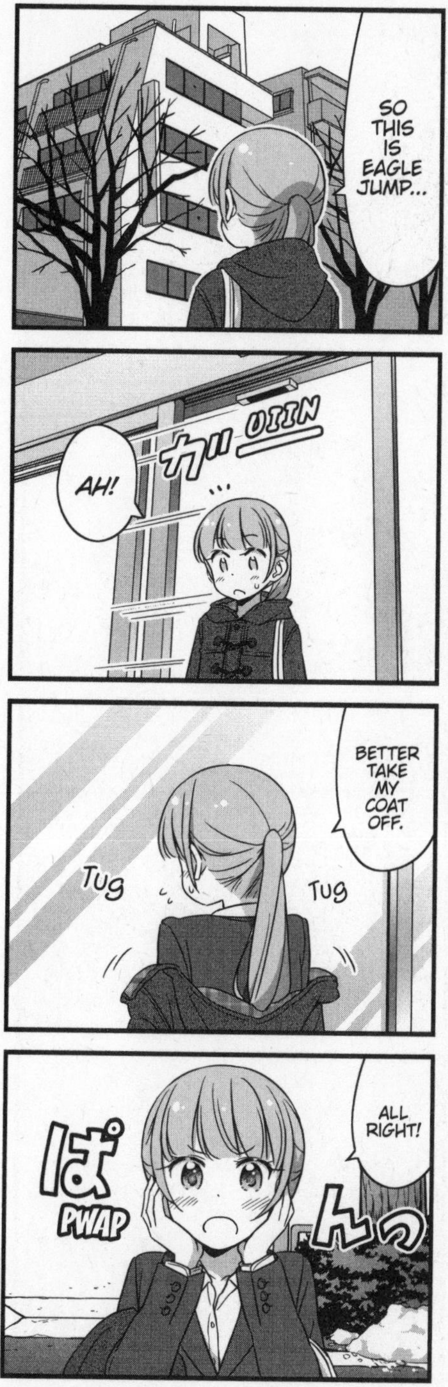
SO THIS IS EAGLE JUMP...
カッ
UIIN
AH!
BETTER TAKE MY COAT OFF.
Tug
Tug
ALL RIGHT!
ぱ
PWAP
んっ

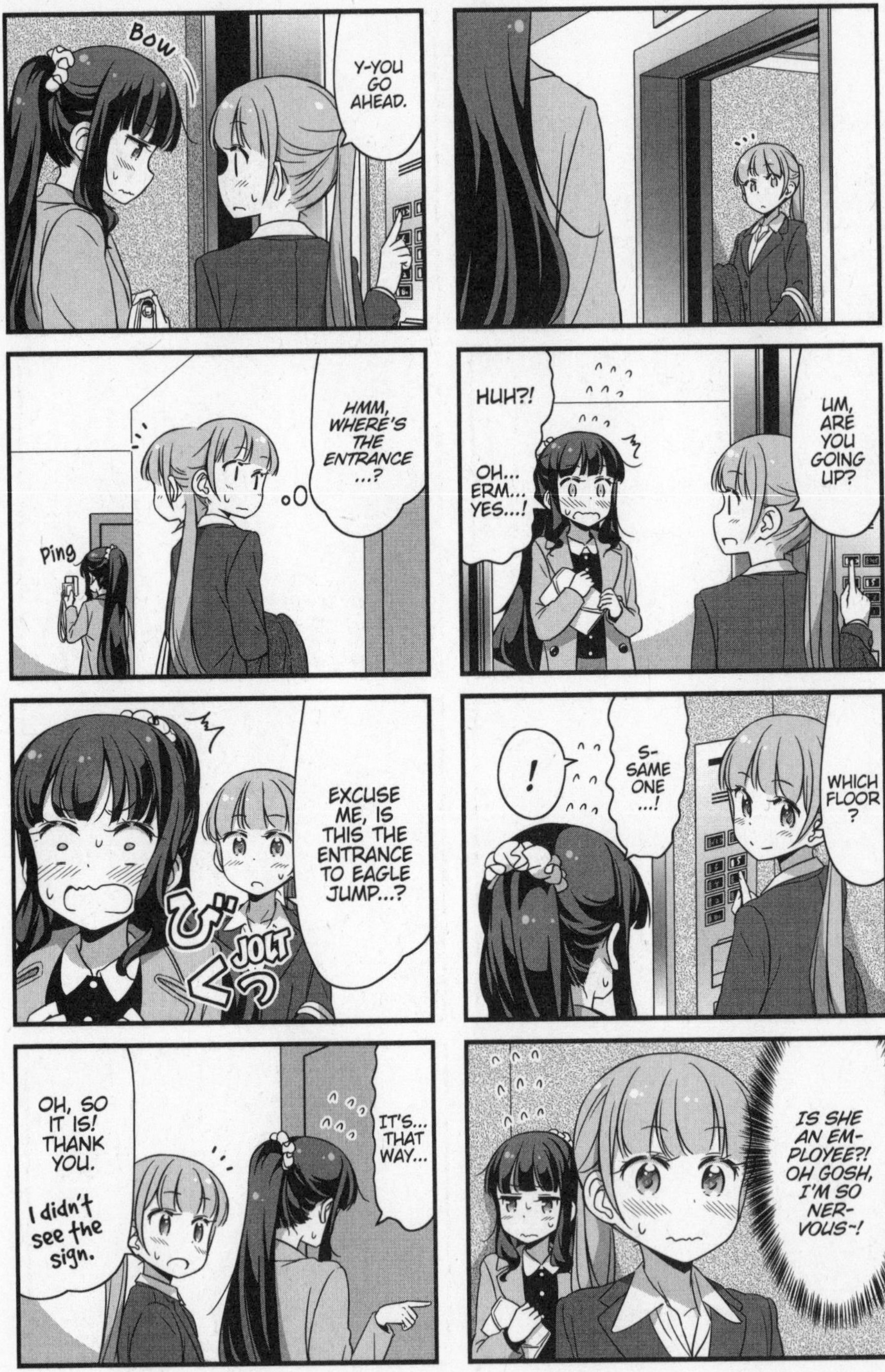
Bow
Y-YOU GO AHEAD.
UM, ARE YOU GOING UP?
HUH?!
OH... ERM... YES...!
HMM, WHERE'S THE ENTRANCE ...?
Ping
WHICH FLOOR?
S-SAME ONE ...!
!
EXCUSE ME, IS THIS THE ENTRANCE TO EAGLE JUMP...?
びくっ
JOLT
IS SHE AN EM-PLOYEE?! OH GOSH, I'M SO NER-VOUS~!
IT'S... THAT WAY...
OH, SO IT IS! THANK YOU.
I didn't see the sign.

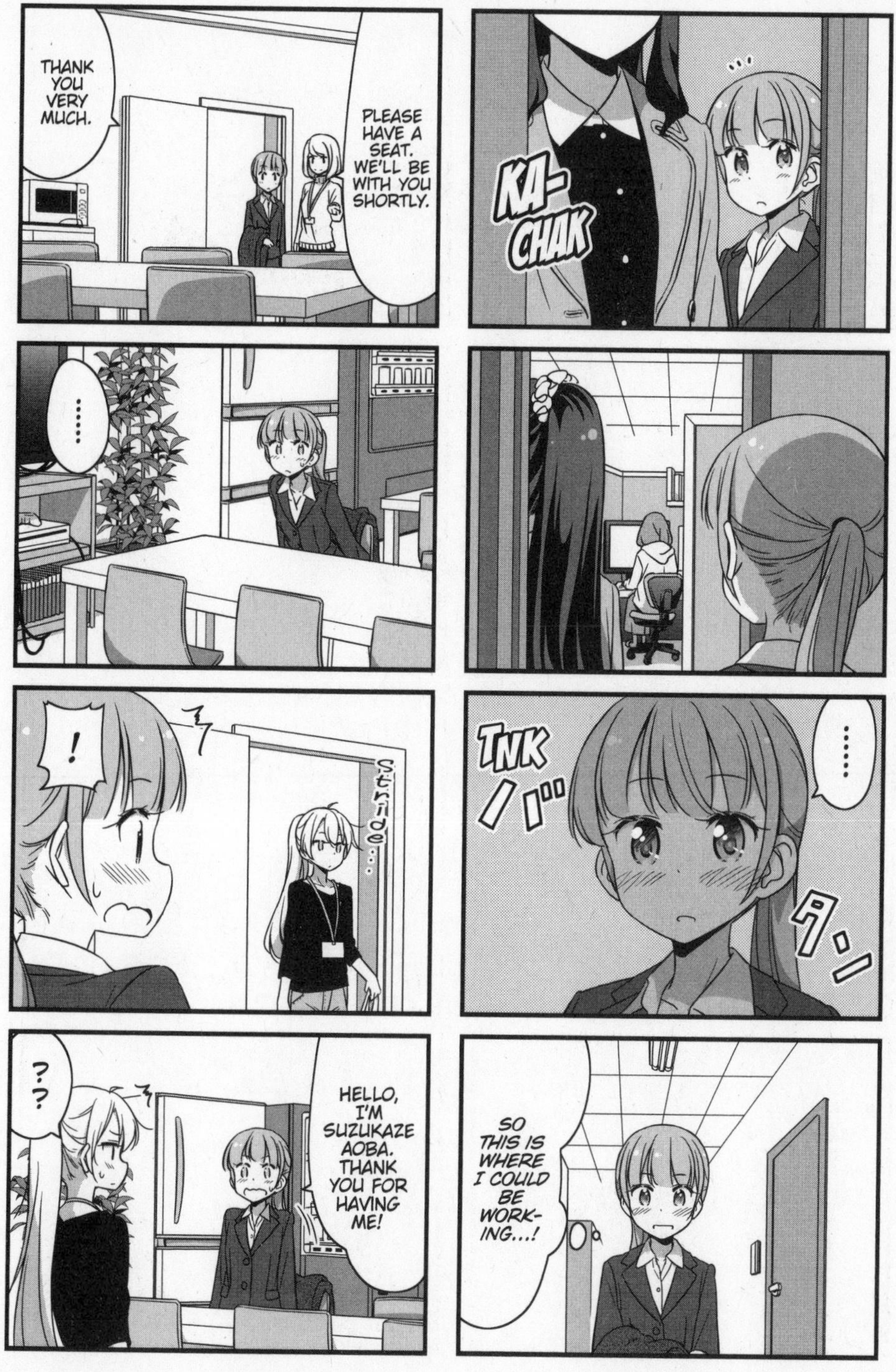

...
KA-CHAK
PLEASE HAVE A SEAT. WE'LL BE WITH YOU SHORTLY.
THANK YOU VERY MUCH.
......
TNK
......
!
Stride...
SO THIS IS WHERE I COULD BE WORKING...!
HELLO, I'M SUZUKAZE AOBA. THANK YOU FOR HAVING ME!
??

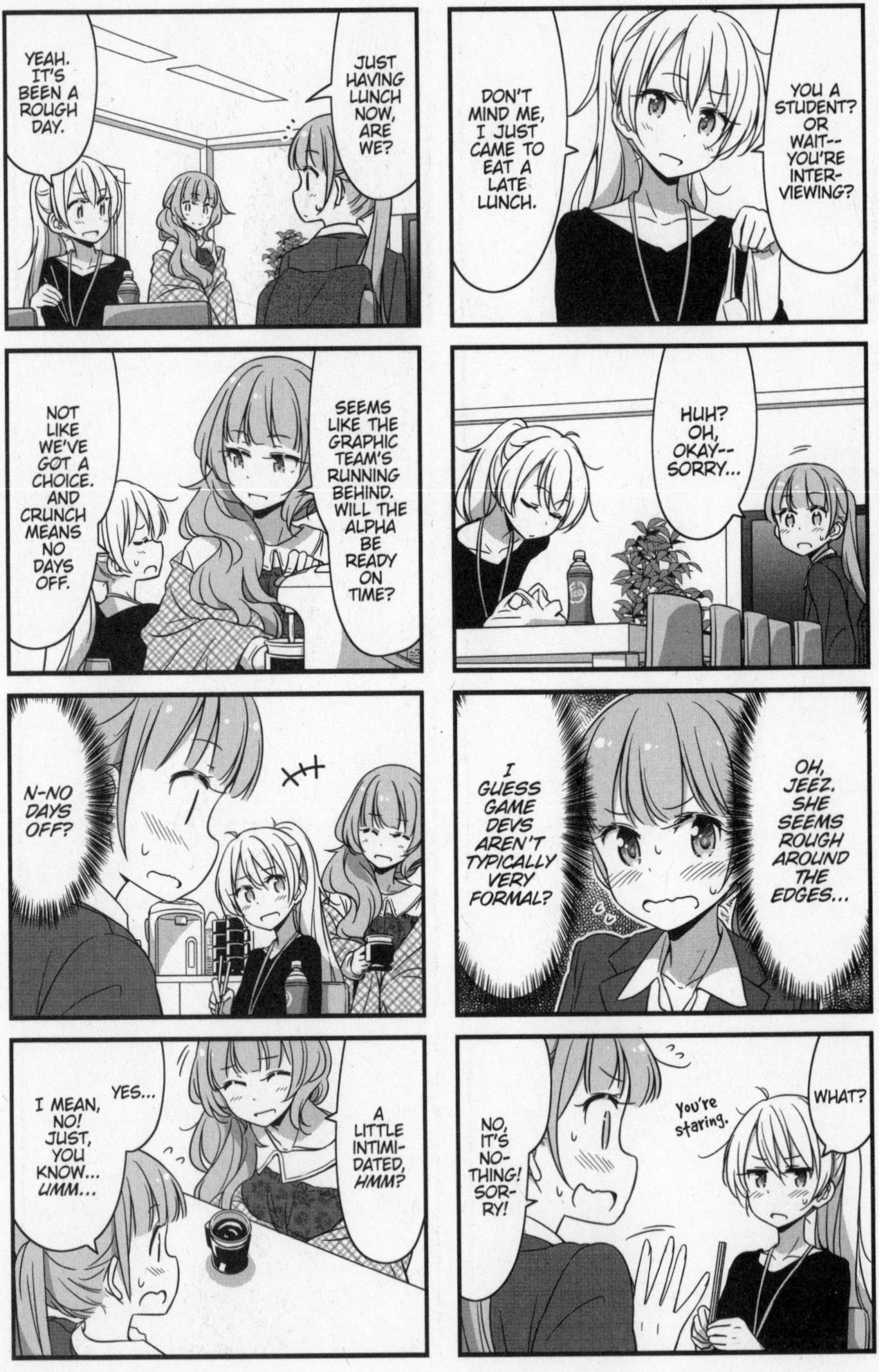
YOU A STUDENT? OR WAIT-- YOU'RE INTERVIEWING?
DON'T MIND ME, I JUST CAME TO EAT A LATE LUNCH.
JUST HAVING LUNCH NOW, ARE WE?
YEAH. IT'S BEEN A ROUGH DAY.
HUH? OH, OKAY-- SORRY...
SEEMS LIKE THE GRAPHIC TEAM'S RUNNING BEHIND. WILL THE ALPHA BE READY ON TIME?
NOT LIKE WE'VE GOT A CHOICE. AND CRUNCH MEANS NO DAYS OFF.
OH, JEEZ. SHE SEEMS ROUGH AROUND THE EDGES...
I GUESS GAME DEVS AREN'T TYPICALLY VERY FORMAL?
N-NO DAYS OFF?
WHAT?
You're staring.
NO, IT'S NOTHING! SORRY!
A LITTLE INTIMIDATED, *HMM*?
YES...
I MEAN, NO! JUST, YOU KNOW... *UMM*...

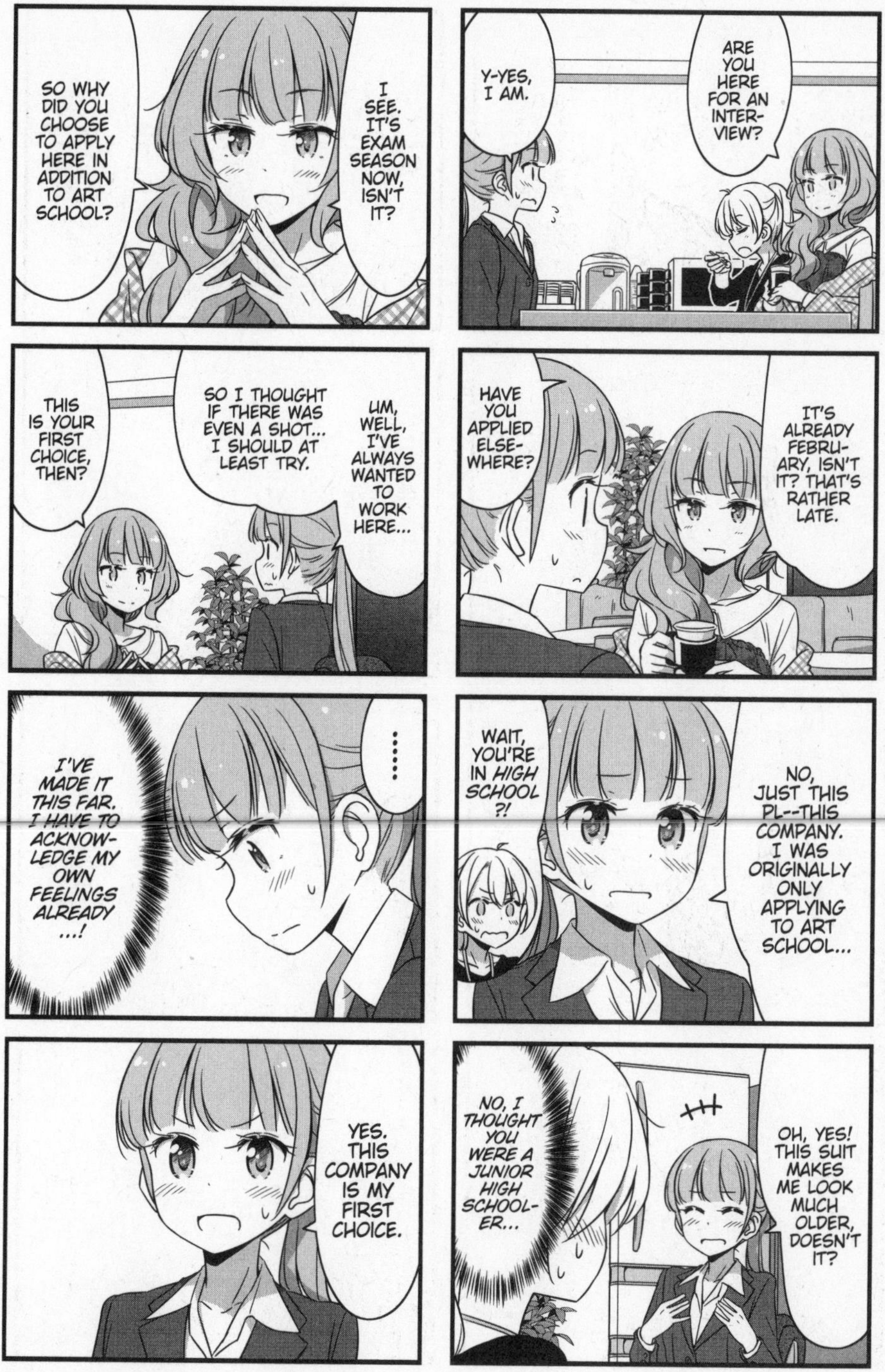
ARE YOU HERE FOR AN INTERVIEW?
Y-YES, I AM.
I SEE. IT'S EXAM SEASON NOW, ISN'T IT?
SO WHY DID YOU CHOOSE TO APPLY HERE IN ADDITION TO ART SCHOOL?
IT'S ALREADY FEBRUARY, ISN'T IT? THAT'S RATHER LATE.
HAVE YOU APPLIED ELSEWHERE?
UM, WELL, I'VE ALWAYS WANTED TO WORK HERE...
SO I THOUGHT IF THERE WAS EVEN A SHOT... I SHOULD AT LEAST TRY.
THIS IS YOUR FIRST CHOICE, THEN?
NO, JUST THIS PL--THIS COMPANY. I WAS ORIGINALLY ONLY APPLYING TO ART SCHOOL...
WAIT, YOU'RE IN *HIGH SCHOOL*?!
......
I'VE MADE IT THIS FAR. I HAVE TO ACKNOWLEDGE MY OWN FEELINGS ALREADY...!
OH, YES! THIS SUIT MAKES ME LOOK MUCH OLDER, DOESN'T IT?
NO, I THOUGHT YOU WERE A JUNIOR HIGH SCHOOLER...
YES. THIS COMPANY IS MY FIRST CHOICE.

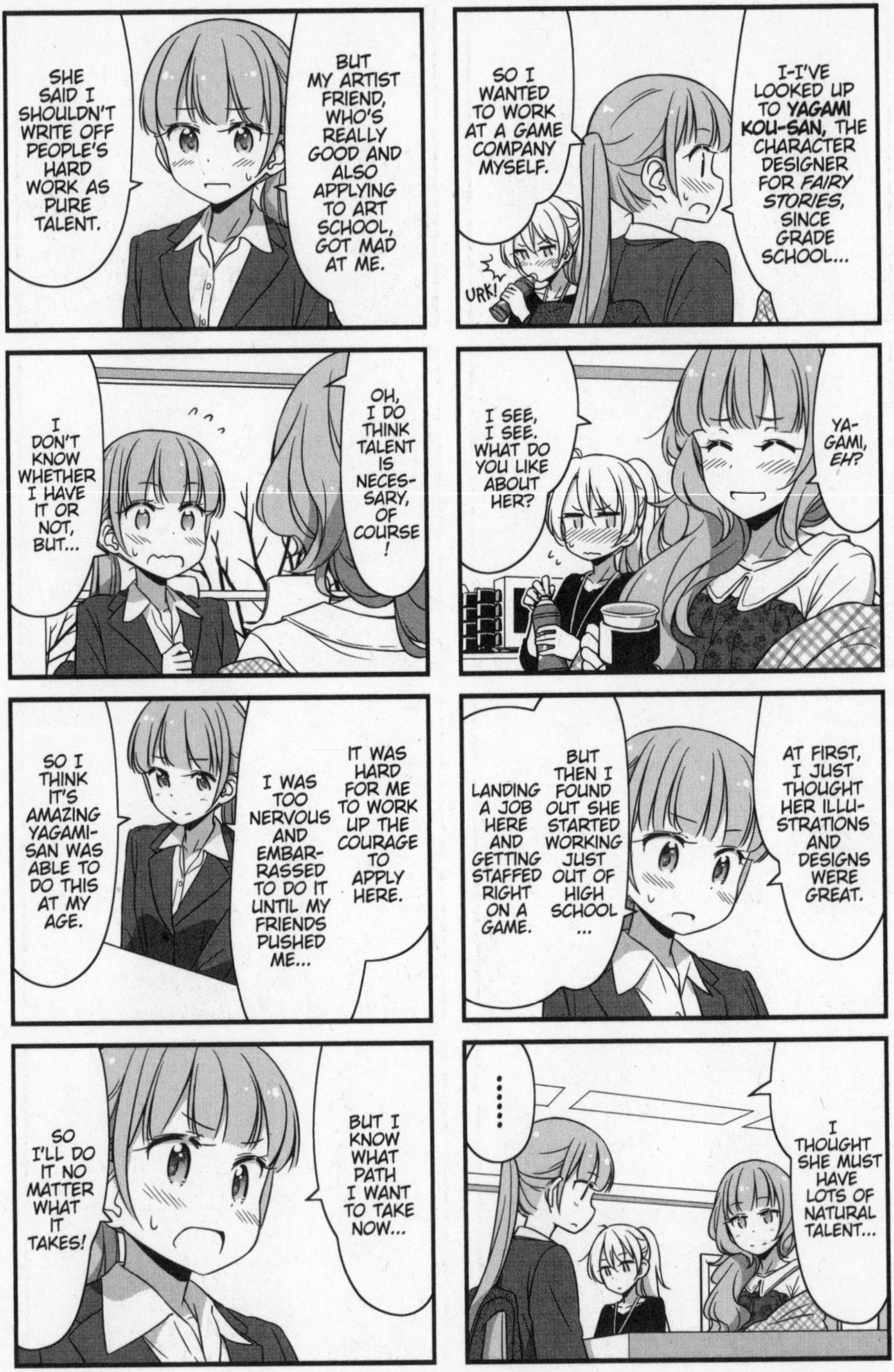
I-I'VE LOOKED UP TO YAGAMI KOU-SAN, THE CHARACTER DESIGNER FOR FAIRY STORIES, SINCE GRADE SCHOOL...
SO I WANTED TO WORK AT A GAME COMPANY MYSELF.
URK!
BUT MY ARTIST FRIEND, WHO'S REALLY GOOD AND ALSO APPLYING TO ART SCHOOL, GOT MAD AT ME.
SHE SAID I SHOULDN'T WRITE OFF PEOPLE'S HARD WORK AS PURE TALENT.
YA-GAMI, EH?
I SEE, I SEE. WHAT DO YOU LIKE ABOUT HER?
OH, I DO THINK TALENT IS NECES-SARY, OF COURSE!
I DON'T KNOW WHETHER I HAVE IT OR NOT, BUT...
AT FIRST, I JUST THOUGHT HER ILLU-STRATIONS AND DESIGNS WERE GREAT.
BUT THEN I FOUND OUT SHE STARTED WORKING JUST OUT OF HIGH SCHOOL...
LANDING A JOB HERE AND GETTING STAFFED RIGHT ON A GAME.
IT WAS HARD FOR ME TO WORK UP THE COURAGE TO APPLY HERE.
I WAS TOO NERVOUS AND EMBAR-RASSED TO DO IT UNTIL MY FRIENDS PUSHED ME...
SO I THINK IT'S AMAZING YAGAMI-SAN WAS ABLE TO DO THIS AT MY AGE.
I THOUGHT SHE MUST HAVE LOTS OF NATURAL TALENT...
......
BUT I KNOW WHAT PATH I WANT TO TAKE NOW...
SO I'LL DO IT NO MATTER WHAT IT TAKES!

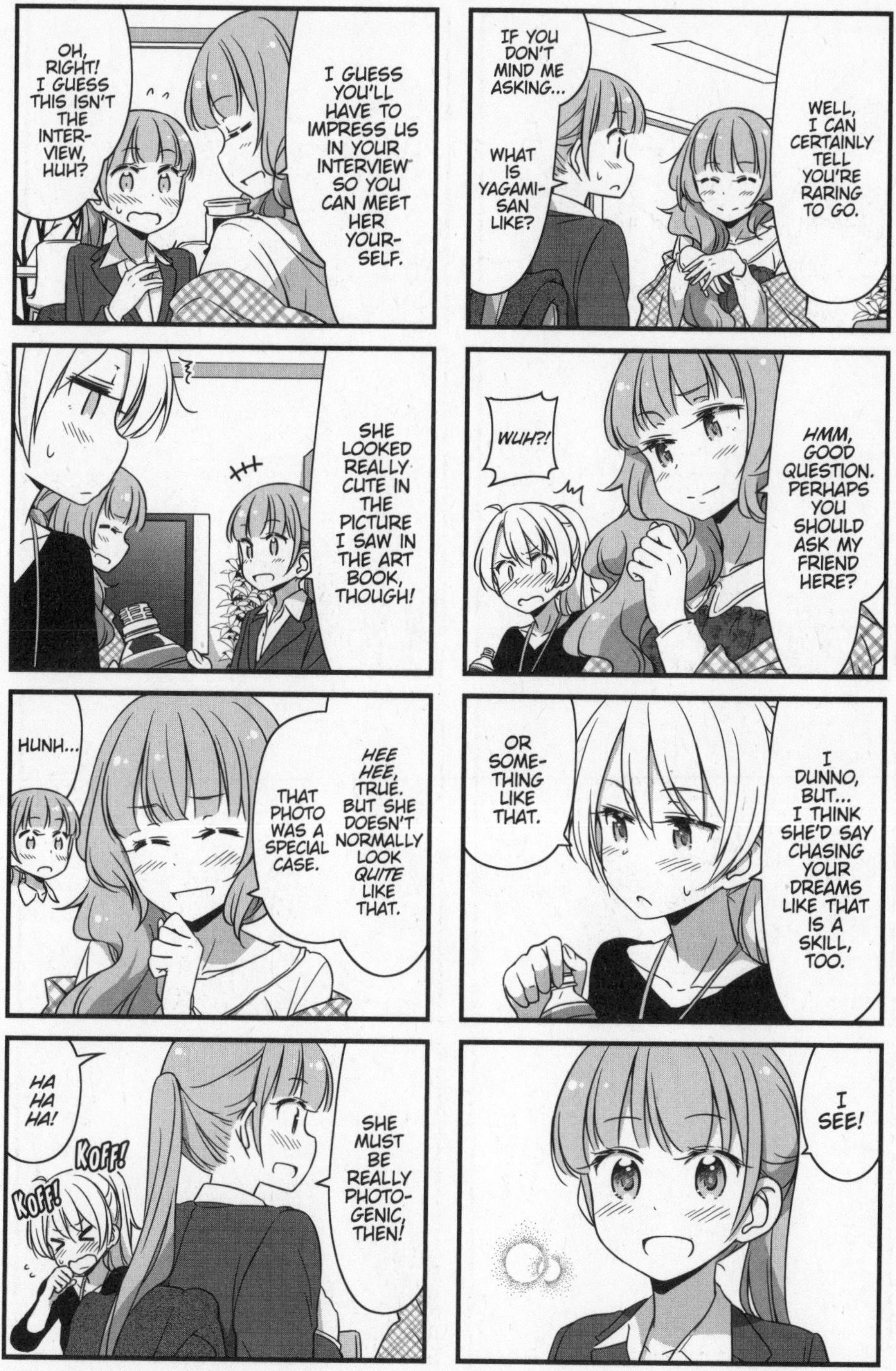
IF YOU DON'T MIND ME ASKING...
WHAT IS YAGAMI-SAN LIKE?
WELL, I CAN CERTAINLY TELL YOU'RE RARING TO GO.
HMM, GOOD QUESTION. PERHAPS YOU SHOULD ASK MY FRIEND HERE?
WUH?!
I DUNNO, BUT... I THINK SHE'D SAY CHASING YOUR DREAMS LIKE THAT IS A SKILL, TOO.
OR SOMETHING LIKE THAT.
I SEE!
I GUESS YOU'LL HAVE TO IMPRESS US IN YOUR INTERVIEW SO YOU CAN MEET HER YOURSELF.
OH, RIGHT! I GUESS THIS ISN'T THE INTERVIEW, HUH?
SHE LOOKED REALLY CUTE IN THE PICTURE I SAW IN THE ART BOOK, THOUGH!
HEE HEE, TRUE. BUT SHE DOESN'T NORMALLY LOOK QUITE LIKE THAT.
THAT PHOTO WAS A SPECIAL CASE.
HUNH...
SHE MUST BE REALLY PHOTOGENIC, THEN!
HA HA HA!
KOFF!
KOFF!

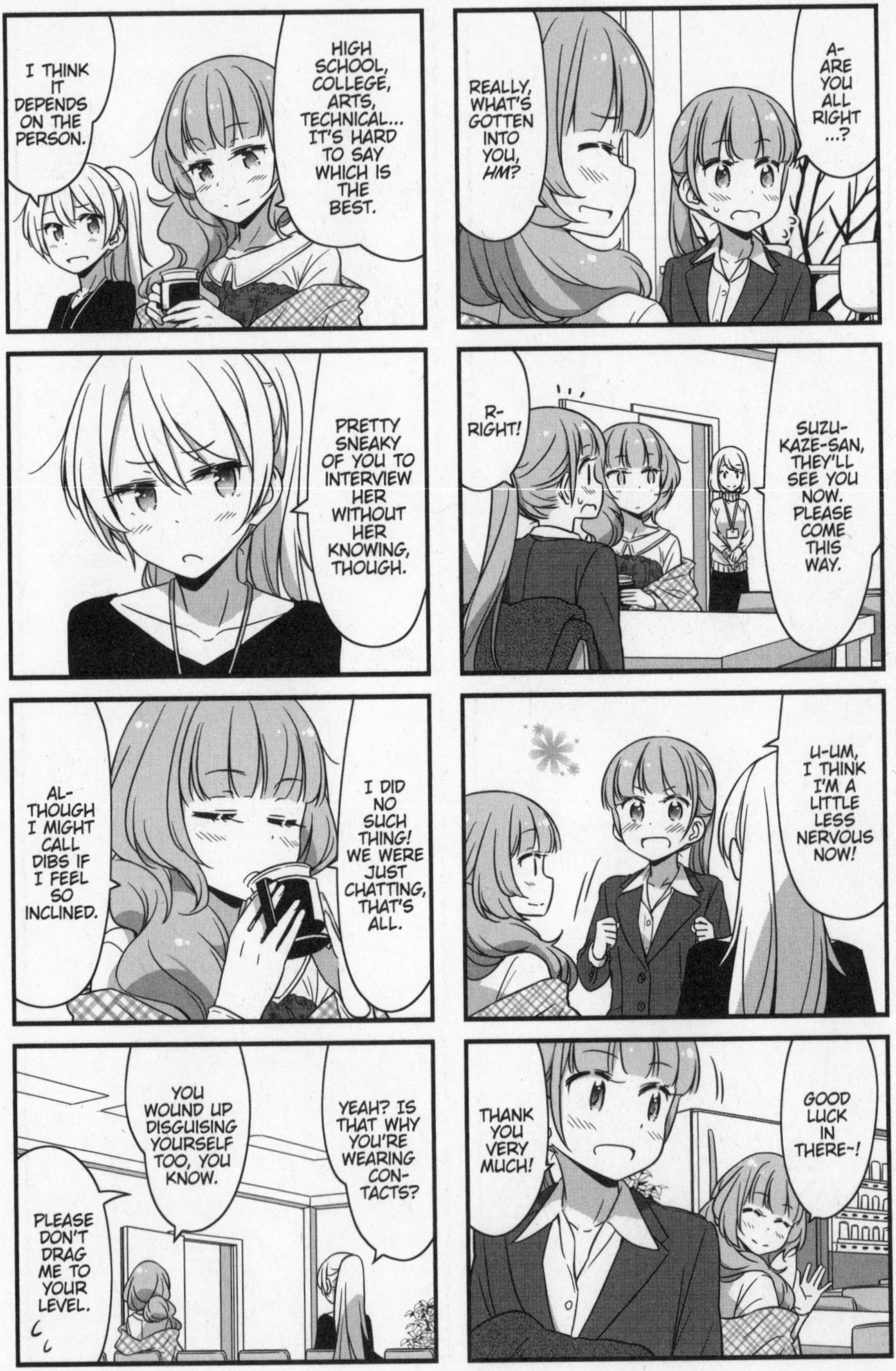
A-ARE YOU ALL RIGHT ...?
REALLY, WHAT'S GOTTEN INTO YOU, *HM*?
SUZU-KAZE-SAN, THEY'LL SEE YOU NOW. PLEASE COME THIS WAY.
R-RIGHT!
U-UM, I THINK I'M A LITTLE LESS NERVOUS NOW!
GOOD LUCK IN THERE~!
THANK YOU VERY MUCH!
HIGH SCHOOL, COLLEGE, ARTS, TECHNICAL... IT'S HARD TO SAY WHICH IS THE BEST.
I THINK IT DEPENDS ON THE PERSON.
PRETTY SNEAKY OF YOU TO INTERVIEW HER WITHOUT HER KNOWING, THOUGH.
I DID NO SUCH THING! WE WERE JUST CHATTING, THAT'S ALL.
AL-THOUGH I MIGHT CALL DIBS IF I FEEL SO INCLINED.
YEAH? IS THAT WHY YOU'RE WEARING CON-TACTS?
YOU WOUND UP DISGUISING YOURSELF TOO, YOU KNOW.
PLEASE DON'T DRAG ME TO YOUR LEVEL.

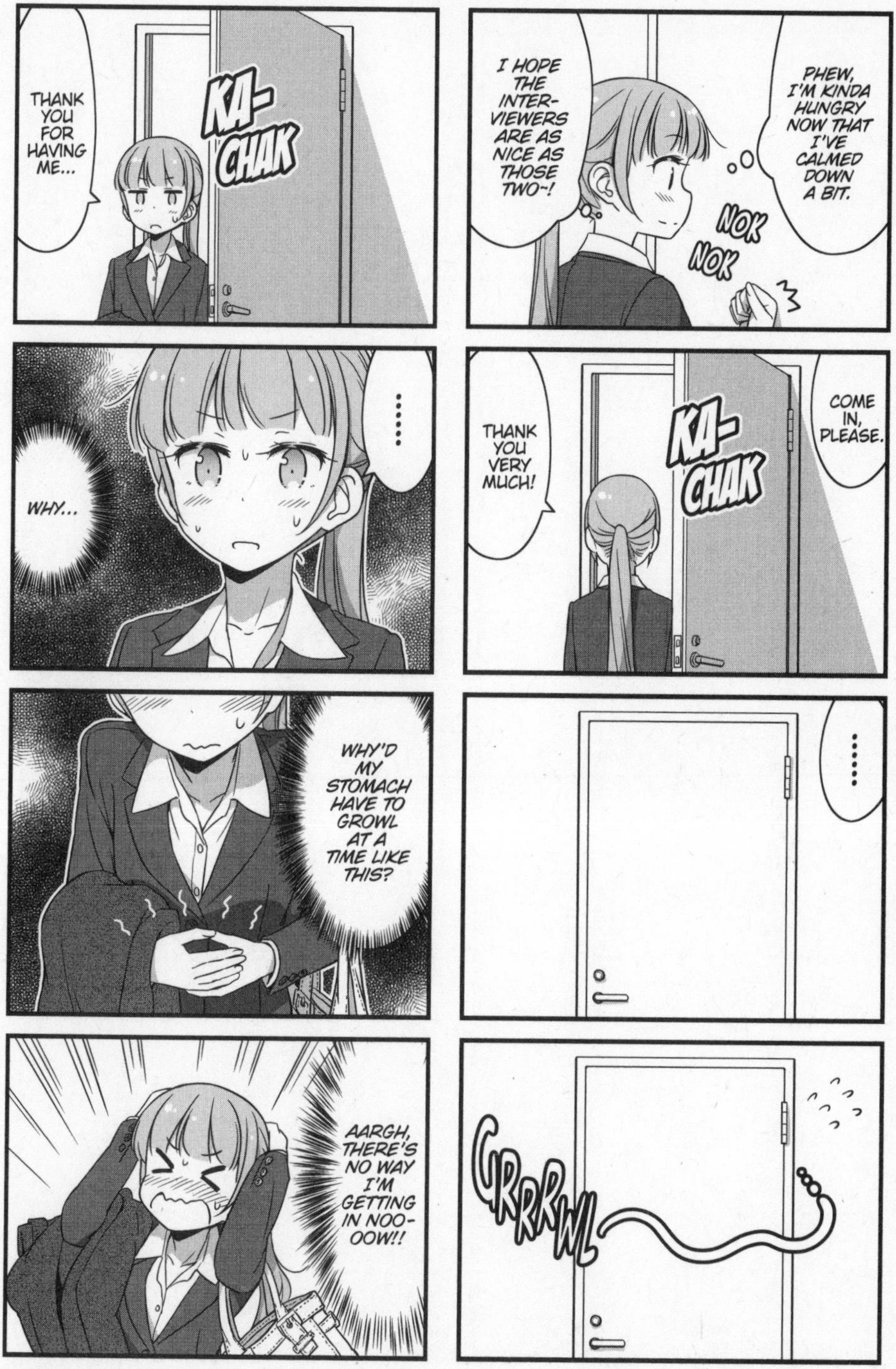
PHEW, I'M KINDA HUNGRY NOW THAT I'VE CALMED DOWN A BIT.
I HOPE THE INTER-VIEWERS ARE AS NICE AS THOSE TWO~!
NOK NOK
KA-CHAK
THANK YOU FOR HAVING ME...
COME IN, PLEASE.
KA-CHAK
THANK YOU VERY MUCH!
......
WHY...
......
WHY'D MY STOMACH HAVE TO GROWL AT A TIME LIKE THIS?
GRRRWL
AARGH, THERE'S NO WAY I'M GETTING IN NOOO-OOW!!

NEW GAME!

NEW GAME!

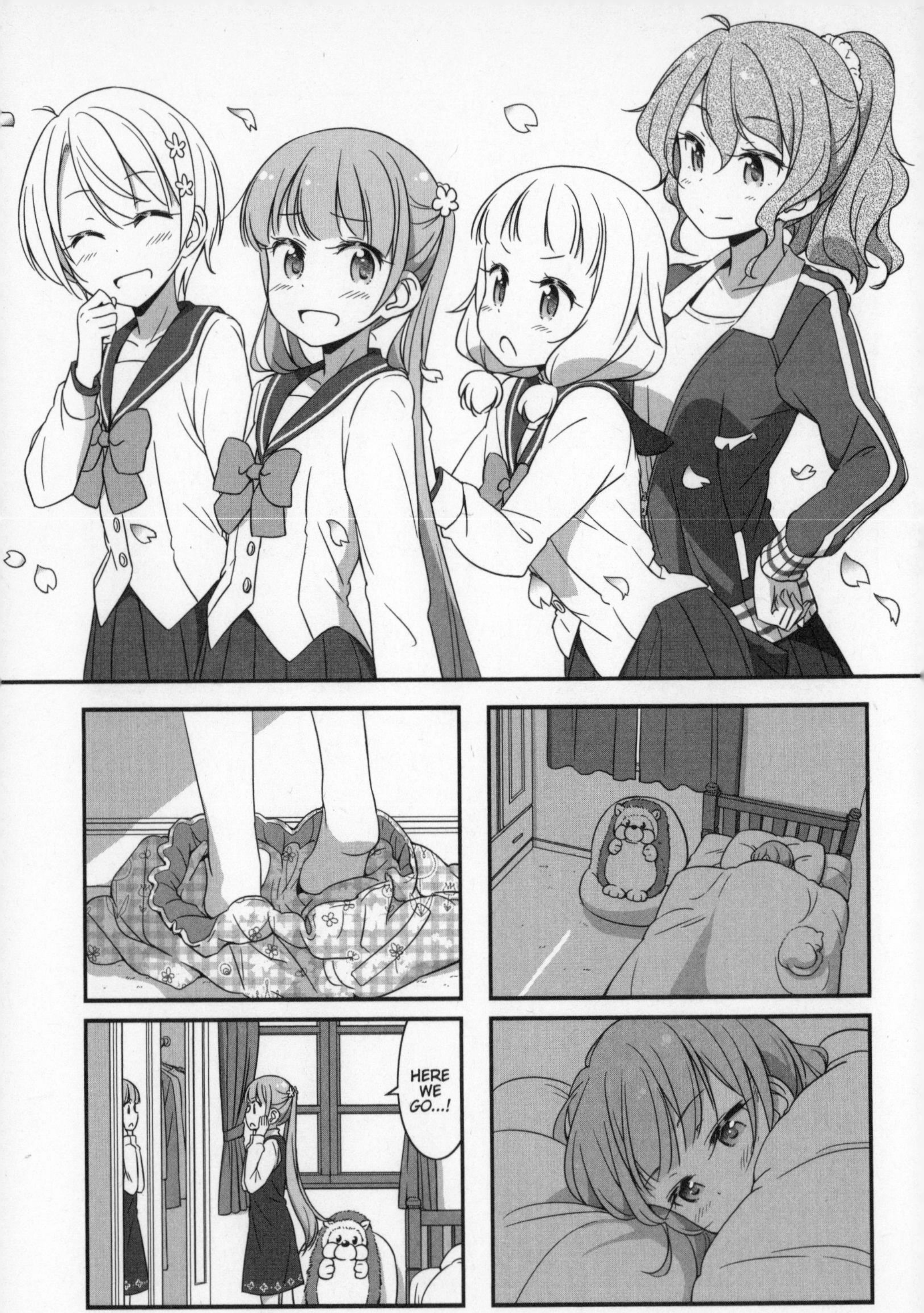
HERE WE GO...!

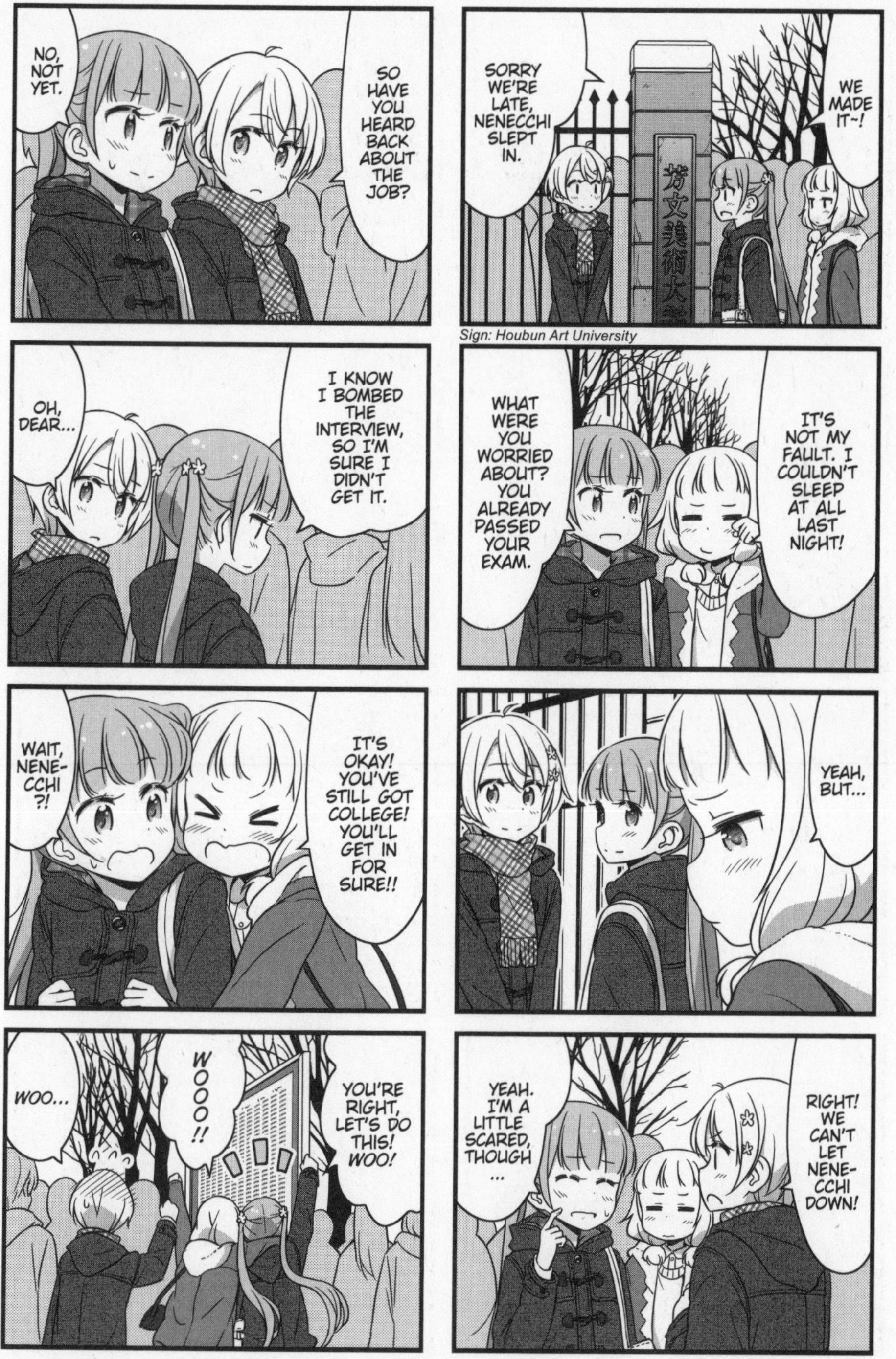
WE MADE IT~!
SORRY WE'RE LATE, NENECCHI SLEPT IN.
Sign: Houbun Art University
IT'S NOT MY FAULT. I COULDN'T SLEEP AT ALL LAST NIGHT!
WHAT WERE YOU WORRIED ABOUT? YOU ALREADY PASSED YOUR EXAM.
YEAH, BUT...
RIGHT! WE CAN'T LET NENECCHI DOWN!
YEAH. I'M A LITTLE SCARED, THOUGH ...
SO HAVE YOU HEARD BACK ABOUT THE JOB?
NO, NOT YET.
I KNOW I BOMBED THE INTERVIEW, SO I'M SURE I DIDN'T GET IT.
OH, DEAR...
IT'S OKAY! YOU'VE STILL GOT COLLEGE! YOU'LL GET IN FOR SURE!!
WAIT, NENECCHI?!
YOU'RE RIGHT, LET'S DO THIS! WOO!
WOOOO!!
WOO...

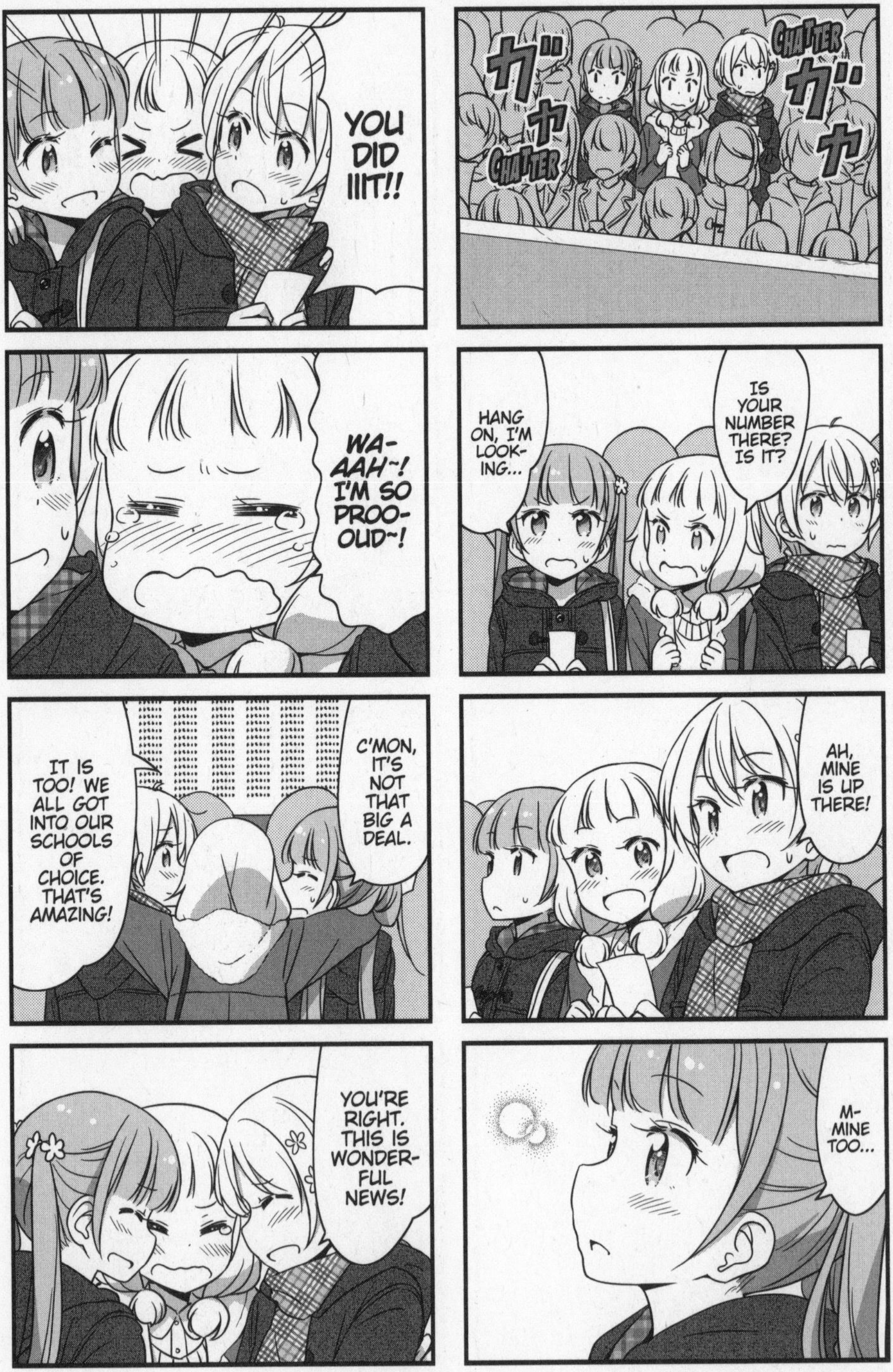
CHATTER
ガヤ
ガヤ
CHATTER
YOU DID IIIT!!
IS YOUR NUMBER THERE? IS IT?
HANG ON, I'M LOOK-ING...
WA-AAH~! I'M SO PROOO-OUD~!
AH, MINE IS UP THERE!
C'MON, IT'S NOT THAT BIG A DEAL.
IT IS TOO! WE ALL GOT INTO OUR SCHOOLS OF CHOICE. THAT'S AMAZING!
M-MINE TOO...
YOU'RE RIGHT. THIS IS WONDER-FUL NEWS!

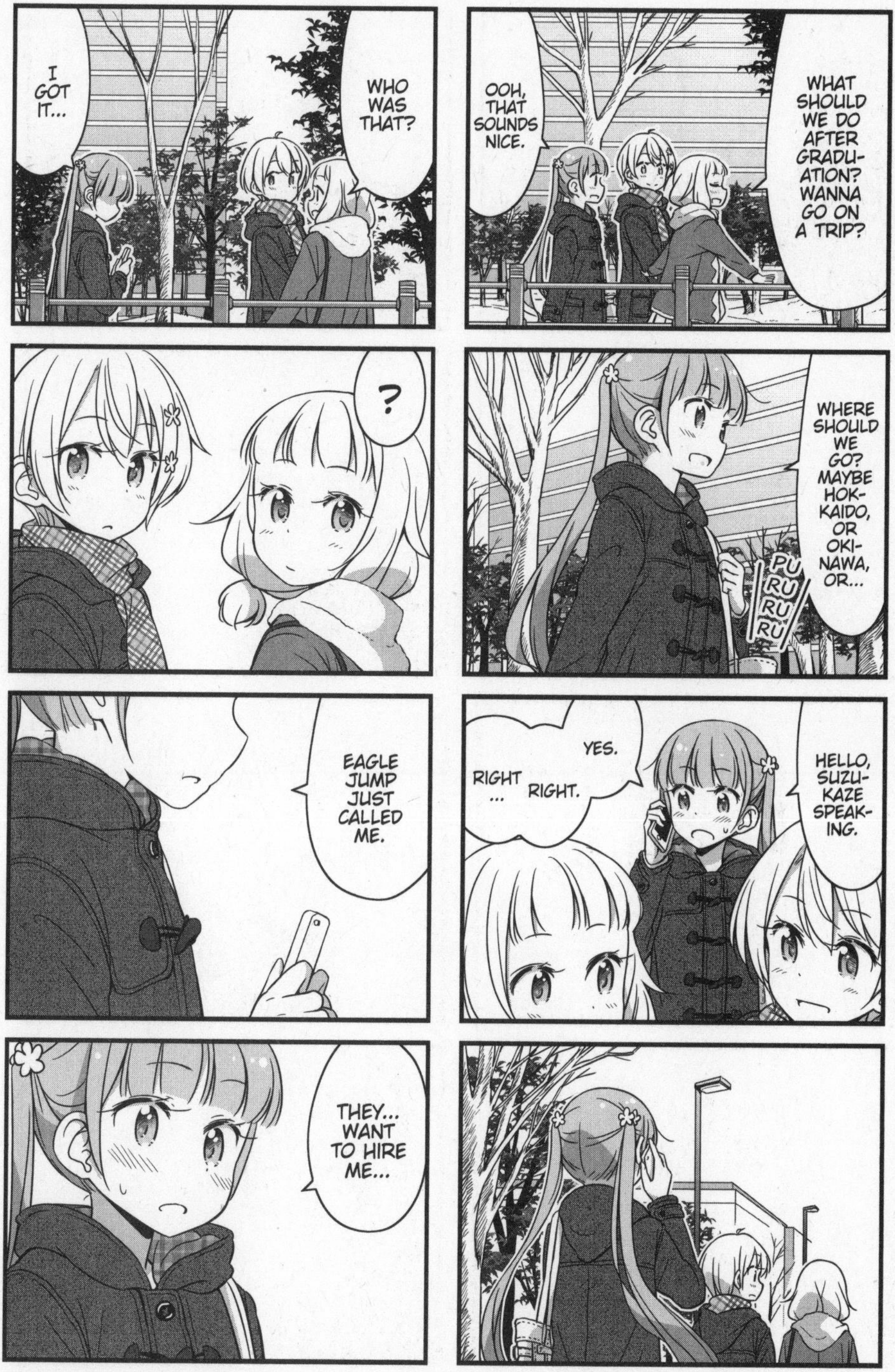
WHAT SHOULD WE DO AFTER GRADUATION? WANNA GO ON A TRIP?
OOH, THAT SOUNDS NICE.
WHERE SHOULD WE GO? MAYBE HOKKAIDO, OR OKINAWA, OR...
PURURURU
HELLO, SUZUKAZE SPEAKING.
YES.
RIGHT...
RIGHT.
WHO WAS THAT?
I GOT IT...
?
EAGLE JUMP JUST CALLED ME.
THEY... WANT TO HIRE ME...

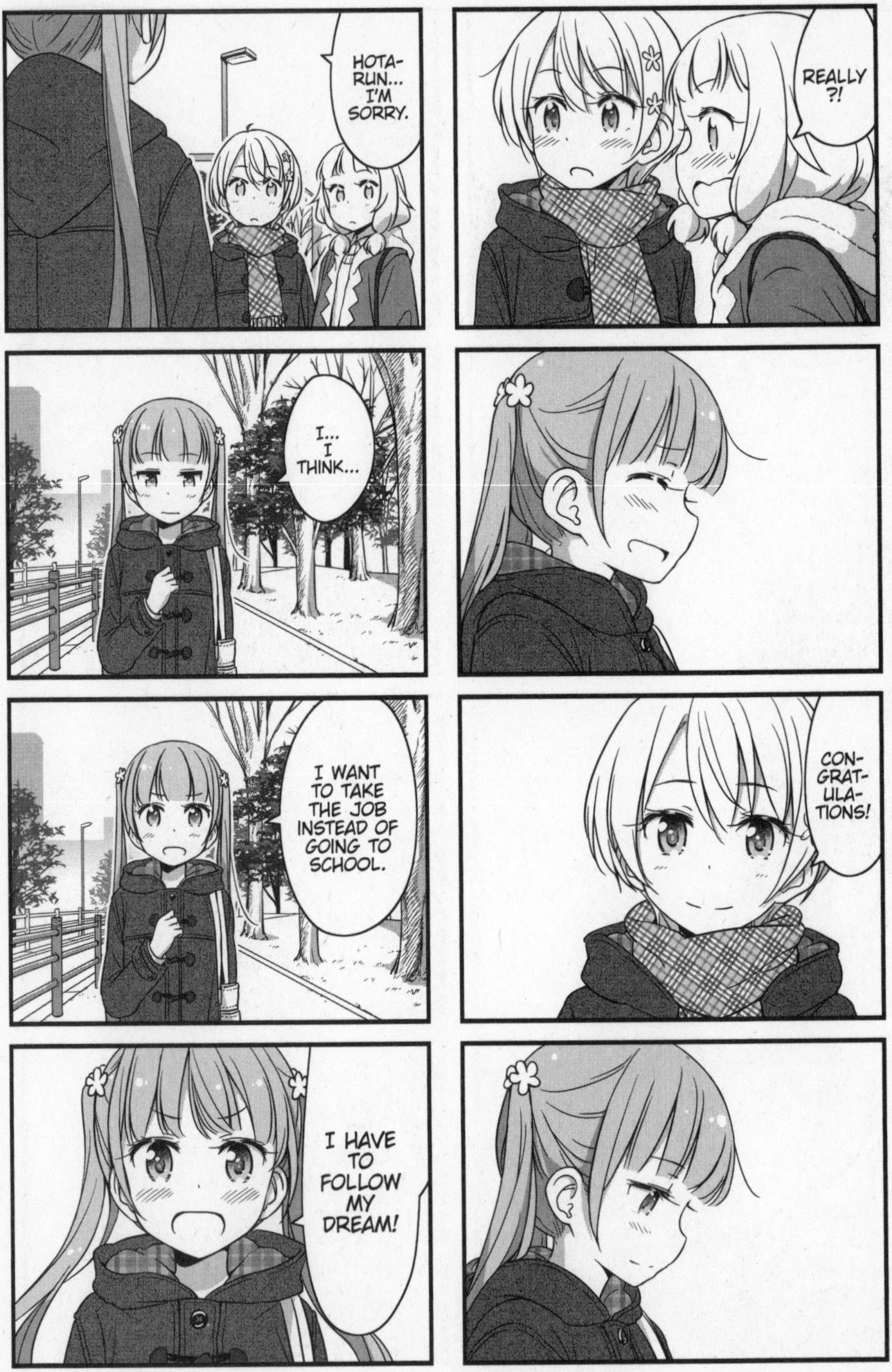
HOTA-RUN... I'M SORRY.
I... I THINK...
I WANT TO TAKE THE JOB INSTEAD OF GOING TO SCHOOL.
I HAVE TO FOLLOW MY DREAM!
REALLY ?!
CON-GRAT-ULA-TIONS!

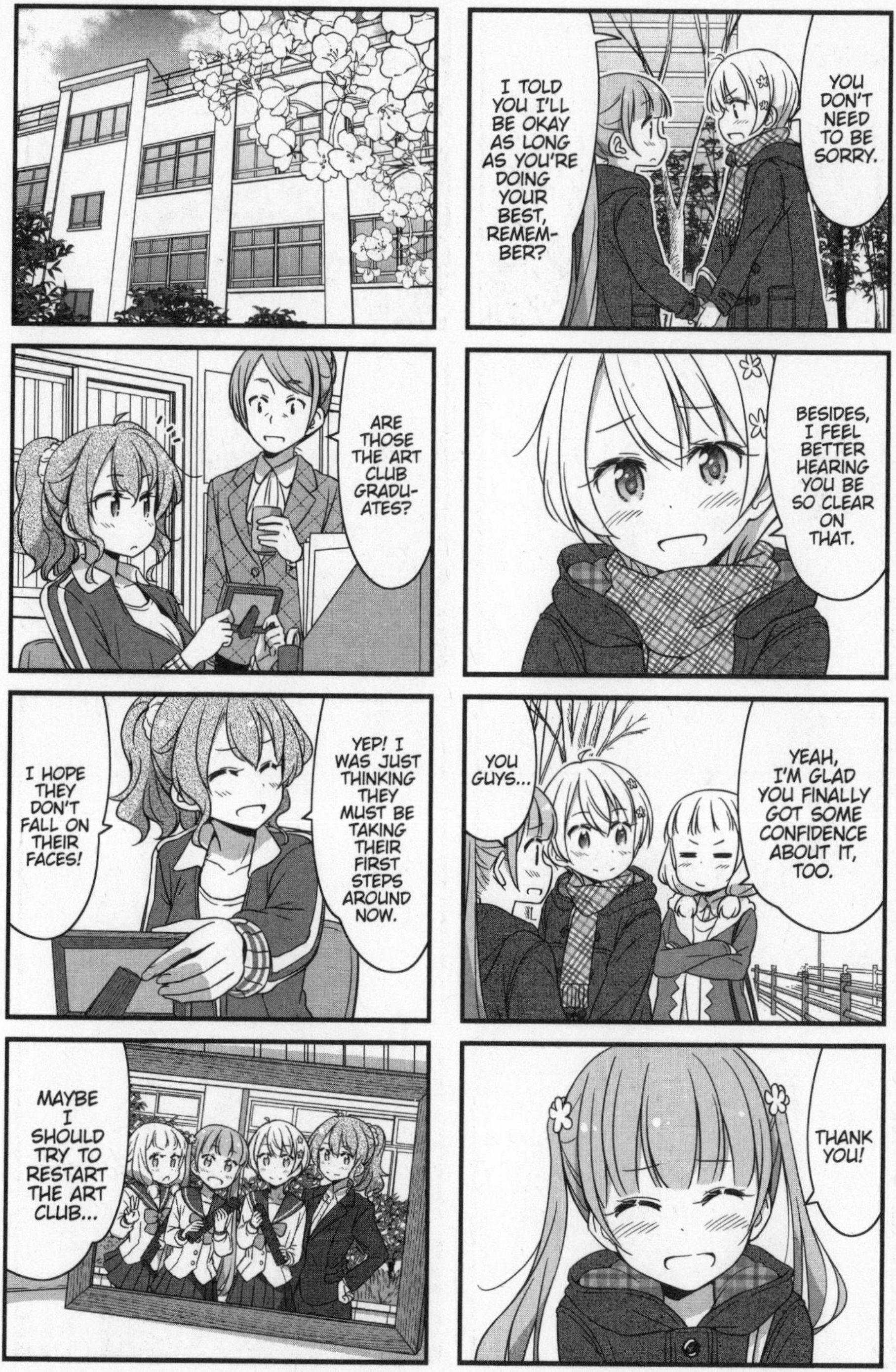
YOU DON'T NEED TO BE SORRY.
I TOLD YOU I'LL BE OKAY AS LONG AS YOU'RE DOING YOUR BEST, REMEMBER?
BESIDES, I FEEL BETTER HEARING YOU BE SO CLEAR ON THAT.
YEAH, I'M GLAD YOU FINALLY GOT SOME CONFIDENCE ABOUT IT, TOO.
YOU GUYS...
THANK YOU!
ARE THOSE THE ART CLUB GRADUATES?
YEP! I WAS JUST THINKING THEY MUST BE TAKING THEIR FIRST STEPS AROUND NOW.
I HOPE THEY DON'T FALL ON THEIR FACES!
MAYBE I SHOULD TRY TO RESTART THE ART CLUB...

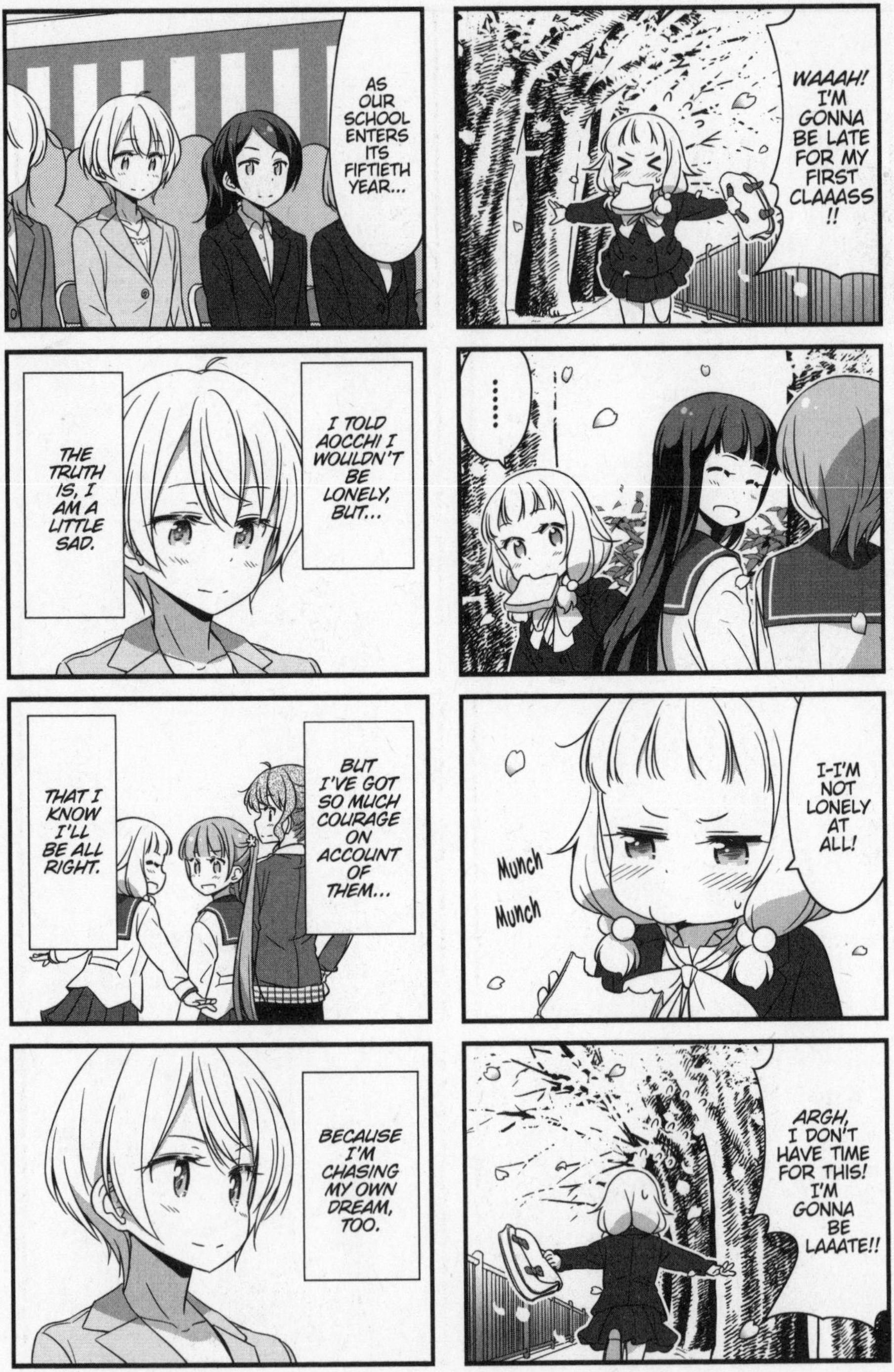
WAAAH! I'M GONNA BE LATE FOR MY FIRST CLAAASS!!
AS OUR SCHOOL ENTERS ITS FIFTIETH YEAR...
......
I TOLD AOCCHI I WOULDN'T BE LONELY, BUT...
THE TRUTH IS, I AM A LITTLE SAD.
I-I'M NOT LONELY AT ALL!
Munch
Munch
BUT I'VE GOT SO MUCH COURAGE ON ACCOUNT OF THEM...
THAT I KNOW I'LL BE ALL RIGHT.
ARGH, I DON'T HAVE TIME FOR THIS! I'M GONNA BE LAAATE!!
BECAUSE I'M CHASING MY OWN DREAM, TOO.

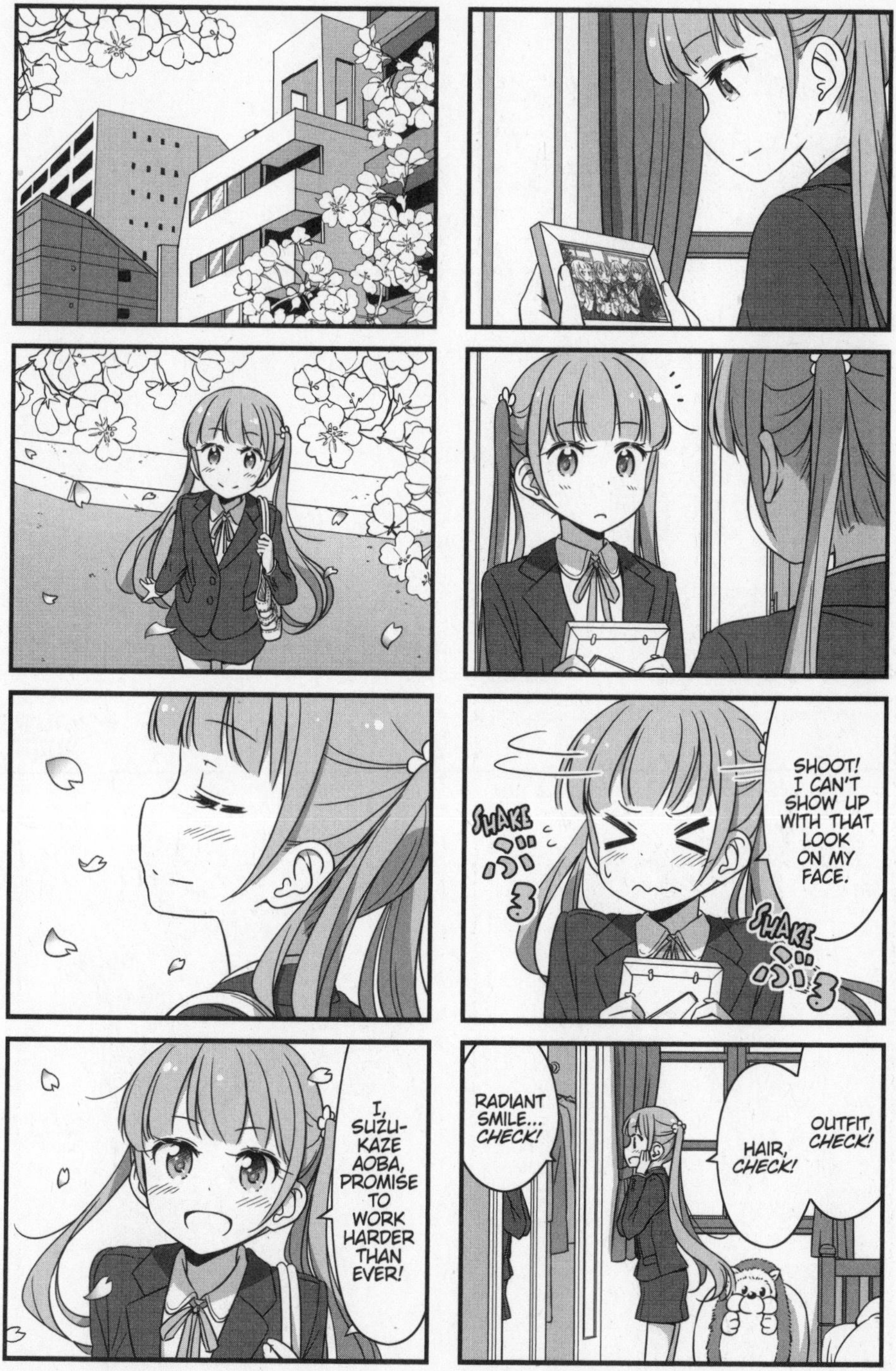
SHAKE
SHOOT! I CAN'T SHOW UP WITH THAT LOOK ON MY FACE.
SHAKE
OUTFIT, CHECK!
HAIR, CHECK!
RADIANT SMILE... CHECK!
I, SUZUKAZE AOBA, PROMISE TO WORK HARDER THAN EVER!

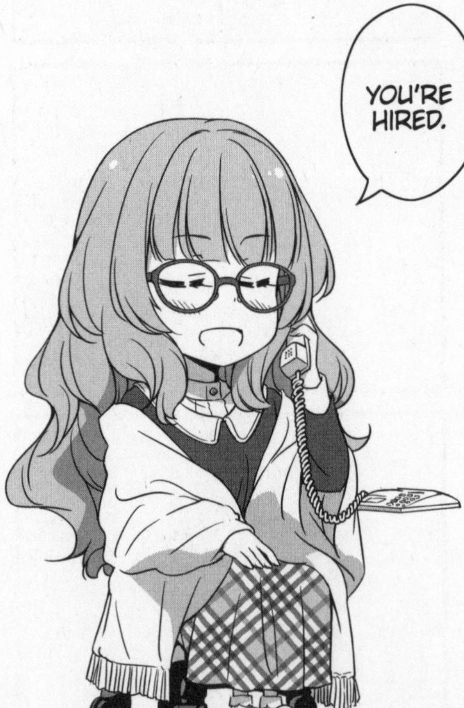
YOU'RE HIRED.

The Hiring Process

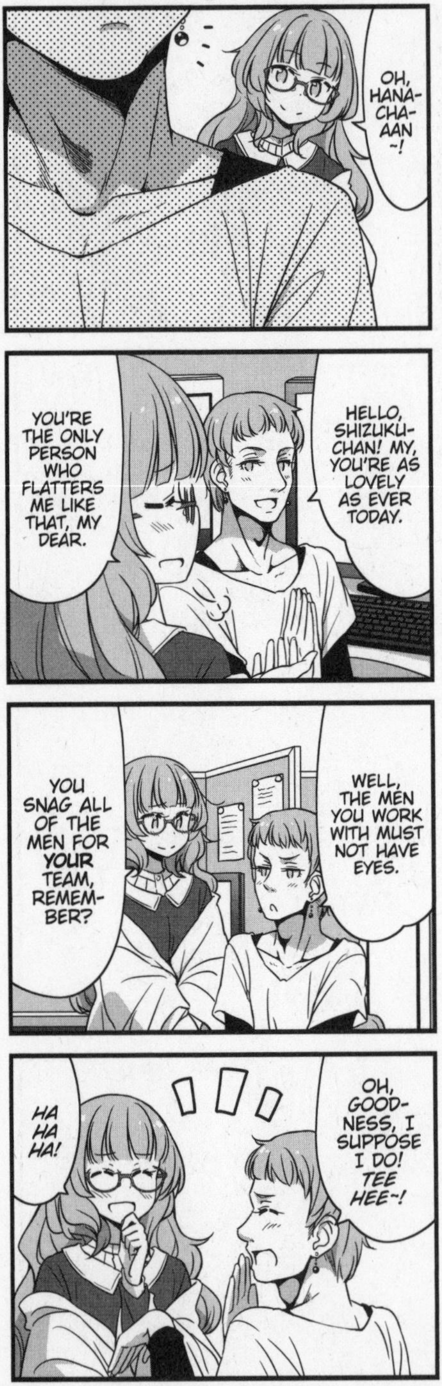
OH, HANA-CHA-AAN~!
HELLO, SHIZUKU-CHAN! MY, YOU'RE AS LOVELY AS EVER TODAY.
YOU'RE THE ONLY PERSON WHO FLATTERS ME LIKE THAT, MY DEAR.
WELL, THE MEN YOU WORK WITH MUST NOT HAVE EYES.
YOU SNAG ALL OF THE MEN FOR **YOUR** TEAM, REMEMBER?
OH, GOODNESS, I SUPPOSE I DO! *TEE HEE~!*
HA HA HA!

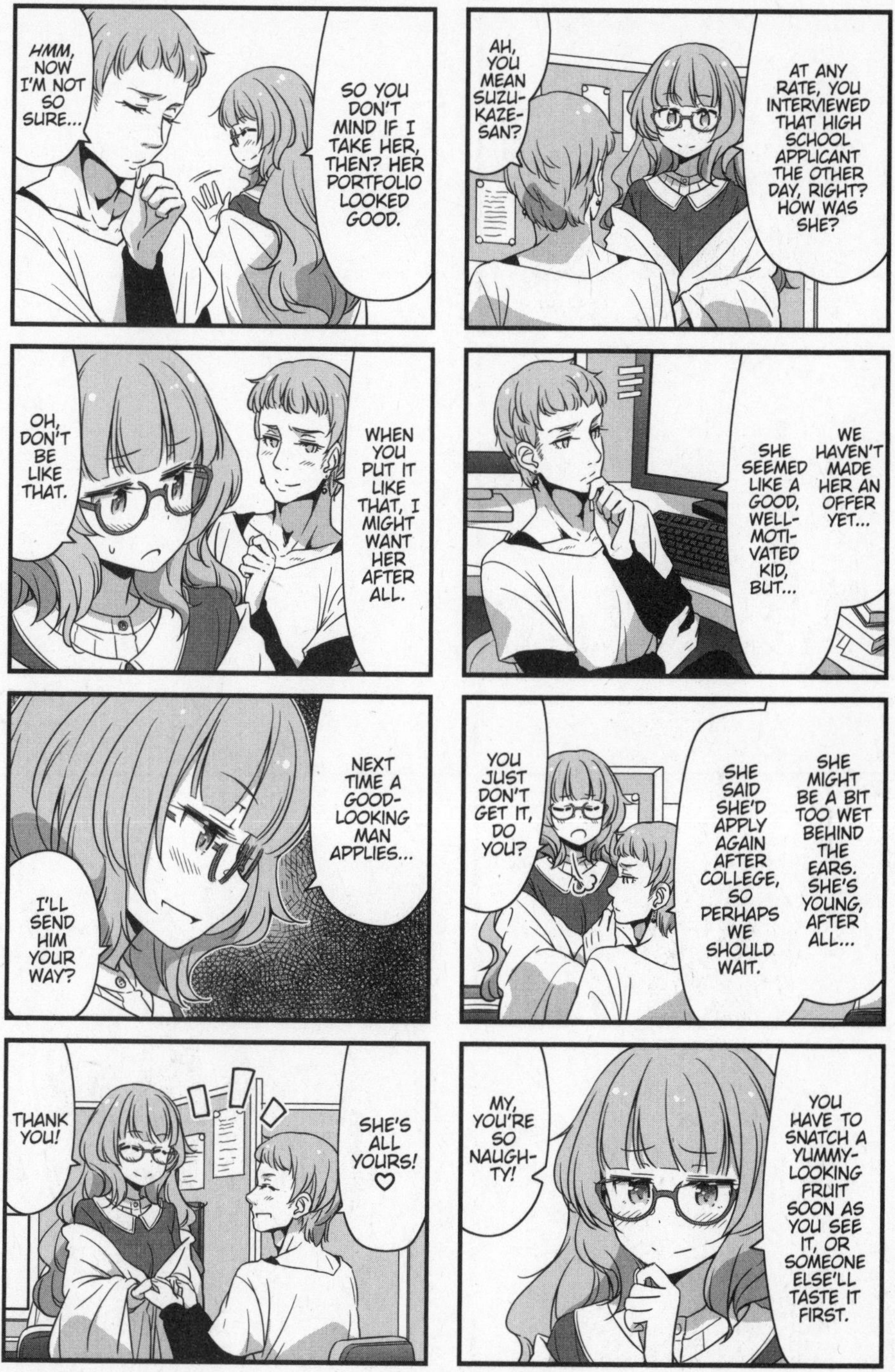
AT ANY RATE, YOU INTERVIEWED THAT HIGH SCHOOL APPLICANT THE OTHER DAY, RIGHT? HOW WAS SHE?
AH, YOU MEAN SUZUKAZE-SAN?
WE HAVEN'T MADE HER AN OFFER YET...
SHE SEEMED LIKE A GOOD, WELL-MOTIVATED KID, BUT...
SHE MIGHT BE A BIT TOO WET BEHIND THE EARS. SHE'S YOUNG, AFTER ALL...
SHE SAID SHE'D APPLY AGAIN AFTER COLLEGE, SO PERHAPS WE SHOULD WAIT.
YOU JUST DON'T GET IT, DO YOU?
YOU HAVE TO SNATCH A YUMMY-LOOKING FRUIT SOON AS YOU SEE IT, OR SOMEONE ELSE'LL TASTE IT FIRST.
MY, YOU'RE SO NAUGHTY!
SO YOU DON'T MIND IF I TAKE HER, THEN? HER PORTFOLIO LOOKED GOOD.
HMM, NOW I'M NOT SO SURE...
WHEN YOU PUT IT LIKE THAT, I MIGHT WANT HER AFTER ALL.
OH, DON'T BE LIKE THAT.
NEXT TIME A GOOD-LOOKING MAN APPLIES...
I'LL SEND HIM YOUR WAY?
SHE'S ALL YOURS! ♡
THANK YOU!

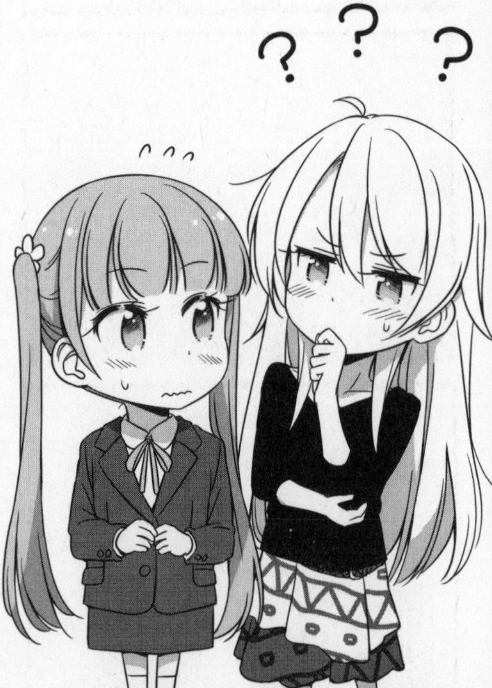
? ? ?

Familiar Face

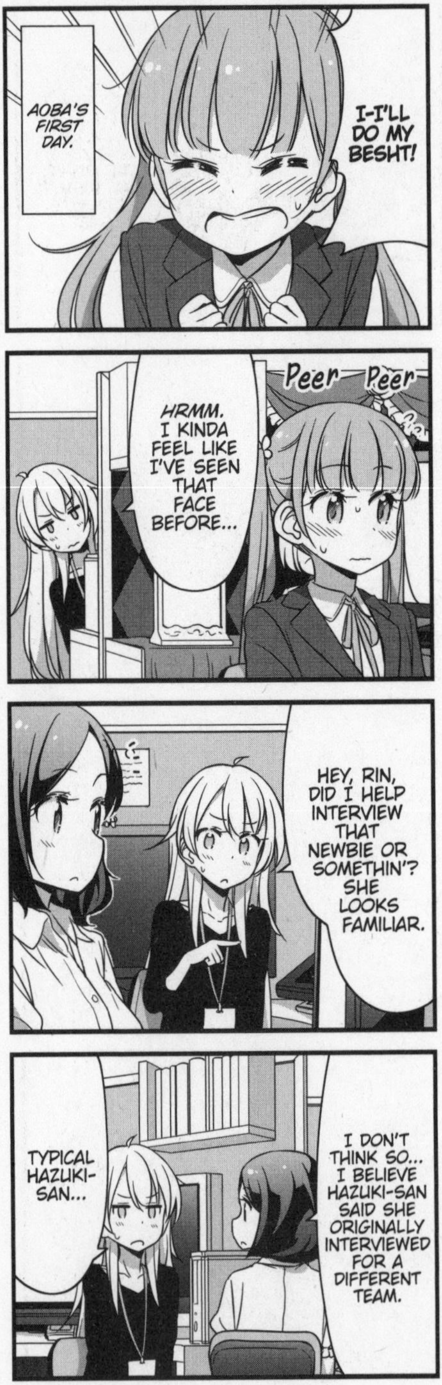
AOBA'S FIRST DAY.
I-I'LL DO MY BESHT!
Peer Peer
HRMM. I KINDA FEEL LIKE I'VE SEEN THAT FACE BEFORE...
HEY, RIN, DID I HELP INTERVIEW THAT NEWBIE OR SOMETHIN'? SHE LOOKS FAMILIAR.
I DON'T THINK SO... I BELIEVE HAZUKI-SAN SAID SHE ORIGINALLY INTERVIEWED FOR A DIFFERENT TEAM.
TYPICAL HAZUKI-SAN...

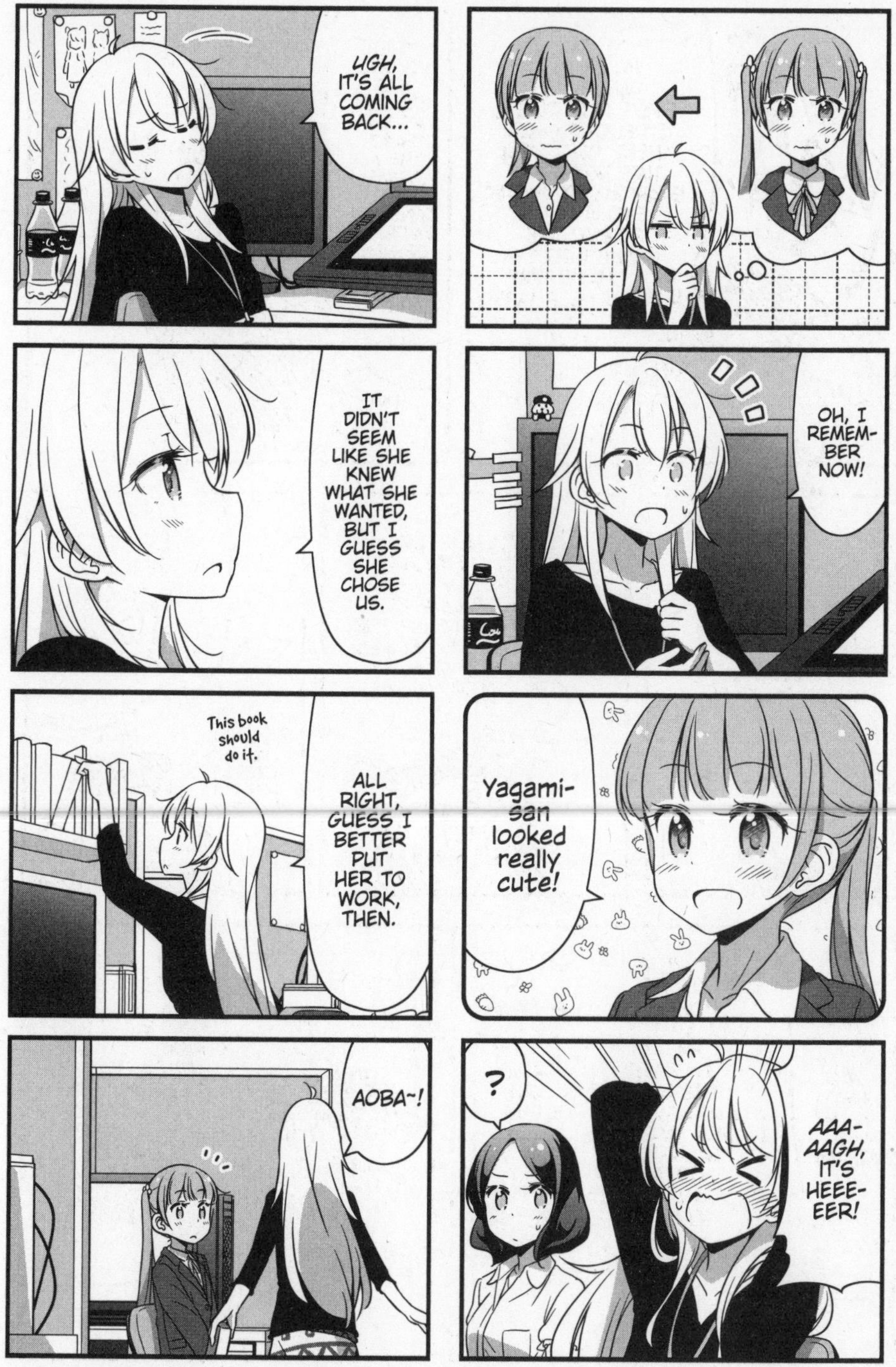
UGH, IT'S ALL COMING BACK...
OH, I REMEMBER NOW!
IT DIDN'T SEEM LIKE SHE KNEW WHAT SHE WANTED, BUT I GUESS SHE CHOSE US.
Yagami-san looked really cute!
ALL RIGHT, GUESS I BETTER PUT HER TO WORK, THEN.
This book should do it.
?
AAA-AAGH, IT'S HEEEE-EER!
AOBA~!

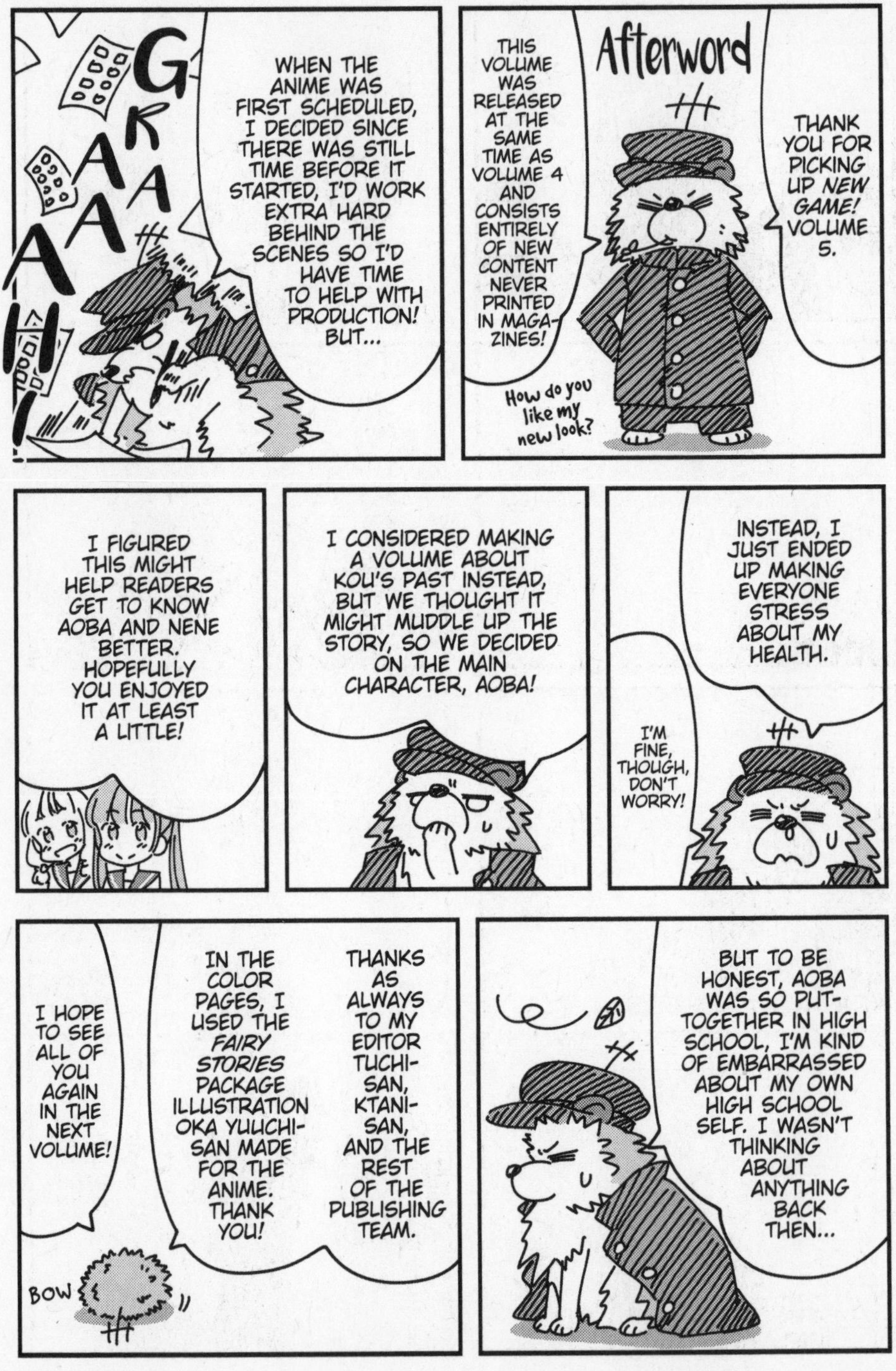
Afterword
THANK YOU FOR PICKING UP *NEW GAME!* VOLUME 5.
THIS VOLUME WAS RELEASED AT THE SAME TIME AS VOLUME 4 AND CONSISTS ENTIRELY OF NEW CONTENT NEVER PRINTED IN MAGAZINES!
How do you like my new look?
WHEN THE ANIME WAS FIRST SCHEDULED, I DECIDED SINCE THERE WAS STILL TIME BEFORE IT STARTED, I'D WORK EXTRA HARD BEHIND THE SCENES SO I'D HAVE TIME TO HELP WITH PRODUCTION! BUT...
GRAAAAH!!
INSTEAD, I JUST ENDED UP MAKING EVERYONE STRESS ABOUT MY HEALTH.
I'M FINE, THOUGH, DON'T WORRY!
I CONSIDERED MAKING A VOLUME ABOUT KOU'S PAST INSTEAD, BUT WE THOUGHT IT MIGHT MUDDLE UP THE STORY, SO WE DECIDED ON THE MAIN CHARACTER, AOBA!
I FIGURED THIS MIGHT HELP READERS GET TO KNOW AOBA AND NENE BETTER. HOPEFULLY YOU ENJOYED IT AT LEAST A LITTLE!
BUT TO BE HONEST, AOBA WAS SO PUT-TOGETHER IN HIGH SCHOOL, I'M KIND OF EMBARRASSED ABOUT MY OWN HIGH SCHOOL SELF. I WASN'T THINKING ABOUT ANYTHING BACK THEN...
THANKS AS ALWAYS TO MY EDITOR TUCHI-SAN, KTANI-SAN, AND THE REST OF THE PUBLISHING TEAM.
IN THE COLOR PAGES, I USED THE *FAIRY STORIES* PACKAGE ILLUSTRATION OKA YUUCHI-SAN MADE FOR THE ANIME. THANK YOU!
I HOPE TO SEE ALL OF YOU AGAIN IN THE NEXT VOLUME!
BOW

Watermelon (1)

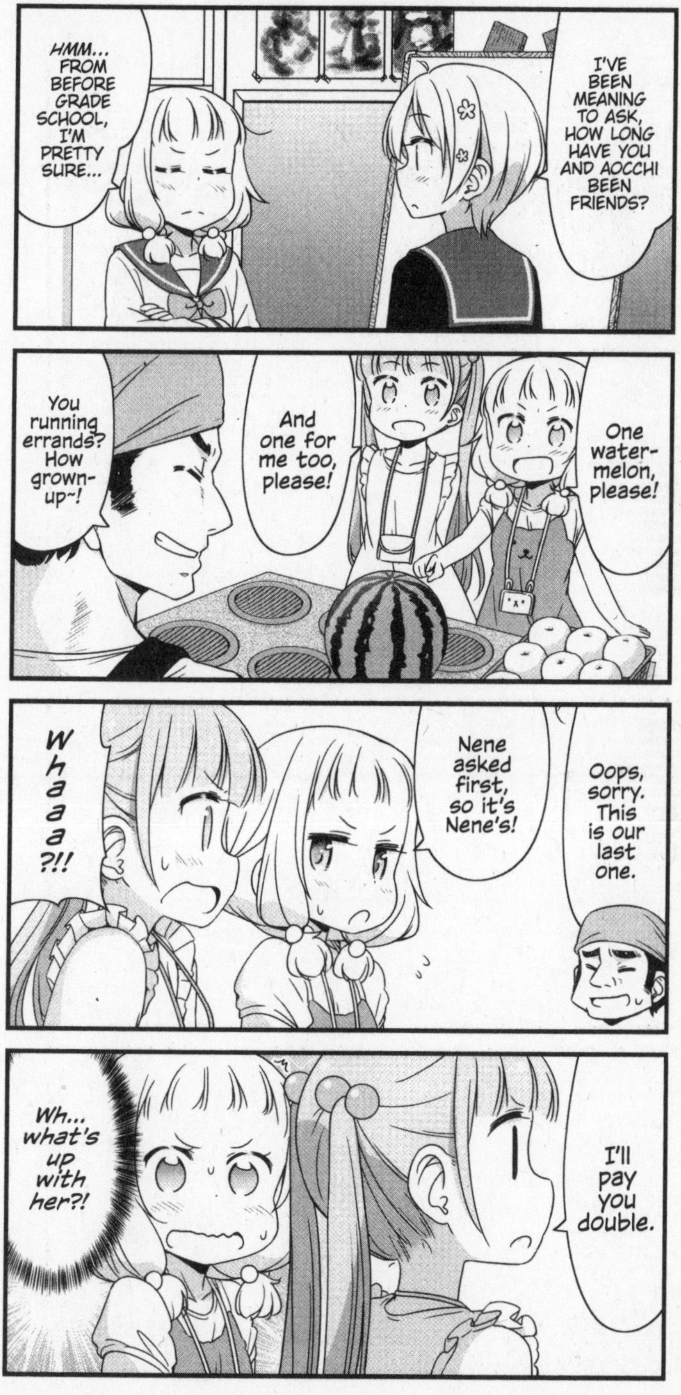
I'VE BEEN MEANING TO ASK, HOW LONG HAVE YOU AND AOCCHI BEEN FRIENDS?
HMM... FROM BEFORE GRADE SCHOOL, I'M PRETTY SURE...
One watermelon, please!
And one for me too, please!
You running errands? How grown-up~!
Oops, sorry. This is our last one.
Nene asked first, so it's Nene's!
Whaaaa?!!
I'll pay you double.
Wh... what's up with her?!